THE CLASSICS
OF WESTERN
SPIRITUALITY

Francis de Sales, Jane de Chantal
LETTERS OF SPIRITUAL DIRECTION

TRANSLATED BY
PÉRONNE MARIE THIBERT, V.H.M.

SELECTED AND INTRODUCED BY
WENDY M. WRIGHT AND JOSEPH F. POWER, O.S.F.S.

PREFACE BY
HENRI J.M. NOUWEN

PAULIST PRESS
NEW YORK • MAHWAH

Cover Art:

JOHN LYNCH, a Franciscan friar, states that in his portrait of St. Francis and St. Jane, his purpose was to capture not only their well-recognized human qualities but also the unique friendship which they shared and which was surpassed only by their love for God. His previous art work for Paulist Press appeared on the covers of the recently published Classics of Western Spirituality volume *John of the Cross* and *Stumbling Blocks or Stepping Stones*.

Book Design by Theresa M. Sparacio.

Acknowledgments

Permission to use three letters of Jane de Chantal has been granted by Les Editions du Cerf, Paris. Direct Scripture quotations are taken from the *New American Bible*, (c) 1970 by the Confraternity of Christian Doctrine, Washington, D.C., and are used with permission. Permission to use letters from the *Oeuvres de saint François de Sales*, the Annecy Edition, and from *Sainte Jeanne-Françoise Frémyot de Chantal, sa vie et ses oeuvres*, the Plon Edition, has been granted by the Order of the Visitation, Annecy, France.

Library of Congress Cataloging-in-Publication Data

Francis, de Sales, Saint, 1567–1622.
    [Correspondence. English. Selections]
    Francis de Sales, Jane de Chantal : letters of spiritual
direction / selected and introduced by Wendy M. Wright and Joseph F.
Power ; translated by Péronne Marie Thibert ; preface by Henri J.M.
Nouwen.
      p. cm. — (Classics of Western spirituality)
    Bibliography: p.
    Includes index.
    ISBN 0-8091-0408-3 : $16.95. ISBN 0-8091-2990-6 (pbk.) :
$13.95.
    1. Francis, de Sales, Saint, 1567–1622—Correspondence.
2. Chantal, Jeanne-Françoise de, Saint, 1572–1641—Correspondence.
3. Spiritual life—Catholic authors—Early works to 1800.
I. Chantal, Jeanne-Françoise de, Saint, 1572–1641. II. Wright,
Wendy M. III. Power, Joseph F. IV. Title. V. Letters of
spiritual direction. VI. Series.
BX2349.F694   1988
282'.092'2—dc19
[b]   88-4390
                                          CIP

Published by Paulist Press
997 Macarthur Boulevard
Mahwah, New Jersey 07430

Printed and bound in the United States of America

Contents

Translator of this Volume
PÉRONNE MARIE THIBERT, V.H.M. is a member of the Order of the Visitation of Holy Mary. She has served as Superior of her community in St. Paul, MN. and as a Councillor for the Second Federation of the Visitation Sisters in the U.S.A. Sister Thibert has done graduate studies at Middlebury College, Marquette University, and the University of Rennes, France. In 1969 she was an official translator for the General Assembly of the Order, and in 1971 was one of the team of Sisters who translated the revised Constitution into English.

Introducers of this Volume
WENDY M. WRIGHT holds a doctorate in Contemplative Studies from the University of California at Santa Barbara. She has taught the history of spirituality, and family spirituality at Weston School of Theology in Cambridge, Massachusetts, and is currently teaching in the graduate program of Christian spirituality at Creighton University in Omaha, Nebraska. Previous publications include *Silent Fire, An Invitation to Western Mysticism.*

JOSEPH F. POWER, O.S.F.S. is an Oblate of St. Francis de Sales who has studied at Catholic University, the University of Fribourg, and the University of St. Michael's College, Toronto. He has taught theology at seminary and college levels before joining the staff of the Center of Renewal at Stella Niagara, N.Y. in 1980. There, in addition to general retreat and renewal work, he established DeSales Resource Center, which offers a research library, a book and tape service, and various programs in the spirituality of Francis de Sales and Jane de Chantal.

Author of the Preface
HENRI J.M. NOUWEN has written widely on modern spirituality. He has taught pastoral theology at Yale and Harvard Divinity Schools and is the author of many books, including *Reaching Out, The Way of the Heart, With Open Hands* and *Out of Solitude.*

Acknowledgements

From its inception this volume has been a shared undertaking. We who have worked most directly on it have shared our various tasks and have worked together as closely as our diverse locations allowed. Furthermore we are very conscious of having been surrounded and supported by a host of others without whom our task would have been impossible. In particular we would like to express our indebtedness to the following:

To Sister Marie-Patricia Burns of the Visitation community in Annecy, France, who contributed immensely to this volume at every step of the way, and whose unique expertise in the correspondence of St. Jane de Chantal was unstintingly shared with us.

To Mother Marie-Agnès Coppé, Superior of the Annecy Visitation, for her kind permission to use the classic Annecy edition of St. Francis de Sales' *Oeuvres complètes* and the Plon edition of St. Jane de Chantal, *Sa Vie et ses oeuvres*.

To Editions du Cerf, the French publisher of a first critical edition of Jane de Chantal's letters, for permission to translate three previously unpublished letters from among those which will appear in that edition.

To Doctor Elisabeth Stopp of Cambridge, England for her inspiring example in Salesian scholarship and for permission to draw on her recently recorded reflections about the two saints she knows so well.

To Father Anthony Ceresko, O.S.F.S., Associate Professor of Old Testament at St. Michael's College in the Toronto School of Theology, for assistance with Francis de Sales' biblical citations.

To the many who suggested improvements in the text at various stages of its development, especially Sister Mary Regina McCabe, V.H.M. of St. Paul, Minnesota, and Roger Bergman in Omaha, Nebraska.

To administrators and colleagues of our respective institutions for understanding and encouragement, especially to Dean Richard Clifford, S.J. of Weston School of Theology, where much of the word-processing was done.

ACKNOWLEDGEMENTS

To those whose typing and computer skills advanced the text from stage to stage, notably to Teresa Busher at Weston, Sister Catherine Gale, O.S.F. at Stella Niagara, Jackie Lynch in Omaha, and several alumnae of the Visitation School in St. Paul.

To Sister Mary Paula McCarthy, V.H.M., of St. Paul, who developed and verified the Index.

Finally and most especially to Father Henri Nouwen for introducing and enhancing this volume with his preface.

PREFACE

When I started reading the letters of Francis de Sales and Jane de Chantal published in this book, I expected to be faced with an old fashioned piety that might be of some historical interest but would not be able to touch the hearts of men and women of the nuclear age. But when I finished, I knew that I had met a man and a woman of such spiritual depth and breadth that the period between 1567, the year of Francis's birth, and 1641, the year of Jane's death, was but a sowing season of their spiritual influence. In fact I am gradually becoming aware that our contemporary predicament allows us to find in these letters what is crucial for our own spiritual survival: a Jesus-centered, affectionate friendship.

This Jesus-centered, affectionate friendship pervades all the letters that Francis and Jane wrote to their correspondents, but the source is clearly the friendship between themselves. Regretfully, most of the letters of Jane to Francis have been destroyed and, therefore, we can only indirectly discern the mutuality of their friendship. Still, there is no doubt that all the letters published in this book—the letters from Francis to Jane as well as the many letters from Francis and Jane to others—are undergirded by the "bond of perfection" that bound them together in a mutual Jesus-centered love.

What is most obvious from this correspondence is that Jesus stands in the center of the lives of both Francis and Jane. The love of God revealed in Jesus Christ pervades every line of the letters they both wrote. They are two people whose friendship is solidly anchored in their common love of God. It is a mediated friendship. There lies the secret of their freedom and their fruitfulness. Francis and Jane are not two lonely people who cling to each other in order to find a safe home in the midst of a fearful world. Both of them have found Jesus as the bridegroom of their souls. He is the fulfilment of all their desires. He himself makes their friendship possible. They have been given to each other as spiritual friends, to enjoy each other's spiritual gifts, to support each other in their commitment to faithfulness, to be of mutual help in their search for perfection and to give shape to a new spiritual family in the Church. In an era in which so much emphasis is put on the interpersonal and so much attention is given to emotions, passions and feelings as the "stuff" that makes or breaks relationships, the Jesus-centered friendship between Francis de Sales and Jane de Chantal is a challenge to us. Without Jesus, friends tend to become possessive of each other and are easily tempted to violence when mutual expectations are not fulfilled. With Jesus there remains ample freedom for the unique ways of the individual persons. Without Jesus, friends tend to close in on each other and ignore the larger world. With Jesus friendships can bear fruit which many can enjoy. Francis and Jane show us clearly that the deepest intimacy among people is an intimacy that finds its origin and goal not in the human partners, but in God who gives people to each other in friendship to be incarnate manifestations of the divine love. Most noticeable in the friendship which Francis and Jane show for each other and the people entrusted to their care is the affectionate quality.

There is a remarkable directness with which affection is expressed in these letters. On June 24, 1604, Francis writes to Jane:

> I know you have complete confidence in my affection; I have no doubt about this and delight in the thought. I want you to know and to believe that I have an intense and very special desire to serve you with all my strength. It would be impossible for me to explain either the quality or the greatness of this desire that I have to be at your service, but I can tell you that I believe it is from God, and for that reason, I cherish it and every day see it growing and increasing remarkably. If it were appropriate, I would say more, and say it in all truth, but I had better stop here. Dear Madam, you can see clearly enough to what extent you may call on me and trust me. Make the most of my affection and of all that God has given me for the service of your soul. I am all yours; give no more thought to the role or to the rank I hold in being yours. God has given me to you; so consider me as yours in Him, and call me whatever you like; it makes no difference.

This is but one of the many expressions of affection which characterize the spiritual letters of these friends. The deep affection they have for each other is generously shared with all the women and men with whom they enter into a spiritual relationship. There is no holding back, no careful distance, no concern about possible misinter-

PREFACE

pretations, no fear for too much too soon. To the contrary, there is a constant encouragement to be open, direct and spontaneous. Both Francis and Jane give and receive affection freely and share it generously with all who are part of their spiritual family.

In a time in which there is so much concern about the right professional distance within a helping relationship and in which there is so much preoccupation with transference and counter-transference, Jane de Chantal and Francis de Sales offer us a fresh perspective on a healing relationship. They dare to take risks with each other and those they care for. Mutuality is the word here. It is the mutuality of the ministry of Jesus the Good Shepherd who says: "I know my own and my own know me" (Jn 10:14). A mutual openness, a mutual sharing, a mutual confession of needs, a mutual confession and forgiveness, a mutual knowing and being known—that is the source of a community where God's strength is made manifest among weak people. The Jesus-centered affectionate friendship between Francis de Sales and Jane de Chantal, generously shared with the many who came to them for spiritual comfort and consolation, is a great gift to our century.

I rejoice in the publication of these letters in the English language. They encourage us to make Jesus the center of all our relationships and then create the space for each other in which we can express our affection without fear in mutual vulnerability. In our distrustful, fearful and fragmented world constantly exploding in violence and destruction, friendships such as lived out by Francis and Jane and expressed in these letters point the way to healing, reconciliation and new life. How to develop and nurture such friendships? This book suggests that writing letters may still be one of the most fruitful ways.

Giving less hours to the dark violent forces of contemporary entertainment and more to writing letters in the spirit of Jesus is a true discipline of friendship. During the quiet peaceful hours that we spend communicating God's love to others in our letters, we build a new community and bring light into the world. This is what Francis and Jane did in their time. This is what we still can do in ours. I have little doubt that the fruits will be plentiful.

Henri J.M. Nouwen

INTRODUCTION

At the head of each of the letters she wrote and throughout the writings he penned the words "Live Jesus!" appeared.[1] This exclamation was for Jane de Chantal and Francis de Sales an emphatic statement about how they saw themselves and what they were about in the world. For them "Live Jesus!" was far more than a cheer of affirmation or a rallying cry in the manner of *Vive le Roi!* It was expressive of the particular vision of the Christian life that they sought to bring to birth in their own persons. To study Salesian spirituality—the spiritual tradition parented by de Sales and de Chantal—is then to reflect on the distinctive way in which this French woman and this man from Savoy allowed Jesus to live in themselves and in those they directed.[2]

Certainly the entire history of Christian spirituality might be said to be the attempt on the part of myriads of diverse personalities situated in differing historical moments and with the particular socio-political, cultural, and theological tools at their disposal to let Jesus live.[3] From this point of departure, Salesian spirituality is but one example of a continuing endeavor. Undergirding all Christian spiritual traditions is the insistence that human beings, to be true to their deepest insights, must follow the way to God opened for them by Jesus of Nazareth, in some way taking on the reality of the life he lived.[4] The essential pattern of that life has generally been under-

---

1. "Vive Jésus" became the motto of the Visitation of Holy Mary, the congregation founded by Francis de Sales and Jane de Chantal. It is also found in the dedicatory prayer that launches de Sales's famous *Introduction to the Devout Life* and in his *Treatise on the Love of God*, Book XII, Ch. 13, as well as scattered throughout his letters and occasional writings.

2. At this time Savoy was an independent duchy governed by Duke Charles-Emmanuel and politically linked with Turin. Culturally Savoy was influenced by France. Jane was from Dijon in Burgundy.

3. One insightful attempt to write just such a history, with the Crucifixion as central organizing principle, is Rowan Williams, *Christian Spirituality: A Theological History from the New Testament to Luther and St. John of the Cross* (Atlanta: John Knox Press, 1980). Cf. also *Une Spiritualité pour tous*, Textes choisis et présentés par Claude Roffat (Paris: Editions du Centurion, 1980), for a brief discussion of the various Christian spiritualities as they relate to the Gospel and to Christ.

4. This statement is especially true of pre-Reformation spirituality and, after the sixteenth century, the Catholic tradition. Mainline Protestant traditions, with differing anthropological assumptions and predominantly theocentric syntheses, tend not to focus upon the

9

stood to be one of self-emptying in order to be filled with God. It is this process of self-emptying and being filled—one's dying and rising—that is known in traditional Catholic terminology as the ascetic life and the mystical life. The entire progress of the human endeavor is thus articulated with a language (both verbal and pictorial) fashioned from the paradigmatic life, death, and resurrection of Jesus Christ. The question "How does Jesus live?" could therefore be asked of any Christian spirituality. The answers would differ depending on the ways in which individuals or groups of believers understand *who* Jesus is and the way in which they envision the process of ridding the self of obstacles that are in the way of Jesus's showing forth. Put another way, each variety of Christian spirituality will project a slightly different asceticism and a somewhat variant mystical perception.

But the motto "Live Jesus!" is more than simply descriptive of a wider Christian contemplative assumption about the human drama and thus aptly applied to the Salesian spirit as well. "Live Jesus" belongs especially to that spirit. The tradition of spirituality that this volume represents and which this introductory essay attempts to analyze is well encoded in the pithy phrase that Jane de Chantal so boldly inscribed as she began each act of correspondence.

To "Live Jesus" was to have—in Francis de Sales's words—the name of Jesus engraved on one's heart.[5] It was to allow that name to become one's own true name, to allow one's entire self—body, thoughts, affections, actions, decisions, work, devotion—to be animated by the reality of the person known by that name. To allow Jesus to live one did not simply learn about Jesus or pray to Jesus or even imitate Jesus. One surrendered the vital center of one's being—

---

activity or cooperation of the human person in "letting" Jesus live. For some insight see Frank C. Senn, ed., *Protestant Spiritual Traditions* (New Jersey: Paulist Press, 1986). The eastern Christian teachings on deification as the central dynamic of the spiritual life also approach the issue of making Jesus live from a different perspective. On this see Louis Bouyer, *A History of Christian Spirituality*, Vol. 3, *Protestant and Orthodox Traditions* (N.Y.: Desclée Co., 1969).

5. *Oeuvres de Saint François de Sales, Evêque de Genève et Docteur de l'Eglise, Edition Complète,* d'après les autographes et les éditions originales . . . publiée . . . par les soins des Religieuses de la Visitation de Iᵉʳ Monastère d'Annecy, 27 vols. (Annecy: J. Niérat *et al.*, 1892–1964), III, 217: *Introduction,* III, 23. Throughout the present volume we will cite the Annecy edition simply as *Oeuvres,* followed by the volume and page; to this we will generally add an indication of the work referred to and its appropriate subdivisions, in this case the *Introduction to the Devout Life,* Bk III, chapter 23, thus making it possible for users of other editions or translations to find the reference.

one's heart, as understood in the wholistic biblical sense—to another living presence.[6] The Pauline dictum "I no longer live but Christ lives in me"[7] is at the core of the distinctive Salesian inscription. Jesus was for the two early seventeenth-century founders of the Salesian tradition a presence to be experienced, a reality to be lived. Authentic human existence was identified by them as the continual and ever-present bringing to life of the living Lord who bears the name Jesus.

Two Sources of the Tradition

To have begun with an exclamation used both by Francis de Sales and Jane de Chantal is to already suggest a distinctive if not unique perspective adopted in the present volume. Typically it is Francis de Sales alone who has been viewed as the originator of Salesian spirituality—as the name itself suggests. Scholarly opinion has held that the Genevan bishop created an eminently personal form of thought which never developed beyond the confines of the shape he gave it.[8] Given this assumption, Jane de Chantal emerges in the secondary literature as a subordinate figure, at the least as a dutiful disciple of a great master who simply handed on his theories or, at best, as the chief artistic creation of his direction, as a woman with a particular (and somewhat untempered) personality who was molded and sanctified by the masterful hand of her guide. We have not held to this view.

First, because of the long intimacy of these two friends and the extent to which each of their own spiritual orientations was radically influenced by their relationship, it is difficult to claim that the spirituality they held in common came from only one of them.[9] In any

---

6. André Ravier writes, "The heart (in the Salesian sense) refers, as it does in the Bible, to that which is most profound, inalienable, personal and divine in us; it is the mysterious center where each person meets God, responds to his call or refuses it." *Un Sage et Un Saint: François de Sales* (Paris: Nouvelle Cité, 1985), p. 128.

7. Galatians 2:20. Another Pauline text underlying Francis's notion of "living Jesus" is Colossians 3:3: "Your life is hidden now with Christ in God." Cf. his commentary in *Treatise on the Love of God*, VII, 6 and 7.

8. Cf. Louis Cognet, *Histoire de la Spiritualité chrétienne*, III, *La Spiritualité moderne* (Paris: Aubier, 1966), pp. 299ff.

9. On their friendship, Wendy M. Wright, *Bond of Perfection: Jeanne de Chantal and François de Sales* (New Jersey: Paulist Press, 1985).

long-term relationship of depth, two persons give birth to each other, creating each other anew in the interaction that transpires between them. This certainly can be said of these two figures. It is true that when Madame de Chantal met Monseigneur de Sales and became his directee he was already well formed in his creative vision. His influence on her was central to her religious experience during the formative early years of their relationship, and she continued to venerate him to the end of her life. Yet, after the initial years of their interaction, during which time Francis was the dominant figure, the two of them entered a period of intense and mutually supportive friendship. During this time Jane was teacher as much as Francis, sharing with him the depth of her inner life with God, enriching his own perceptions of the Christian life through her experience and collaborating with him in the creation of their community, the Visitation of Holy Mary.

Indeed, aside from his initial vision of the community and his conscientious but periodic spiritual direction sustained by either his actual presence or through his written works, the nurturance of the Visitation was very much up to Jane de Chantal. In that context, the spirituality that they shared was worked out in a specific and quite unique way as it had not been by de Sales himself. Salesian spirituality as it became known in the only religious community that the bishop was instrumental in founding was very much a matter of Jane de Chantal's handiwork. As such, it bears the imprint of her own personality and religiosity in a unique way.

There are then, in our opinion, two primary historical forms in which Salesian spirituality is embodied. One is in the person of Francis de Sales: active bishop, spiritual director, writer, preacher, correspondent with persons in all walks of life, reformer, advocate of lay devotion, preacher to the royal court. The other is found in the person of Jane de Chantal and the community of the Visitation: a quasi-monastic women's congregation formed by a woman who identified closely with her roles as wife and mother, and peopled by women attempting to live out a vision of mutual charity in imitation of and interior intimacy with the humble, gentle Jesus. It is from these two distinct yet interconnected vessels that that tradition flows into the stream of history, and it is these two vessels which are given to the historian as sources to examine when trying to discern the shape and texture of what it means to "Live Jesus."

INTRODUCTION

To put it somewhat differently, Salesian spirituality contains more variety, more richness and nuance than has previously been acknowledged. The two springs from which that spirituality flows have much in common; there is a basic gestalt that identifies both as Salesian. But these parents of the tradition lived out their common spirit in quite different vocational circumstances. Furthermore, they were very distinctive personalities and brought to their shared views their own life histories, capabilities, and religious perceptions. Jane and Francis employed essentially the same religious language, but in fact that language, in function, tone, and assimilation, was not identical, as will be shown later. It is arguable that past efforts have insufficiently explored the wealth of religious insight or the complexity of the spirituality that this language, viewed in more than one form, can yield.

Letters of Spiritual Direction

The Salesian tradition parented by Francis and Jane is observed most clearly in the place where it "lives" most vigorously. Like other spiritual traditions, it is essentially a lived experience, which only secondarily produces and is nourished by a written expression. It is a tradition known by assimilation, internalized only gradually through personal contact and communication. Among the various vital exchanges between persons, the practice of spiritual direction has held a privileged place in the Salesian tradition from its very origins.

A preliminary description of spiritual direction may be helpful here, although much can be gleaned from the letters themselves. Salesian direction was not simply the passing on of a system of ideas or methods of prayer. It was first and foremost a process of intuitive response practiced between two persons. The director was one who authentically lived the vocation of Christian. The style envisioned for this vocation was firmly rooted in the cultural context of early seventeenth-century Catholicism. The directee came to the director seeking some of the authenticity perceived there. To put it in the historical terminology: he or she felt called to the devout life lived in the name of Jesus and came to discover how such a life might be fashioned. The directee brought the nascent yearning of his or her heart and the director then helped that person to learn to identify those promptings, to "lean toward" the center of the self, to distinguish movements of the heart that seemed to be from God from those which seemed to be aligned to purposes alien to God, and to propose possible practices that might encourage the free expression of those God-born impulses as well as practices that might curb the impulses born of other sources.[10] Salesian direction was always personal and unique to each directee. It was concrete and adapted to the particular temperament and life circumstances in which a given individual found himself or herself.

The director in this situation did not see himself or herself as a professional dispensing information to the uninformed but as a fellow Christian walking the same road as the directee. In such a context all director/directee relationships might be viewed as spiritual friendships although the intensity and mutuality of the actual friendships Jane and Francis enjoyed differed greatly according to the parties involved.

Such was, in general outline, the lived reality of spiritual direction as practiced by Francis and Jane, and, if it has been possible to reconstruct something of that context, it is largely due to the letters they have written as a means of continuing the process of direction while at a distance.

"Letters of spiritual direction" has come to constitute a genre of spiritual literature, a formalized mode of communicating general spiritual advice, so it is important to stress that the letters in this volume do not fit into that category. In a way they preceded the genre, and arose as the only way of continuing the kind of direction process just sketched when the two people were separated. As such they are spontaneous, personal, and as varied as the relationships they sustained and nourished. Each of them was written for the person addressed, and none of them was written with the thought of publication.

At the same time, these letters embody an art and a style of their own, an unselfconscious art that tends to hide itself, and a style that is closer to the dialogue of spoken language.[11] This seems true

---

10. Francis Vincent, *St. François de Sales, Directeur d'âmes: l'éducation de la volonté* (Paris: Gabriel Beauchesne, 1923), is an older but comprehensive study of the Genevan bishop as director.

11. On the unique style of Francis's letters, see André Ravier, *Un Sage et un saint, François*

of all of Jane's writings, and it can help account for the differences in style and vocabulary between Francis's letters and his published works. Francis, who knew well the importance of writing for the age in which he lived when he wrote for publication, wrote more freely when he penned these letters, and he encouraged his correspondents to do the same: "Don't pay any attention to how well your letters are constructed before you send them to me."[12]

Thus letter-writing was one method by which spiritual direction might legitimately be carried on. As such, it was a creative as well as a descriptive medium with the power to be formative for both writer and reader. In this sense, the letters reproduced here, while obviously literary in the general sense, are also primary sources for what is not at root a literary enterprise.

The Genevan bishop once wrote to Madame de Chantal that he believed that the reason persons are in the world is

> . . . to receive and carry the gentle Jesus: on our tongue by proclaiming Him; in our arms by doing good works; on our shoulders by supporting the yoke of dryness and sterility in both the interior and exterior senses. . . . [13]

The same might be said of the pen in hand.[14] It is through the living exchange of letters that Jesus might be carried more faithfully by the correspondents both individually and together.

To focus on the letters of direction as a means of plumbing Salesian spirituality is not meant to detract from other writings where it can also be found, notably in the published works of both saints. Francis's works especially have enjoyed wide popularity, and deservedly so. But in addition to all the intrinsic reasons flowing from the nature of the letters themselves, the choice of letters rather than other works for this volume was prompted by two practical considerations. On the one hand, de Sales's published works are available

---

de Sales (Paris: Nouvelle cité, 1985), pp. 127–129, and Elisabeth Stopp, St. Francis de Sales, Selected Letters (New York: Harper, 1960), pp. 35–39.

12. Oeuvres, XVIII, 400: Letter MDXXIX.

13. Oeuvres, XIV, 211: Letter DLV.

14. Francis de Sales, it should be noted, is officially the patron saint of Catholic journalists.

in accurate English translations.[15] On the other hand, some of the writings published under the name de Chantal, because they were never written for publication and because they were in fact written down from memory by her sister Visitandines, are of uneven aesthetic quality and questionable authenticity.[16] The great exception to this is her letters of direction which constitute an extensive, authentic, and personal witness to her spirit. In this they are a fitting counterpart to the letters of Francis, which she collected, edited and published a few years after his death. Hence from a textual point of view, their respective letters are the most apt means of entering into the vision and the spirituality they shared.

Jane's letters begin with the expansive outburst, "Live Jesus!" Who was this Jesus who was entreated to live? What was the face Francis and Jane hoped to see alive in the faces of those they directed? Who was the person they hoped would animate their own lives? To begin to answer these questions three efforts must be made. First, it is necessary to suggest the various contexts in which the Salesian spirit came to be: the socio-political context, the biographical context of its founders' lives, and the evolving context of western Christian spirituality as it flowed in and around them. Second, it will be necessary to paint a picture of the whole of Salesian spirituality. This will be done somewhat impressionistically, portraying what is Salesian not as a logical system of thought—for such an attempt surely must fail to capture the depth and color that is there—but by suggesting six thematic clusters that, when viewed as a whole and at something of a distance, create an effect suggestive of the living spiritual reality. Third, it will be necessary to distin-

---

15. See especially *Introduction to the Devout Life*, trans. John K. Ryan (New York: Doubleday, 1982) and *Treatise on the Love of God*, 2 vols., trans. John K. Ryan (Rockford, Ill.: TAN Books, 1974).

16. This is particularly true of the *Traité sur oraison* which bears her name but actually may be a collection of spiritual sayings garnered from diverse sources by Visitandines of the eighteenth or nineteenth century. Her *Entretiens* and *Conférences* bear the marks of oral reflections that have been recorded by a variety of listeners. These are all found in her collected works, Ste. Jeanne Françoise Frémyot de Chantal, *Sa Vie et ses oeuvres*, édition publiée par les soins des Religieuses du Premier Monastère de la Visitation Sainte-Marie d'Annecy, 8 vols. (Paris: Plon, 1874–79), which also contains the *Life* of Mère de Chaugy, a reliable, if secondary, historical source. Perhaps the best example of her authentic writing is the *Responses* which is not included in the Plon collection but published separately as *Réponses de Notre Sainte Mère, Jeanne Françoise Frémiot, Baronne de Chantal sur les règles, constitutions et coutumier de l'Institut* (Annecy: Imprimerie de Aimé Burdet, 1849).

guish between the unique spiritual styles of Jane de Chantal and Francis de Sales, looking to several central ideas they held in common to perceive how each one understood and lived out those ideas.

This impressionistic portrait, whose main features have been culled from the experiences of both Jane de Chantal and Francis de Sales, and known to us, the editors and translator, variously through historical inquiry and present affiliation, will, we hope, serve as a useful introduction to the letters of Salesian spiritual direction presented here.

The Historical Context

The time was the turn of the seventeenth century. The place was eastern France and the neighboring duchy of Savoy. In the preceding three-quarters of a century Christian Europe had experienced the birthpangs of an entirely new era: the emerging nation states of the continent were torn in bloody warfare—nation against nation, king against prince, Roman against Reformed Christian, emperor against pope, peasant against ruler, family dynasties against each other; modern vernacular languages were in their adolescences; the scientific discoveries of Copernicus and Galileo were reshaping the mental map of western thought as were the philosophic ideas of Montaigne, Ronsard, and Rabelais; the powerful critique of Christendom leveled by Luther, Calvin, Zwingli, and other reformers rocked the foundations of society; on the radical fringe of the magisterial reformation fresh attempts were made to realize the fullness of Christian community in sectarian terms; biblical exegesis was given a new direction through the infusion of the sense of historical perspective so congenial to the Renaissance mind; the Catholic consolidation at the Council of Trent gave energy to a new militant and reformed Roman Church; Ignatius Loyola, Angela Merici, Teresa of Avila, John of the Cross, Philip Neri, and Pierre de Bérulle put their formidable talents behind the creation of new religious communities destined to infuse the religious atmosphere of Europe with their vital spirits.

It was that hinge time, much neglected in English historiography, between the medieval and modern worlds. It was a time of violence motivated especially by religious intolerance, the era of what have become known as the "wars of religion." Into this world Francis de Sales and Jane Frances Frémyot were born.[1] The country

---

1. The most accessible biographies of the two saints in English are, for Jane, Elisabeth Stopp, *Madame de Chantal: Portrait of a Saint* (London: Faber and Faber, 1962) and, for Francis, Michael de la Bedoyere, *François de Sales* (New York: Harper and Bros., 1960). French biographies include Henri Bremond, *Sainte Chantal* (Paris: J. Gabalda, 1912), André Ravier, *Un Sage et un saint: François de Sales* (Paris: Nouvelle Cité, 1985) and E.M. Lajeunie, *Saint François de Sales, L'homme, la pensée, l'action* (Paris: Guy Victor, 1966, 2 vols.). An English translation

of his birth was Savoy, of hers, France. He was the son of an aristocratic family claiming loyalty to the Savoyard duke and exercising limited but influential service within the duchy's mountainous regions. She was the daughter of a Dijonese lawyer, a member of the rising class of "nobles of the robe" who secured their place and imprint in French society through legal and diplomatic channels.

From 1567 and 1572 respectively until 1604 their two lives did not intersect. Francis was the first-born child of Francis de Boisy and his young wife. A much gifted boy, beloved especially by his mother, Francis was prepared for a distinguished career. At the age of eleven he was sent to Paris to school. He pressed his family to let him attend the Jesuit college of Clermont, an institution noted not only for its academic excellence but for the depth of the religious and moral vision it promulgated.[2] There he followed the humanist curriculum, becoming instructed in the literary and communicative arts, reading philosophy, and perfecting his skills in horsemanship, fencing, and dancing. Following his own bent, he also took courses in theology beyond his own curriculum. He received the nourishment of the Greek and Latin classics leavened with the agent of Christian principles. On his own initiative he began the study of scripture, following the lectures of Gilbert Génébrard, who in 1584 was commenting on the *Song of Songs*.

It was in Paris between 1586–87 that he underwent a great spiritual crisis that eventually yielded to the religious insights that were to be formative in his thought for the rest of his life. The issue was predestination, a theological topic hotly debated in both Catholic and Reform circles. For the young de Sales the crisis over predestination presented itself as a personal dilemma. Was he fated to be parted forever from the God, the good, he loved so ardently? The pain of the crisis was particularly acute because from childhood he had enjoyed a radiant sense of loving and being loved by God. The fear of separation from this most central and unifying focus of his life was devastating. It has been suggested that his anguish arose from an interior conflict.[3] Entranced by the charms of Parisian

---

of this last work is in progress at present. Vol. I is available: *Saint Francis de Sales, the Man, the Thinker, His Influence* (Bangalore, India: S.F.S. Publications, 1986).

2. Cf. Elisabeth Stopp, "St. Francis de Sales at Clermont College" in *Salesian Studies*, 6 (Winter 1969) pp. 42–63.

3. Ravier has a helpful treatment of the Paris crisis in his Preface to the Pléiade edition,

womanhood, urged on by the adolescent escapades of companions, the young Savoyard seems to have discovered within himself a leaning that was at variance with the morally disciplined life he had set out to cultivate. This and a sudden recognition of human limitation may have fanned the fires of his doubt. He plunged into a period of despair, fell ill, and was unable to eat or sleep. The crisis came to a head as he came to perceive his God-given ability to love in the present. The issue, felt at a deep emotional level, was the realization of radical human dependence. Francis needed to abandon himself unconditionally to the mercy of God. To do that involved accepting the idea that he might indeed, in some unforeseen future, be eternally damned. Once he had done just this and cast away the anxious attention he was giving to protecting himself from such a fate, he was able to perceive the gift that was given. Now, regardless of what the future might hold, he was utterly free to love to the fullest of his capacity. And love he would in joyous celebration of the potential of the present moment.[4]

But de Sales's insight did not stop there. The focus in his struggle had been wrongly directed. He had labored too much under the sense of his own inability to attain salvation. He had failed to look to the God revealed in the figure of Jesus. The theological dimension of his crisis came to the fore at Padua where the young Savoyard went in 1588 to continue his graduate studies.[5] The university there was at the time the center of Italian humanist currents of thought. Students from all over Europe came to sit at the feet of the acclaimed faculty. In accord with paternal ambition, Francis took up the study of law, a discipline which he found somewhat tedious. Under the spiritual direction of Jesuit Fr. Possevin, he continued to immerse himself in private theological studies as well. It was at this time that the predestination issue took on formal theological overtones. Francis had been

---

Saint François de Sales, Oeuvres (Paris: Gallimard, 1969), pp. xxviii–xxxiii. It is Lajeunie, Vol. I, pp. 138ff, who suggests that adolescent sexuality might have been part of Francis' crisis.

    4. Francis' own words about the crisis are reported by his earliest biographer on the testimony of his tutor and other witnesses in the canonization proceedings.

> Will I be deprived of the grace of the One who has so kindly let me experience his delights, and who has shown himself so loving to me? . . . However that may be, Lord, at the very least let me love you in this life if I am not able to love you in eternal life—for no one praises you in hell (cf. Ps. 6:5).

Oeuvres, XXII, 18–19. A similar text is given, *ibid.*, pp. 19–20.

    5. Cf. Ravier's Preface to the Pléiade edition, pp. xxxiii–xxxv, on the Padua crisis.

studying Thomas Aquinas and Augustine. He regarded them as luminaries. But on the issue of predestination he parted their company. "Prostrating himself at the feet" of the two fathers he adopted a position which affirmed that the will of God was to save all of humankind. In a heartfelt account he recorded his struggle to rest in conscience with this decision, proclaiming his intention to glorify and exalt the divine name which had revealed itself on the cross not as "he who condemns" but as "Savior." Ready at any time to be informed about his possible error in this matter, Francis in fact worked out for himself a theological opinion that was in harmony not only with gospel teaching but with his experienced sense of the unconditional love of God that creates, sustains, and desires to redeem all humankind as well as with his felt sense of the freedom of the human will to choose or not to choose to respond to this love.

There is a way in which this second phase of the Savoyard's crisis both confirmed and deepened the insight gained in the first phase in Paris. The initial enlightenment involved grasping the truth of the freedom of the human person to love or not to love. It involved seeing that this was a possibility at every moment. It was a receiving of that gift. It was also a recognition of the responsibility that this gifted state implied. The next enlightenment came with the realization that, although this gifted freedom is real and expansive (thus emphasizing the power of human choice), the compassion and mercy of the divine life are prior to such freedom. God's love sustains, draws forth, and perfects all that is within the power of human beings to do. And God's mercy is ultimately greater than the choices the human person may make. This dual knowledge—of human freedom and the loving will of God toward humankind—formed forever after Francis de Sales's vision of the Christian life.

In fact, the theological point of view that de Sales adopted was the position that was being worked out by the Jesuit Molina in his *Concord of Free Will with the Gift of Grace*, published in 1588, and taken up by Jesuit followers. The emergence of this idea engendered several decades of heated debate, the first portion of which was carried on by Molinists and Thomists; the second was carried to the highest levels of Dominican and Jesuit theological dispute.[6] The fra-

---

6. Lajeunie shows that the position rejected by Francis is not that of Thomas himself but of his interpreters. See *Saint François*, Vol. I, p. 153.

cas was never settled in favor of either opinion but laid to rest by a firm papal warning to cease disputation issued in 1606. In fact, Francis de Sales, by then a noted churchman, was consulted in the process of papal discernment.

At Padua the young de Sales delved deeply not only into current theological controversy but into contemporary philosophy, especially the philosophy of beauty, which was so much a part of the intellectual climate of the Italian town.[7] The writings of Marsiglio Ficino, Giovanni Della Casa, and Pierre Charron contributed to this climate. They taught that inherent in the human soul was a longing for beauty and a love of the good. The source of this longing, indeed the source of all beauty and goodness itself, is (for Ficino especially) God. The contemplation of all that participates in beauty and goodness leads to the contemplation of God. Thus there developed an entire aesthetic of the person which aimed at making the person beautiful through the cultivation of wisdom. The excellence and perfection of humanity lay in the creation of a beautiful whole: interior, exterior, thought, action, and movement. De Sales's approach to Christian living, to the free response that the person made to the liberty and the prior love that came from God, was to be deeply indebted to this philosophy of beauty current at Padua during his years there.

Returning in 1592 to his paternal home in Savoy, the youthful Francis expressed his desire to become a priest. This was not the career his father had in mind for his talented son but, with his mother's persuasive aid, he was granted the familial blessing to thus dispose his life. Despite the fact that he had never been in a seminary nor followed a program of theology, it was felt that, because of his private study and close supervision by spiritual directors, he was ready for the priesthood. He accepted the post of provost of the Church of St. Peter of Geneva (a more lofty first position than he would have preferred but one that satisfied his father's ambitions). He was assistant to the bishop, Claude de Granier. At this time the bishop exercised his diocesan functions not from the traditional seat of the diocese, Geneva, but from the mountain village of Annecy some fifty miles south. Geneva had for some time been a Calvinist

---

7. Cf. James Langelaan, O.S.F.S., *Man in Love with God: Introduction to the Theology and Spirituality of Saint Francis de Sales*, unpublished paper, Hyattsville, MD, 1976.

stronghold, recognizing a theocratic system of government that could not allow for religious pluralism or even the limited exercise of a variant faith. All Catholics had been banned from Geneva in 1568 and much of the territory traditionally under the administrative and spiritual influence of de Granier's see no longer admitted Roman worship. In his inaugural sermon the new provost pledged himself to the task of winning Geneva back to Catholicism, and he urged his fellow clergy to assist—not by force of arms, as would be attempted in the abortive "escalade" of 1604—but by reforming themselves and by unleashing the power of love.

As a matter of fact a change in the political control of the Chablais, a region south of the Lake of Geneva, had prompted Duke Charles Emmanuel of Savoy to ask Bishop Granier to send missionary preachers into the area. Francis immediately volunteered, and spent four difficult years there. He preached, wrote, and witnessed to the faith he professed. His manifest skills of persuasion aided the successful campaign. De Sales saw himself in his missionary role as reconquering by love and as restoring rightful peace to a wartorn Christian family.[8] While his persuasive efforts were often accompanied and reinforced by the less pacific encouragement of political maneuvers, he nonetheless carried out his own evangelization using only the weapons of pen and tongue. As part of his activity he also traveled to Geneva to take part in several secret dialogue sessions with the noted Reformed spokesman, Theodore Beza, and he published his *Defense of the Standard of the Holy Cross*, a work representing the fruits of reflections forged while thick in the fray of Protestant/Catholic debate.

The provost desired to reconquer Geneva and restore the unity of the Christian faith within the confines of his diocese. He also saw as his long-range tasks the application of the reforms of the Council of Trent and the building up of a wide community of "devout souls" who would live out the life of Christian perfection in all their varied states and vocations. When he became bishop in 1602, it was to see the culmination of these desires that de Sales applied administrative pressure and persuasive skill. All clerics in his diocese were to be theologically educated, morally sound, and function as true shepherds to their spiritual flocks. They were to be resident at their posts

---

8. Francis as peacemaker is treated in E.J. Lajeunie, *Saint François*, Vol. II, pp. 99ff.

and preach the gospel. Monasteries were to observe the purity of their rules and, reforming their sometimes decadent practices, become springs of spiritual sustenance for the entire community. Francis de Sales himself took these obligations most seriously. He preached, often and with charismatic fervor. He administered the sacraments. He taught, personally attending to the instruction of children. He wrote voluminously for the instruction, edification, and reformation of the Christian community.

All men and women were encouraged to become authentic Christians, to realize the gospel with their lives. One means by which this was to be done was through spiritual direction. Francis became director for many individuals yearning to realize authentic Christian lives. He also encouraged others to direct and to seek direction. Exemplary of those he came to direct was Madame de Charmoisy, wife of a courtier at the decadent French court. This young woman sought to live out her religious desires to realize a greater love of God and to live in accord with that love. De Sales saw no obstacle to her, or any Christian for that matter, in achieving a life of authentic devotion and true love of God. His *Introduction to the Devout Life*, which was soon enthusiastically received all over France, was a structured reworking of the letters he had written to Madame de Charmoisy and others like her who sought him out for direction. He saw himself as building up the larger Church by giving wings to the religious aspirations of the laity, aiding in the creation of a community of true devotion that would animate the body of Christ.

In this desire to refresh the Church with new sources of life de Sales was very much a part of his times. Europe and especially France was witnessing an era of profound renewal. Laity and clergy alike were hungry for spiritual nourishment. Devotional classics, newly translated into the vernacular, began to circulate freely. New spiritual writers gained popularity. There was a thirst for the ascetic, the mystical, and the visionary.

Representative of this atmosphere was the Parisian Salon of Barbe Acarie. Madame Acarie was an aristocratic housewife who possessed rare spiritual capacity. The luminaries of the religious elite of her day were drawn to her home, there to imbibe some of her own wisdom and to exchange ideas with each other. Pierre de Bérulle, founder of the French Oratory, Benedict of Canfield, exponent of the French school of spirituality which taught a union of divine and human will through "anéantissement" (annihilation), and Francis de Sales were among those frequenting Madame Acarie's salon.[9]

Following the death of Bishop de Granier, de Sales succeeded to the episcopal post. In his duties he continued to spend himself in the service of Christian unity, Tridentine reform, and the creation of a true community of devotion. In March of 1604 he met Jane Frances Frémyot, Baroness de Chantal. She, a young widow, had come with her father to hear Monseigneur de Sales preach a series of Lenten sermons in Dijon. Jane had, since the death of her beloved husband several years previously, been struggling with an emerging sense of vocation, of being called to give herself utterly into the service of God. But with four small children and the responsibilities that her position as Baroness de Chantal entailed, she was floundering between desire and the painful and taxing facts of her daily life. Born the second child of Bénigne Frémyot, a Dijonese lawyer, Jane had never really known her mother who died in childbirth when she was just eighteen months old. She and her sister and brother (who survived the birth his mother did not) were raised by their supportive father and an aunt to be knowledgeable of practical, financial, and legal affairs, to retain a firm loyalty to the Catholic cause (her father was aligned with the Holy League which defended the Catholic succession to the French crown in opposition to the claims of Protestant pretendants) and to be a wife and mother befitting her station in life. She was married at twenty to Baron Christophe de Rabutin-Chantal, a handsome, somewhat high-living but reflective man only a few years her senior. It was a happy match. Jane was a devoted companion, a lively hostess, and she undertook the financial rehabilitation of the Chantal family's troubled estates. This she did with skill but not without initial trepidation and not without reaping the weariness that this long task wrung from her.

The couple gave birth to six children, four of whom survived infancy: Celse-Bénigne, Marie-Aimée, Françoise, and Charlotte. It was a mere two weeks after Charlotte was born that Christophe was killed in a freak hunting accident. He had been at home for some

---

9. For a useful overview of Post-Reformation Catholic spirituality which includes sections on Bérulle and Canfield, see Louis Cognet, *Post-Reformation Spirituality*, N.Y.: Hawthorn Books, 1959.

time, on leave from his soldier's duties, retired from royal service as a result of ill health and a public quarrel which effectively ended his career. Jane had been nursing him back to health. His unexpected death sent her into a grief process so deep and long that she was only beginning to emerge when she met de Sales several years later. In her widow's despair she had begun to discover new depths of religious aspiration, a new sense of hunger for God. She began to sense that she wished not to marry again but to give herself wholly to a life of prayer and service. During this time she was called by the capricious will of her father-in-law from the baronial estates where she had lived with her husband to the Chantal rural properties where the old man resided. Under threat of having her children disinherited, Jane took up residence there.

It was during the loneliness of her widowhood and during his rise to public service and visibility that Jane and Francis met. He became her director and began the process of enabling her to achieve spiritual liberty, that inner freedom that allows one to perceive and then to respond to the deepening layers of awareness of God's constant and challenging presence. The relationship of director and directee soon blossomed into a lasting friendship.[10] This friendship, born of their common love of God, was nurtured by their shared delight in each other's spiritual gifts and their mutual quest for perfection. Over the next six years the two of them discerned together both the future of Madame de Chantal's spiritual aspirations and the shape of a new project that would speak to the dreams of both their hearts. In 1610 they co-founded the Visitation of Holy Mary in Annecy in Savoy, a congregation for women who felt drawn to a life of religious commitment but who were not sufficiently young, robust, or free of family ties to enter one of the austere reformed women's communities or who were simply not attracted to the physical austerity of these houses or to the lukewarm religiosity of the older lax religious orders.

The Visitation offered to women such as these a home—simple and modest in its physical ascetic demands yet rigorous in its interior pursuit of authentic Christian charity—where they could flower and become "daughters of prayer." The women were to follow a simplified monastic routine, saying a shortened version of the

---

10. For a detailed treatment of this see Wright, *Bond of Perfection*.

daily office, engaging in modest work. They were women called to great intimacy with God who would realize a community of true charity among themselves. With graciousness, gentleness, and tender concern they were to lead each other to pure love of God. Women who had completed the novitiate were to express their love of God to neighbor by making visits to the poor and infirm in the surrounding neighborhood. There was also provision made for a limited number of laywomen to come within the community for brief periods of refreshment and retreat.

In part, the Visitation was one facet of de Sales's program for the building up of a society infused with the spirit of true devotion. In part, it was the culmination of the widow de Chantal's deepest personal longings to find a way to both uncompromisingly abandon herself to her religious impulses while still caring for the needs of her children and her extended family. Her then-youngest daughter Françoise went with her and stayed within the community (Charlotte had recently died); her eldest daughter Marie-Aimée, recently married to Francis's own brother, Bernard, resided nearby. Jane was free to move in and out of the community cloister as her maternal duties required. During the years that followed she was able to arrange for her son's and daughter's education and marriages and settle the estates left by her father and father-in-law, not neglecting these responsibilities but not having her religious aspirations set aside because of them.

After the foundation of the Visitation, Jane de Chantal found her life as much defined by her position as superior of a budding community as her friend Francis found his determined by his role as bishop. Both were considered spiritual leaders of their day. Both were concerned with the continuing spiritual revitalization of their society. Both to this end gave themselves in spiritual direction, wrote, spoke, and continued to grow in their own faith.

Between 1608 and 1616 Francis de Sales worked on the most ambitious of his written works, the *Treatise on the Love of God*, a voluminous "history of the birth, progress, and decay of the operations, characteristics, benefits, and excellence of divine love."[11] This seminal work represented the fruit of its author's theological reflection and spiritual penetration, drawing as it did upon the gathered

---

11. *Oeuvres* IV, 8: *Treatise*, Preface.

wisdom of the Church's contemplative tradition and contemporary religious thought.

Indeed, it is almost possible to see in de Sales's writing, especially in the *Treatise*, a reflection and synthesis of the entire wisdom of the Christian past. His sources are many and eclectic. He cited classical authors, appreciated Montaigne, was inspired by contemporary writer Honoré d'Urfé's *Astraea*, was dependent upon the thought of his Benedictine mentor Génébrard in his profound insight into the *Song of Songs*. De Sales read his fellow theologians, especially the Spaniards, venerated the mystical theology of Dionysius the Pseudo-Areopagite, knew by heart the maxims of medieval spiritual writers like Anselm, Bernard, and Bonaventure, always kept a copy of Laurence Scupoli's *The Spiritual Combat* in his pocket, breathed the rarified air of the mystical theology of the Rheno-Flemish school of spirituality, knew the writings of Teresa of Avila that were then available in France, was formed in the spirit of Ignatius Loyola when at Clermont and under the direction of Fr. Possevin and other Jesuit directors, and exhibited rare familiarity with the bible and the exegetical tradition of the Church.[12]

The *Treatise* and the *Introduction to the Devout Life* were de Sales's most popular works, those prepared most specifically for wide public circulation. But his other writings, most notably the *Spiritual Conferences*, compiled from informal conversations held with the Visitation community in Annecy in its years of infancy, are full of grace and insight. Jane, too, produced written works but for the most part she did not write for publication.[13] Nor did she care to sit down and write a formal statement of her teachings on any given topic. Instead, she preferred to spontaneously answer questions put to her by her sister Visitandines who recorded by memory what she said. It is in the letters that she wrote, as is the case too with Francis, that Jane's living spirit is captured. For the letters sprang naturally out of the duties and rhythm of their daily

---

12. Cf. *Dictionnaire de Spiritualité ascétique et mystique*, article "François de Sales," Vol. V, pp. 1057–1097 and Antanas Liuima, *Aux sources du traité de l'amour de Dieu de St. François de Sales*, 2 parts, Rome: Librairie Editrice de l'Université Grégorienne, 1960.

13. Jane did, however, work over her *Responses* for several years and sent her manuscript to several superiors for comments before allowing them to be privately printed. The first edition is *Responses de nostre tres honoree et digne Mere Jeanne Françoise Fremiot sur les Regles, Constitutions et Coustumier de nostre Ordre de la Visitation Saincte Marie* (Paris, 1632).

lives. As a busy bishop Francis was often on the road traveling in the service of this or that episcopal responsibility. He served in the train of the French court and acted as arbiter in several public disputes both theological and political; he oversaw the reform of monasteries and other religious communities, restored pilgrimage sites, preached often outside his diocese and made constant rounds of his own diocese in regular pastoral visits. He founded the Academy Florimontane (1607) with his friend Antoine Favre for the purpose of establishing an educational institution on the soil of Savoy which would provide an arena for the dissemination and discussion of current philosophical and theological ideas, drew up plans for Ursuline education of young girls to be introduced in his native land and developed a catechism for the Christian instruction of the very young.

His day was always full—there was correspondence to attend to, officials who came on business, there were liturgical and pastoral duties at all times, and always the Genevan bishop received whoever wished to see him about personal spiritual matters. His episcopal ante-rooms were always crowded with those seeking his advice. He is reported to have received them all with equal concern: women, men, poor, rich, ignorant, learned, the spiritually impoverished and the richly endowed. He wrote his letters during several hours in the early morning before the activity of the day closed in upon him. Each letter was highly personalized; the directees were addressed exactly at the point where they found themselves, in the concrete circumstances of their lives and at the particular moment of their spiritual development. For that was where, in Francis's perception, one was met by God.

Jane's letters too reflect this understanding of the spiritual enterprise. And she, like Francis, wrote to her correspondents amid the routine of her own day at the Visitation. Ordinarily, that day was punctuated by the monastic rhythm of prayer—the community said the little Office of Our Lady daily; there were periods for work, for recreation, for individual prayer, for community interaction. Jane penned her hasty letters often with the help of a secretary— especially for formal correspondence. Letters of direction were generally written in her own hand, jumbling together bits of news, requests, informal advice, with what might be called more formal spiritual counsel. Her life and the lives of her directees were embraced as one whole. One went to God in the context of the events in which one found oneself. Jane's letters reflect this mixture of the banal and the practical with the highest ideals of Christian life.

The Mother Superior of the Community of the Visitation was not always within her monastery, however. The vision that the two friends had for religious life also captured the imagination of French society. During her lifetime Jane saw the establishment of over eighty houses of the Visitation. The foundations of many of these she supervised herself. This necessitated that she too travel extensively. It also required that she utilize all the financial and administrative skills she had learned in her father's home, had tested while restoring the impoverished Chantal estates and had perfected when she arranged for her own children's futures and when she settled the affairs of her father and father-in-law after their deaths.

All the busyness was not to her real liking but Jane accepted the burdens of responsibility gracefully. There were many difficult times. As early as 1615 when the Visitation first flowered on French soil—in Lyons—major obstacles were encountered. The bishop of the diocese, de Marquemont, following the directives of the Council of Trent to the letter, perhaps not in their larger spirit, felt, among other things, that he could not allow a community of women who did not observe strict enclosure to reside under his jurisdiction. In a long and eloquently debated correspondence he and de Sales went back and forth. The original plan for the Visitandines had been to exercise the two arms of charity—the love of God in prayer, and in service to others. Now the community structure had to be modified to adapt to changing circumstances. With the Lyons foundation the congregation became a formal order observing permanent and solemn vows and the excursions out of the cloister were curtailed in favor of practicing charity within the house itself. Nevertheless, the essential purpose and spirit of the community remained unchanged—to establish a place for women to be "daughters of prayer" and cultivate a deep interior intimacy with God even if, by temperament, age, or constitution, they might be prevented from joining already established women's foundations.[14]

There were many other difficulties that presented themselves

---

14. The original purpose in founding the Visitation is clearly outlined in the first edition of the *Constitutions*. Cf. *Oeuvres*, XXV, 51–53.

to the burgeoning order. Individuals were attracted to the Visitation who lacked an affinity for its spirit and who failed to understand the religious motives behind the Salesian "gentle" demeanor or who could not abandon themselves to the demands of charity lived in community. Such a one was the young widow Marie-Aimée de Morville. This woman's escapades were many and notorious and the surviving letters to her that we have attest to the depth of the parental vigilance and solicitude that she wrung from Jane and Francis. The letters of direction of Monseigneur de Sales and Madame de Chantal, rooted as they are in the specific daily experience of their directees, provide a glimpse into the complex world of seventeenth-century society and religious sensibilities. A case in point is Francis's correspondence with Angélique Arnauld, the impassioned young abbess, whose name later became associated with Jansenism.[15] These missives paint a picture of a religious climate in which the lines of distinction between what were to become the various strands of French spirituality were not yet clearly drawn.

De Sales did not survive to witness the course of Angélique Arnauld's history nor live to share the labors of creating a network of Visitandine houses throughout France with his friend Jane. In Lyons in 1622, exhausted by the continual labors exercised in the service of the French court, he fell ill and died of apoplexy. This was not before he met with Jane de Chantal one last time. She too was on the road, seeing to the details of a new foundation. The friendship they had begun in 1604 had blossomed over the years into a union of immense richness that led them individually and together to their full spiritual potential. All the reserves of affection and desire of which they were capable had been exquisitely gathered up into their shared desire for perfect love of God. The beauty of the correspondence they exchanged is witness to their bond. It was not a bond without its aspects of suffering and denial, however. In 1616 they underwent a change in what until this time had been primarily an experience of unity. Still joined in their mutual quest to seek God they "let each other go," releasing the other to depend utterly on God alone. In 1622 at Lyons they had not seen each other for three

---

15. On Angélique Arnauld's Salesian connections refer to Louis Cognet, *La Mère Angélique et Saint François de Sales, 1618–1626* (Paris: Editions Sulliver, 1951).

years. Their last interview was taken up in considering the business
of the rapidly expanding Visitation order that they had given birth
to twelve years before.[16]

After Francis's death, Jane de Chantal continued with her work
of overseeing the large family of religious to whom she was chief
spiritual mother. This she did up until her own death. In this work
she relied on the counsel of many of the spiritual friends she enjoyed, notably Vincent de Paul who was for her a confidant and confessor. Primary among her concerns was the continuation of the
pristine spirit in the Visitandine houses, many of whose residents
had never met their founding parents. She called a first general
chapter meeting of superiors in 1624 and helped to draw up a defin-
itive Custom Book which would provide guidelines for practice
within the diverse communities. She wrote ardent letters to superiors, novice-mistresses and novices which reflect her struggle to institute a way in which the authentic Salesian spirit might come to
be observed everywhere.

In her letters of particular direction, where her concern is to
stay close to the very Salesian spirit of beginning right where one is
and with the facts at hand, Jane de Chantal continues to show herself, until her death, as a masterful director of souls. She brought to
this task her own particular life-experience and temperament. The
fact of her motherhood is chief among those experiences. Since her
youth she had been engaged in the art of biological mothering, since
midlife she had exercised her spiritual maternity. The correspondence she kept with the superiors of the Visitation reflects a self-con-
scious cultivation of attitudes and skills she believed congruent with
maternal care. Superiors were enjoined to be true mothers, tenderly
attentive to the nurturing of their young, tolerant of their children's
weaknesses, encouraging their small steps, never overly ambitious
for their advancement until they themselves grew into the maturity
of spiritual wisdom.

The task of cultivating and disseminating this spirit of motherly
direction occupied Jane de Chantal for many years. It was part of
her long-term effort to ensure the survival, both institutional and
spiritual, of the Salesian charism in its manifestation as the order of
the Visitation. Over the years, many challenges to this goal arose.

---

16. Refer to Wright, *Bond of Perfection*, pp. 159–98.

INTRODUCTION

One specific challenge may serve as a case in point. Ecclesiastical authorities tried for many years to press upon the communities the institution of apostolic visitations, a practice which she felt would severely compromise the autonomy from other than episcopal authority that was intended for the order. Her long correspondence on this topic has survived and shows Jane as a persistent and far-seeing defender of the Salesian vision as she believed it should be lived out.[17] She continued her labors in the service of this vision until her death in 1641.

---

17. See Roger Devos, "Le testament spirituel de sainte-Jeanne Françoise de Chantal et l'affaire du visiteur apostolique" in *Revue d'Histoire de la Spiritualité*, Vol. 48 (1972), pp. 453–76 and Vol. 49 (1973), pp. 199–266 and 341–66.

Salesian Spirituality: Six Themes

Theme I

"I am as human as anyone could possibly be." (Francis de Sales in a letter to Jane de Chantal, *Oeuvres* XIII, 330)

Any spirituality rests upon, or better yet, includes a set of assumptions about God and humankind and about how they are related to each other. Salesian spirituality, historically situated as it is in French Counter-Reformation Catholicism at the turn of the seventeenth century, carries within itself a view of the human-divine drama that is consonant with the theological and devotional atmosphere of that period and place. This was an era in which Christian humanism, which had taken recent impetus from the humanist revival of the preceding century, was in full flower.[1] In general, this orientation approached theological questions from the human point of view, affirming the innate dignity of the person. It believed that human nature, while wounded, was not corrupted by the fall, and thus retained a natural orientation to God as its supernatural end; that humans could and must cooperate with divine grace in the accomplishment of saving works; that God does not predestine individuals to salvation or damnation absolutely but "foresees" their appointed ends by taking into consideration their efforts and merits, which are in turn the fruits of (relatively) free human choice.

With these general assertions providing a backdrop against which Salesian spirituality was played out, it is easy to see from whence the often-used term "Salesian optimism" takes its origin.[2]

---

1. On Christian humanism in this period consult the classic Henri Bremond, *Histoire littéraire du sentiment religieux en France depuis la fin des guerres de religion jusqu'à nos jours*, Vol. I (Paris: Bloud et Gay, 1921), English translation: *A Literary History of Religious Thought in France from the Wars of Religion Down to Our Own Times* (New York: Macmillan Co., 1930); Julien Eymard d'Angers, *L'humanisme chrétien au XVIIᵉ siècle: St. François de Sales et Yves de Paris* (LaHaye: Martinus Nijhoff, 1970); Louis Cognet, *De la dévotion moderne à la spiritualité française* (Paris: Librairie Arthème Fayard, 1958).

2. For a discussion of the origin of Francis de Sales's optimism see Henri Lemaire, *François de Sales, Docteur de la confiance et de la paix* (Paris: Beauchesne, 1963), pp. 19–30. Also, William Marceau, CSB, *Optimism in the Works of St. Francis de Sales* (Visakhapatnam, India: SFS Publications, 1983).

INTRODUCTION

The God beheld and entrusted with human destiny is, for Francis de Sales and Jane de Chantal, first of all a God of love and merciful compassion. De Sales in fact constructed his most ambitious work, *The Treatise on the Love of God*, around this Christian humanist portrait of divinity. In book two of that lengthy tome he describes, in lively fashion, the loving God who from all eternity desired to be in intimate communion with the creation. Despite the fall of humankind, which resulted from free choice and which God foresaw, God nonetheless reached into the heart of creation and offered it redemption through the loving sacrifice of the Son. Moreover, God, out of the fullness of abundance, gives to each creature grace sufficient freely to participate in his or her own salvation. And God desires greatly that each person be drawn to the intimate communion for which he or she was created.

> See the divine lover at the gate. He does not simply knock once. He continues to knock. He calls the soul: come, arise my beloved, hurry! And he puts his hand on the lock to see whether he can open it. . . . In short, this divine Savior forgets nothing to show that his mercies are above all his works, his mercy is greater than his judgment, that his redemption is copious, his love is infinite and, as the Apostle says, he is rich in mercy and so he desires that all should be saved and none perish.[3]

In humankind Salesian thought sees a corresponding impulse to respond to the love lavished upon it by its God. God touches each individual with grace, a gratuitously given invitation to union. It is up to each person to respond. The *Treatise* treats in detail the Genevan bishop's theoretical understanding of the reception, growth, consummation, and possible deterioration of the love in the soul for its God. Throughout, the over-arching impression is one of the generosity, liberality, and affective quality of the human-divine courtship to which all are invited.

This radical view of a lovingly inclined God had implications for the Salesian understanding of who was called to authentic Christian life. Put bluntly, all were called. Clerics, vowed religious, lay persons, men and women in all walks and states of life were intended

---

3. *Oeuvres*, IV, 114: *Treatise*, II, 8.

to exercise their deepest human capacities in a unique and creative marriage with the God who created them.

For in Salesian thinking the human person is believed to be made in the divine likeness and image. Drawn to union with divinity by the affinity of natures and propelled by the power of mutual love, the human person, no matter what his or her visible vocation, had a more compelling and far-reaching vocation—to realize his or her fullest capacity for love of God. There is in this a wholistic understanding of the way this love of God comes to be lived out in each person. This love has, to use de Sales's own phrase, two arms. One arm is the affective love of God known especially in prayer. The other is the effective love of God known by the loving actions directed toward neighbor, and also described as conformity to the will of God.[4] With the whole of his or her inner and outer capacities, a man or a woman responds to the essential truth of human nature, a nature created and, though wounded by original sin, still capable, through an ever-increasing identification with the living Jesus, of realizing the divine marriage to which it is drawn.

Implied in this optimistic view of human capacity is an appreciation for the created world and for the human arts. There is little in Salesian thought that could be pronounced world-denying in the sense that matter itself or the society of other people or the works of human hands are in and of themselves suspect from a religious point of view. The vaguely anti-material bias which haunts much of Christian spirituality is virtually absent from Salesian thought. For a Christian humanist such as de Sales love and the appreciation of beauty went hand in hand. Beauty is order and harmony; it is an intrinsic grace which has its origins in the divine beauty. All that is beautiful, harmonious, good, and graceful in the world participates in God by virtue of those qualities. The contemplation of beauty, then, for the humanist tradition that Francis became acquainted with at Padua, can lead to the contemplation of God. Salesian spirituality is marked in its celebration of whatever in the created order participates in the beauty evocative of God.[5]

---

4. On this see *ibid.*, Books VIII and IX.

5. An interesting discussion of the Italian Renaissance background to de Sales's Christian aesthetic as well as an analysis of the idea of beauty in the *Introduction* is found in James S. Langelaan, OSFS, *Man in Love with God: Introduction to the Theology and Spirituality of St. Francis de Sales* (Hyattsville, MD, unpublished paper, 1976).

INTRODUCTION

As has been noted previously,[6] part of that beauty was to be found in the person—"l'honnête homme"—who cultivated both an interior and exterior gracefulness. Francis de Sales was indeed the embodiment of the man whose human capacities were consciously cultivated to most clearly mirror and direct others' focus to the graciously inclining God. Jane de Chantal and the daughters of the Visitation also moved within the world of Christian humanism but their reflection of that tradition was not identical to that of their friend and founder, Francis. It perhaps has not been appreciated that in the Renaissance humanist tradition there were assumptions about the education and character development of women that corresponded to the assumptions held about men. The formation of the feminine character was felt to be primarily an affair of moral shaping and not of intellectual pursuit for its own sake.[7] The general picture that emerges from treatises circulating at the time indicates that education for women consisted in the inculcation of the moral qualities considered necessary to female innocence: humility, simplicity, modesty, piety, patience, obedience. While most of these virtues are also foundational virtues in the traditional monastic view of the Christian life, within the Visitation they became the key virtues to be acquired. These qualities came to be incorporated into the order as its own specific charism, the quality of piety and personal deportment that made the order distinctive.[8] Francis and Jane referred to them as the "little virtues." It was, looked at from this perspective, a very "feminine" and "humanistic" charism. The attainment of other Christian virtues—such as courage, fortitude or justice—while not entirely absent from the ideals of the Visitation, were sub-

---

6. See Historical Context.

7. Cf. Phyllis Stock, *Better Than Rubies: A History of Women's Education* (New York: G.P. Putnam's Sons, 1978), pp. 29–40. The Renaissance and the Reformation were periods in western culture that saw the development of women's education. There were a number of stated reasons for this: to instill moral character, to raise male children more conscientiously, to be suitable companions to learned men, to encourage authentic piety. While there were champions of women's intellectual equality, for the most part, the motives underlying women's education were, by modern standards, questionable. See Paul Rousselot, *Histoire de l'éducation des femmes en France* (New York: Lenox Hill Pub.–Burt Franklin, 1971. Orig. pub. 1883), Georges Snyders, *La Pédagogie en France aux XVIIᵉ et XVIIIᵉ siècles* (Paris: Presses Universitaires de France, 1965), and Gabriel Compayre, *Histoire critique des doctrines de l'éducation en France depuis le seizième siècle* (Geneva: Slatkine Reprints, 1970. Orig. pub. 1879).

8. Cf. Wendy M. Wright, "St. Jane de Chantal's Guidance of Women" in *Salesian Living Heritage*, Vol. I, No. 1 (Spring 1986), pp. 16–28.

ordinated to the qualities deemed in the humanist tradition proper for the attainment of authentic and graceful womanhood.

Salesian spirituality was not simply humanistic in the technical sense of belonging to those spiritualities that are rooted in Christian humanist thought. It was also a very "human devotion" in the ordinary sense of that phrase. Francis and Jane both had a very human touch. Their thoughts and advice on things of the spirit were generally down to earth. They had what has been termed "inspired common sense"[9] and their letters of direction were as often as not concerned with the practical implementation of their spiritual principles within the ordinary context of ordinary lives. Neither otherworldly nor world-denying, they saw the life of devotion as something that should enhance everyday human experience and, in turn, human experience as something that should ground and inform devotion. One is struck by the practical nature of the suggestions Jane de Chantal gives to her own natural daughter about marriage and family life, advice that is no less spiritual and grounded in a radical Christian vision for its being given in such a practical, and ordinary manner. One is also struck by the common-sense maternal wisdom that guides Jane as she directs her spiritual daughters within the community of the Visitation.

Human and divine were, in Salesian thought, inextricably entwined. Francis's famous phrase "I am as human as anyone could possibly be" does not suggest a modest appraisal of his own capabilities, but suggests rather that in his mind his very humanity was in fact the vessel which could contain the miracle of divine life.[10] To be human meant in the Salesian world to have a deep interest in all that is human—especially in the affections, in people's hearts. Whatever is deeply personal and most heartfelt is the stuff of Salesian spirituality. To become fully human one plumbs the resources that one has been given, one searches through the deepest loves of one's heart. There one finds affirmed the fact that there is a corre-

---

9. Elisabeth Stopp in her introduction to Francis's letters, pp. 33–34, coins this phrase. Cf. *St. Francis de Sales. Selected Letters* (N.Y.: Harper & Bros., 1960).

10. Francis's phrase "Je suis tant homme que rien plus" has not generally been translated in this way. Given his use of "si . . . que rien plus" in other places and emboldened by Henri Lemaire's *Lexique des oeuvres complètes de François de Sales* (Paris: Editions A. G. Nizet, 1973), p. 382, we have struggled to find an English equivalent that suggests something of the subtlety of the saint's terse phrase.

spondence and a similarity of the human and divine realities. The methods and concerns of Salesian spirituality, its vision of the nature of God and of humankind, its whole tonality is vibrant with this intuition.

Theme II

"So let us live courageously between the one will of God and the other." (Francis de Sales, *Treatise on the Love of God*, Book 9)

The goodness of God—the sense of that goodness permeating all of creation, of the dynamic thrust in the center of created reality that inclines toward its Creator—is basic to the Salesian spirit. Humankind is created to know and love God and to do God's will. But the discernment of and response to that will is not always a simple matter. The traditional sources of revelation—Church teaching and Scripture—provide a framework within which the individual seeks that will. Beyond that, Christian writers before de Sales had dealt with the issue of discernment in myriad ways.[1] Particularly rich in its analysis of discernment, the Ignatian tradition, as cultivated by the Jesuits and known to Francis from his student days, had established guidelines for the subtle interior art of distinguishing good and evil spirits in order to better know the will of God for each individual life.[2] Moreover, the contemplative tradition known to the Savoyard through the spiritual classics taught a self-abandoned love of God and a heroic obedience to God's will as revealed in that love.

Drawing on the wisdom of received tradition, Salesian spirituality found its own point of spiritual equilibrium by "living between" what Francis de Sales described as the two wills of God.[3] God's will was, for the bishop, in fact only one. But he saw God's essence as so transcending human capacity that it could not be known in its simple unity. God could be known only through the revelation of the divine will. And that will, as humans perceived it,

---

1. Cf. Jacques Guillet, et al., *Discernment of Spirits* (Collegeville, MN: Liturgical Press, 1970).

2. See Stopp's article, "St. Francis de Sales at Clermont College," and F. Charmot, S.J., *Ignatius Loyola and Francis de Sales, Two Masters, One Spirituality* (St. Louis, MO: B. Herder, 1966), pp. 41–115.

3. This analysis of living between the two wills is based primarily on the *Treatise on the Love of God*. Francis's other works, while reflecting similar theological foundations, do not always use the same terminology. It is especially the architecture of the *Treatise* that suggests this. Books VIII and IX treat respectively of the two wills and of the appropriate response to each, the love of conformity and the love of submission.

had various forms. People attached different names to God's will according to the different ways in which it appeared to them. God's two wills are, in Salesian terminology, the "signified will of God" ✓ and the "will of God's good pleasure." The first of these is God's will *to be done*. It is known to persons through what God says, directs, and inspires. The individual, discerning carefully his or her own heart and carried in the arms of the Christian community with its store of traditional wisdom, seeks to discover this signified will for his or her own life. Scripture, Church teaching, devotional literature, private and communal prayer, spiritual direction: these are places where such a will would likely manifest itself. Here de Sales sees human liberty in its widest parameters. The person makes life choices based on the discerned knowledge of this will of God, relying on his or her powers of judgment and movements of heart to detect what that will might be. The person thus is, in a sense, a cocreator of God's will under these circumstances. Francis taught that, even in cases when one could not clearly discern the divine will, one must rely upon one's powers of decision making and, after consultation with other reputable persons, act upon one's decisions with the vitality one would bring to carrying out a clearly perceived manifestation of divine will. Once perceived, the person begins to align himself or herself with that will by observing and loving the indications received. This volitional response the Genevan bishop terms "love of conformity" (i.e., conformity of a human will to a divine will thus revealed).

One example of the cultivation of this will might suffice. When first under Francis's direction, Jane de Chantal, then a widow with four small children, began to discern the emerging shape of her future vocation. She felt she was called to a life of chastity and "withdrawal from the world." Her mentor urged her to have confidence in her nascent inspirations despite the fact that her extended family and the society of her day could only look askance at such longings. He directed her in her growing intimacy and conformity to the signified will of God. He even confirmed her in the practice of imaging her own spiritual world with monastic imagery. For example, she took the Virgin Mary as the Abbess of the cloister of her own heart.

But God's full will does not, in Salesian thought, reside solely in the received inspirations of either individual or community. God's will is also manifest in the events, facts, and existing realities of one's immediate situation. The "will of God's good pleasure"—God's *will done*—for de Sales happens independently of human consent. Where one finds oneself, one's particular situation, is also revelatory of the divine will and must be taken into account and lived with creativity if one is to be truly responsive to the unique will of God. It is especially in painful situations or events—inner or outer—that might seem to thwart one's own sense of God's will that this will of God's good pleasure can be felt. The term "good pleasure" may be misleading.[4] The bishop does not mean to imply that God *causes* all events and existing realities but that whatever *is* is in some way within God's providence; it is not outside of the loving embrace of the creative and redemptive process. God is found wherever one finds oneself. It also means that the totality of the will of God is not to be found in any one place—either in individual discernment or in the factual situations that seem at variance with that discernment. It is not that one is God's will and the other isn't until an impasse causes one to change one's sense of the shape of divine will. It is rather that living *between* the two wills—maintaining a creative tension that refuses to limit God to one expression or another—is in itself more consonant with the immensity and simplicity of the essence of a God whose wholeness can never be contained in any one part of creation.

The widow de Chantal's situation is a case in point and in the bishop's direction of her can be seen the way in which one is to live courageously between the two wills. Validate her emerging desires to give herself utterly to God, he did. Encourage her to be responsive to the will she sensed emerging uniquely in her, he did. But throughout the first five years of his direction he spent the majority of his effort impressing on his ardent and impatient friend the fact that the situation in which she found herself—her widowhood with its familial responsibilities—was the place in which she was, at present, called to love and know God. There could be no undue "yearning ahead" of herself, no serious anxiety about not being somewhere else. God's will for her at this time was to be lovingly accepted in the facts of her motherhood and her uneasy situation in her father-in-law's household.

---

4. This traditional term, used by the saint in a unique way, is most likely based on Matthew 11:26.

Human response to this will of God that has already been done was termed by de Sales, "the love of submission." A nuanced concept, love of submission had a number of forms. The acceptance of God's good pleasure could be undertaken in more than one way. Existing situations, the trials that overtake one, could be received merely with patience and tolerance, what he deemed "resignation." Or they might be embraced with a more responsive and flexible love, with what he termed "holy indifference" or better, "holy disinterestedness." This grace-filled attitude of acceptance of what is beyond one's control was for the Savoyard a mark of Christian character. For God's will he felt was known not only in the promptings and dreams of one's own heart but also in the present, often painful, reality in which one lives; not only in the "how it should be" but in "the way it is." It is somewhere between these two facts that moral choice, loving surrender and authentic human life are discerned.

Thus Salesian spirituality steers a fine course between the otherworldliness and the fatalism that haunts much of Christian thought. To live courageously between these two wills, to engage in the constant and unending interplay between the two, is to begin to live in harmony with the unique will of God. The implications of this foundational Salesian position for a Christian vocation are manifold. By identifying the will of God with what one might call both prophetic and worldly voices Salesian spirituality allows the Christian to engage wholeheartedly in the facts of real life—to see the social and political arenas as legitimate spheres for Christian action. Yet the Salesian spirit does retain its prophetic quality by emphasizing equally the importance of inspiration and individual discernment in the Christian life. It allows for great freedom—what one might call a spirit-led approach to religion—while placing that liberty firmly within the scriptural, dogmatic, ascetic, and mystical traditions of the Church.

Theme III

"Let us belong to God . . . in the midst of so much busyness."
(Francis de Sales, Letter to Mme de Cornillon)

✓ The classic spirituality of Christendom, growing as it does out of what might be termed a "desert" impulse, tends to locate authentic religious experience primarily outside the life of "the world."[1] There is a marginal overtone to the desert voice, a prophetic ring that is discordant when played against the values that ring pleasing in the ears of ordinary society. There is in the silence, solitude, and withdrawal of the desert a challenge to the noisy activity of the marketplace and household. There is a warning that those in the world might well look closely at the lives, both private and communal, that they have fashioned and scrutinize them with the lens of the desert critique. There can also be in the desert spirit a subtle (or not so subtle) devaluation of the world and those who remain there, an insistence that the busy noisy life necessitated in making the social order continue is incompatible with a true discernment of the voice and will of God.

Salesian spirituality, while retaining much of the interior spirit of the desert, in the sense that a radical call from God does indeed claim and refashion the human heart, did not at all assert that that voice could only echo clearly in the stillness of the hermit's cave or the monastery cloister. That voice might also be raised and heard in a life lived in the midst of the world. Francis and Jane insisted that all Christians were called to find God. Seekers after God did not have to abandon the pursuits in which most persons ordinarily engaged. Some individuals might be pursued by the call of the desert and adopt some form of alternative lifestyle. But the vast majority of Christians would be called to find God precisely in the midst of the tasks and circumstances of day-to-day existence. All walks of life

---

1. For a contemporary look at Salesian spirituality as an alternative to desert spirituality see Joseph Power, "Marketplace Spirituality," in *Praying*, No. 19 (July–August, 1987), 14–16. Thomas Gannon and George W. Traub also treat the same issue from the point of view of Ignatian spirituality in *The Desert and the City: An Interpretation of the History of Christian Spirituality* (New York: Macmillan 1969).

provided suitable means for fashioning an authentic Christian way of being. A vocation to a devout life was offered to all: layperson and cleric, man or woman, celibate or married. All were invited to a full participation in the human/divine existence found in Jesus. For this they were created.

It was precisely in the midst of all the busyness of worldly life that God could be found. As Francis encouraged Mme de Cornillon, his own younger sister who was also his directee and "daughter,"

> Let us all belong to God, my daughter, in the midst of so much busyness brought on by the diversity of worldly things. Where could we give better witness to our fidelity than in the midst of things going wrong? Ah, dearest daughter, my sister, solitude has its assaults, the world its busyness; in either place we must be courageous, since in either place divine help is available to those who trust in God and who humbly and gently beg for His fatherly assistance.[2]

It was there, in the midst, that God had planted the householder, the worker, the statesman, the merchant, the courtier. There, among family and work, the will of God—God's good pleasure—was revealed. The implications of this insistence on the religious value of all life callings are great. Jesus was seen to live in each Christian heart that opened to him and was believed to be carried truly on the lips, arms, and shoulders of sailor, housewife, greengrocer or advisor of kings.[3]

Devotion—making Jesus live—was not in the Salesian world something that necessarily took one away, either physically or psychologically, from one's daily experience. It recognized that true Christian life could be realized anywhere. And insofar as one recognized the call of God, the will of God, in where one was and what one was, any situation could be embraced wholeheartedly. No facet of life was thus alien or indifferent: all of the ordinary things and

---

2. *Oeuvres*, XIV, 339: Letter DCXIV.

3. This did not mean that Francis, being a child of the Counter-Reformation, did not view the priesthood with special respect. On the place of the priesthood in de Sales's thought and the high regard he had for the episcopal office, seeing it as taking its authority directly from the mandate of Christ and not from the papacy, see André Ravier's introduction to *L'Introduction à la vie dévote* in Saint François de Sales, *Oeuvres* in *Bibliothèque de la Pléiade* (Paris: Editions Gallimard, 1969), pp. xl–xliv.

actions had value in themselves and could express love of God and neighbor, notably by the compassion and competence that were brought to them.

The Salesian spirit is thus contextual. It is also relational. Being in the midst does not mean simply trying to pray in the brief silences that emerge amid the noise. It means that making Jesus live is not something that occurs solely in the isolated individual vis-à-vis his or her own God. It is not something that is forged only out of the solitary vigil of silence represented by the hermit monk. The word monk itself comes from the root "monos" or "alone." A better word to portray the Salesian spirit might be "between." It is what goes on between persons, in their relationships, that is of the essence in making Jesus live. This interpersonal dimension of the Salesian spirit deepens the importance of the insight that it is in the midst that one loves God. For it is not that one glimpses God despite the persons around one but that one finds God precisely through and with those persons.

Relationships then are central in the Salesian context. They are neither inimical to nor peripheral to one's love of God. It is in relationships between persons, in loving neighbor, that love of God is shown.[4] Francis and Jane's own relationship is a case in point. It was between these two friends that the simultaneous expression of human and divine love was so deeply explored. Their own ardent and poignant bond which spanned nineteen years drew them together into a mature love of God. It was precisely in the midst of that friendship with all the powerful dynamics of interaction between male and female that they both learned what it was to make Jesus live fully. And they extended themselves in friendship to a wide circle of intimates giving credence to the Pauline assertion that friendship is the bond of perfection.[5]

Within Salesian thought the *way* one is with others is of central importance to the art of letting Jesus live. Francis's gentle demeanor, his graceful way with words, the intuitive skill with which he directed others was not social artifice. It was intrinsic to the realization

---

4. Cf. Wright, *Bond of Perfection*, pp. 102ff. on love of God and of neighbor.

5. *Ibid.* on friendship. See also André Ravier, ed., *François de Sales, Correspondance: les lettres d'amitié spirituelle* (Paris: Bibliothèque Européenne, Desclée de Brouwer, 1980). Ravier makes the point that all of Francis's relationships of spiritual direction were also spiritual friendships and he entitled his collection accordingly.

of who Jesus is. Jesus is seen *among* persons, in the grace-filled way they gently lead each other to greater love and conformity to the will of God. Likewise, Jane's motherly guidance of her spiritual daughters was born not solely of her own maternal experience but also out of the recognition that it is in such guidance that the presence of God is felt and the face of the gentle Jesus known. The way one is, the way one loves one's fellow human beings, the atmosphere of mutual charity this creates, marks one as a Christian.

Over and over in the two friends' correspondence is found the insistence that affection and mutual regard are essential means by which the spirit of devotion is manifest. Which is to say, devotion is not so much a matter of how or how long one prays as much as how one enters into relationships with God and neighbor. It is instructive to look at the congregation of the Visitation founded by the bishop and the widow in order to see the way in which they envisioned this relational spirituality being worked out in practice. The Visitation of Holy Mary was established as an institute for women who were drawn to a life of contemplative prayer but who might not be suitable candidates for existing religious communities because of their age, health, or temperament. They formed an unobtrusive congregation not notable for any striking charism but intent on living hidden lives of great interior intimacy with God and on manifesting that intimate union precisely in and through the community of charity that they were. The emphasis was on the shared cultivation of such a group ethos. In Francis's words:

> Since this congregation does not have as many austerities or as indissoluble bonds as formal orders and regular congregations, the fervor of charity and the force of a deep personal resolution must supply for all that and take the place of laws, vows, and jurisdiction; so that in this congregation might be realized the saying of the Apostle which affirms that charity is the perfect bond.[6]

The sisters were to be a perfect union of charity, the Pauline vision of love governing all their relations. This was to be true within each Visitandine house. It was also, as the institute grew, to

---

6. *Oeuvres*, XXV, 216: *Constitutions 1613*. It should be noted that after the writing of this piece, the Visitation was converted into a formal order with solemn vows. Cf. *supra*, p. 30.

be the commanding principle directing the relationships between monasteries. No formal institutional means were established to achieve unity and continuity of spirit. Mutual regard and the bond of love itself, nourished on the founders' examples and expressed in the rule, were to reign as the principles of union.

In the Salesian world one loved God in the midst: in the busy bustle of what might be a "worldly" vocation and in the interpersonal exchanges of family, community, and friends.

Theme IV

"Walk in the presence of God in holy and absolute liberty of spirit." (Jane de Chantal, *Letter to a Superior*)

The Salesian experience of God is in the midst. But the quality of that experience, while contoured by the busyness and the personal relationships that surround it, is not wholly defined by the bustle, noise, and impingement that must necessarily be found there. The Salesian spirit instead bespeaks a God that bestows a spacious liberty on humankind. A fundamental assumption that underlies Salesian thought, and one which marks that thought as especially Catholic and especially early Counter-Reformation, is this idea of the centrality of human freedom in the divine scheme of things.[1] Essential to the nature of the person is the freedom to choose and act. God never, in this view, violates that principle of integrity. Human beings, to be truly in God's image and likeness, are never simply puppets in a marionette show that plays out some remotely devised drama of predestination. Rather, each person cooperates freely in his or her own salvation. Christian humanism, beginning as it does from the point of view of human experience, asserts that human beings are saved, brought into the fullness for which they were created, not despite, but according to their intrinsic nature. That nature is free.

The liberty of the children of God that Jane and Francis taught their friends and which, in their own relationship, was one of the chief insights that he gave to her, was such a vision of freedom of choice. Each person, they thought, could exercise that freedom by the way he or she chose to love. The choice was: to love for self-serving ends, for the self-satisfaction that love brings or to love with a "pure love," a love that is modeled on the unconditional love given to humankind by God. Each person could choose objects of love. The choice here was between objects that could, by their nature or

---

1. An excellent study of Christian humanism and one which places Francis de Sales firmly within that tradition (as opposed to Henri Bremond whose classic *Histoire Littéraire* describes de Sales as a "devout humanist") see Julien-Eymard d'Angers, *L'Humanisme Chrétien au XVIIe-siècle: St. François de Sales et Yves de Paris* (La Haye: Martinus Nijhoff, 1970).

by association, lead one either away from or toward God. Finally, each person could choose to love or not to love the facts of their lives, the unique situation in which he or she found himself or herself. And each could choose the way in which he or she accepted all events that occurred.

To love purely meant to love in a way that did not always come easily. True, human nature, in the Salesian view, was created with the desire for good and the inner dynamic of love that moves toward conformity to the divine will. But human nature, in that view, is also wounded. To recover the ability to love purely was the essential task of human life. The Christian tradition of spirituality had long spoken of pure love contrapuntally with the terms "indifference" or "detachment."[2]

While indifference could mean a devaluation of creation, a sort of blindness to or even recoiling from all that was seen as non-spiritual, at its best indifference was the ability to love creatures deeply without attaching oneself to them unduly. It was about seeing God in all things, about attending to what is of God in all things. It was about perceiving each person solely in the hope of the wholeness to which they were created. This did not necessarily devalue creation but treated creation as a product of God's loving hand to be appreciated but not used for self-serving ends. Pure love of creatures and of God went hand in hand. Negatively stated, no created thing was to stand in the way of one's love for God. Positively stated, one's love for God and thus for God's created order was to be shown in the respectful way in which one dealt with it. Within creation human persons, above all, were not to be possessed but loved in such a way that they were freed to be fully themselves in God.

In practice, "indifference" was central to Salesian spirituality. It was the virtue which, when realized, freed one for the liberty of the children of God. It can be seen in de Sales's teaching on living between the two wills of God, especially in his insistence that "submission" to the will of God's good pleasure is as essential as "con-

---

2. St. Bernard of Clairvaux and Catherine of Genoa are among those whose thought centers on the pure love of God. The basis for this was ultimately, of course, biblical, and Francis de Sales utilized the *Song of Songs* extensively to construct his vision of the human-divine interaction. Likewise, in his *Spiritual Exercises*, Ignatius twice asks his retreatant to develop the virtue of indifference: in the foundations and in the exercise preparatory to election. On Francis and Ignatius on indifference, see Charmot, *Two Masters, One Spirituality*.

formity" to the signified will of God. The Salesian emphasis on indifference can also be seen in the directorial process both in the way in which the director was encouraged to view direction and in the way in which the directee was enabled to pray.

First, as directors, Jane de Chantal and Francis de Sales did not see themselves as superimposing a set of ideals or a set method of devotion on a directee. They saw themselves as enabling the person to respond fully to the spirit of God that speaks and lives uniquely within. There can be no constraint in this. Directees should not be utterly dependent on a director, should not substitute a director's advice for an authentic experience of the presence of God. There may be as many faces and forms to that presence as there are directees. Directors then should not attach themselves too firmly to their own methods of prayer but foster a sensitive awareness to the diverse movements of God within the great variety of persons.

Mirroring this indifference in the directorial process is the practice of prayer in the Salesian tradition. No one method, no one type of prayer—either meditative or contemplative—was seen to be superior to other types. Indifference should extend to the loving acceptance of whatever prayer to which one is drawn. Jane is quoted as saying:

> The great method of prayer is to have no method at all. When the Holy Spirit has taken possession of the person who prays, it does as it pleases without any more need for rules or methods. The soul must be in God's hands like clay in the hands of a potter so that he might fashion all sorts of parts. Or the soul must be like soft wax to receive a seal's impression, or like a blank tablet upon which the Holy Spirit can write the divine will.
>
> If, going to prayer, one can become pure capacity for receiving the spirit of God, that will suffice for any method. Prayer must happen by grace not by artfulness. Go to prayer by faith, remain there in hope and go out only by charity which requires simply that one act and suffer.[3]

This "methodless prayer" in fact became a distinctive feature of the Visitandine charism. While novices were encouraged to re-

---

3. *Sa Vie et ses oeuvres*, III, 260. Cf. Francis's Letter to Mme de Granieu (*Oeuvres*, XVIII, 237–240); cf. below, p. 166.

spond individually to the ways in which they were drawn in prayer, they did seem as a group to have a special predilection for a simple waiting before God. Jane described it well.

> I have recognized that the almost universal attraction of the daughters of the Visitation is to a very simple practice of the presence of God effected by a total abandonment of themselves to Holy Providence. . . . Several are attracted this way from the beginning and it seems as though God avails Himself of this one means to cause us to achieve our end, and the perfect union of our soul with Him.[4]

In such an attitude before God one does not attach oneself unduly to how one feels, or to what the results of prayer might be. One might in fact affectively experience nothing. Yet, if the focus in the prayer is upon waiting before God in loving attention, then the receiving of "gifts" like warmth, spiritual thoughts, and attractions will be secondary. Jane herself experienced this type of prayer. It was the dominant chord of the whole of her inner reality. Its harmonies were often discordant for she found herself always wanting to "feel" something. In his direction of her, Francis encouraged her to cultivate a state of indifference to such feelings. In a letter of 1612 he wrote:

> It is the height of holy disinterestedness to be content with naked, dry, and insensible acts carried out by the superior will alone. You have expressed your suffering well to me and there is nothing to do to remedy it but what you are doing: affirming to our Lord, sometimes aloud and other times in song, that you even will to live and to eat as the dead do, without taste, feeling or knowledge. In the end, the Savior wants us to be His so perfectly that nothing else remains for us, and to abandon ourselves entirely to the mercy of His providence without reservation.[5]

Salesian teaching on indifference, that true liberty of the children of God, is summed up in Francis de Sales's oft-quoted maxim: "ask for nothing, refuse nothing." It is this kind of liberty, which

---

4. *Ibid., Conseils de direction*, 337.
5. *Oeuvres*, XV, 198: Letter DCCLXIV.

neither seeks a specific result nor rejects what in fact is, that characterizes the free human response to God and God's world. Human liberty resides, *not* in not caring about what happens (were that possible) but in caring more that God's results be accomplished whatever the outcome.

Salesian liberty, in terms of practice, becomes a freedom to serve. The Genevan bishop was famous for his generosity with time and advice. His episcopal apartments were daily open to all who sought his counsel. The poor, the powerless, the tedious and overly scrupulous, were received equally with (and sometimes to the chagrin of) the rich, powerful and magnanimous of spirit. This personal generosity of service was a result of the Savoyard's profound internalization of the liberty of the children of God. Such a freedom rested upon a non-attachment to his own particular notions of results.

In the bishop's personal life and in the spirituality that bears his name, this indifference extends even to the realms of sanctification and salvation. In this view such concerns were, as a matter of continual attention, best left up to God. Human freedom resided not in being able to ferret out the inscrutable mysteries of divine judgment, not in being able to "earn" one's place in heaven or assure oneself of one's perfection. Freedom was instead found in the cultivation of non-attachment, even to these assurances so dear to religious personalities. If the focus of attention in one's relationship with God became one's own ultimate good as one's own felt acquisition of some ideal state, then the focus would not be upon God.

Salesian spirituality, as has been mentioned, is deeply relational in its operations. One comes to God in the midst of worldly vocation and of interpersonal relations. But one must be in the midst as a child of God. One must cultivate a holy freedom that truly loves all things. One must have a clarity of perception that sees the purpose in all things, that sees their origin and destination. One loves, one realizes the kingdom proclaimed in Jesus when, free from the desire to possess anything, even one's own ultimate good, one enters into the service of the created order desiring only the manifestation of the will of God. In this, Jesus lives.

Theme V

"Since the heart is the source of all our actions, as the heart is, so are they" (Francis de Sales, *Introduction to the Devout Life*, III, 23)

Classic desert spirituality, while pointedly concerned with the Christian renovation of the whole person and stressing the importance of the interior dimension of religion, is notable for the extent to which it emphasizes the exterior dimension of the spiritual life. The hermitage, the monastery, celibacy, the religious habit, the cloister all witness to the counter-cultural quality of desert spirituality, to its emphatic insistence that to be made anew in the image of Christ one must be visibly changed. The outward signs of new life are both a witness to the world that its values are overturned by the new covenant and a means by which the interior change that challenges those worldly values might be facilitated. The desert ascetic flees society, the person entering a religious community takes a new name, they submit themselves to a discipline of life, they undergo mortification, fasting, penance. All these practices are formative for the individual. They are the hallowed means by which a growing conformity to Jesus Christ is achieved.

The desert experience begins by calling one out of the world. Salesian experience does not. For Madame de Chantal and the Monseigneur of Geneva the location of that process is first and foremost interior. It is hidden in the heart. It is only after the slow and dramatic change of person has been engraved in the center of one's being that the issue of that metamorphosis can be seen. To impress this idea on his readers, Francis relied upon the metaphor of the almond tree (an image shaped by the particular botanical knowledge of his day).

Men engaged in horticulture tell us that if a word is written on a sound almond seed and it is placed again in its shell, carefully wrapped up and planted, whatever fruit the tree bears will have that same written word stamped on it. For myself . . . I cannot approve the methods of those who try to reform a person by beginning with external things, such as bearings, dress or hair. On the contrary, it seems to me that we should begin inside. "Be converted to me with your whole heart," God said. "My child, give me your heart." Since the heart is the source of actions, as the heart is, so are they. . . .

For this reason . . . I have wished above all else to engrave and inscribe on your heart this holy, sacred maxim, LIVE JE-SUS! I am sure that your life, which comes from the heart just as the almond tree comes from its seed, will after that produce all its actions—which are its fruits—inscribed and engraved with this sacred word of salvation.[1]

Francis drew on the desert ascetic tradition but taught that mortification was an activity best hidden in the heart. Thus the desert practices which facilitated the profound renovation of character became translated, in the Salesian context, into interior realities which then might be realized exteriorly in a variety of ways depending on the setting in which the devotee finds himself or herself—for example, how to practice poverty while in the possession of wealth.

The *Introduction to the Devout Life* is based on the assumption that a fully authentic Christian devotion can be realized in virtually any circumstance. De Sales wrote this early work as a result of his direction of persons like Madame de Charmoisy, a young noblewoman of Savoy who consulted him about integrating her religious practices and aspirations with her duties as the wife of a courtier serving at the opulent French court. For "Philothea" (the addressee of *The Introduction*), devotion is primarily an interior practice, something that occurs first in the heart and secondarily makes itself known in a visible way. Which is not to say that making Jesus live is simply a private, personalized matter which need not affect anyone else. Far from it. The almond seed does flower into a tree with real fruits. But devotion should not, in Francis's view, interfere with the rightful fulfillment of the duties of one's state in life. The spiritual life is not intrusive. Rather, it springs organically from the central core of the person and adapts itself to the unique life circumstances in which he or she finds himself or herself. Philothea can integrate her devotional longings with the reality of life at the

---

1. *Oeuvres*, III, 216–217: *Introduction*, III, 23.

French court because authentic devotion is simply a true love of God which makes one quick to do good and which perfects all vocations and professions.

The fruits of living Jesus will not then necessarily result in a religious posture that looks monastic and celibate. The fruits will be uniquely imprinted on each individual life, lived out differently on each pair of lips, shoulders, and arms. The flexibility and liberality of the Salesian spirit is seen concretely in this assumption that the living Jesus has as many and as varied faces and dwelling places as there are human hearts open to his presence. The devout wife of the courtier will move modestly attired among garish finery, attend dances and theatre without attachment to the frivolity and licentiousness that sometimes accompany these diversions, fast on prescribed days but otherwise eat moderately of foods set before her, pray fervently but only as often and as long as the discharge of her familial duties recommends, cultivate friendships that are based on mutual religious aspirations and practice the unobtrusive virtues of meekness, temperance, integrity, and humility.[2]

Even when an individual is called to a more traditional form of religious life, the devotion practiced there must be primarily interior to be Salesian in spirit. This is the case with the Visitation. This women's congregation founded by the bishop and the widow had as its raison d'être the tilling of a spiritual garden for the raising of "daughters of prayer." The Visitation takes its name from the account in the gospel of Luke where the Virgin Mary, newly pregnant with the child Jesus, calls on her cousin Elizabeth who is also with child. The story is one of ordinary human interaction. No special heroic or dramatic display is portrayed. Yet hidden within the person of Mary, the miracle of divine life grows. So too, the Visitation community was not to be known by the visible, exterior mortifications they practiced nor by the heroic works they performed. Their lifestyle was to be extremely moderate by seventeenth-century ascetic standards. Instead, dying to self and letting Jesus live took the form of surrender to the demands of living in a community of charity, faithfully carrying out its rule, visiting the poor of the neigh-

---

2. Cf. *Introduction*, Book III.

borhood, practicing the life of the humble Jesus, becoming daughters of prayer.[3]

The Salesian stress on interiority, that is, on beginning from the inner, hidden life, and working outward in whatever setting or circumstances, finds eloquent expression in de Sales's language of the heart. To live Jesus meant to engrave that name on the human heart. For in Salesian spiritual anthropology, the heart is the vital core of the entire personality.[4] It is there, through the heart, that one comes to know and love God, for it is especially by virtue of the heart that humankind can be said to be made in the divine image and likeness.[5] There, at the crossroads of heaven and earth, the living Jesus becomes formed. The heart is the most adequate image Francis finds for human love for God. His is not a static picture of heart but a dynamic one. The heart is a living, ceaselessly pulsing organ which in one movement draws in God's goodness and life and in another, breathes forth his praise. The alternating movements, in which the heart alone finds rest, symbolize the two movements of love which Francis, in his own special use of traditional language, calls "love of complacence" and "love of benevolence."[6]

Throughout his writings, Francis de Sales used marvelously inventive language to describe his central intuition that it is hidden in the heart that the living Jesus comes to be. At the root of his perception, and at the deepest point of wisdom of Salesian spirituality, is the assumption, which derives in part from the Christian human-

---

3. When the Visitation was converted to a formal order in 1618 it became enclosed. The sisters no longer went outside the community to visit the poor. The emphasis in living Jesus came to be upon the cultivation of an absolute interior conformity to the will of God.

4. Drawing on medical, philosophical, and biblical notions of the heart, de Sales developed an entire theology based on the symbolism of the heart. See John A. Abruzzese, *The Theology of Hearts in the Writings of St. Francis de Sales* (Rome: Institute of Spirituality, Pontifical University of St. Thomas Aquinas, 1983), pp. 20–55. Not only was the heart considered the most important organ of the body but the source and meeting place of the life forces and the world spirit within a person, the source of fire or body heat, the seat of intelligence, will, the passions, as well as the location of all noble emotional and intellectual human qualities.

5. This assertion is not normative in the Christian tradition. For many of the great spiritual writers the image and likeness to God in the human person is found in the mind. See *Oeuvres*, IV, 136: *Treatise*, II, 15.

6. *Oeuvres*, IV, *Treatise*, Book V. A clear analysis of these two loves, of benevolence and complacence, which at first reading of the *Treatise* are confusing items, is found in Joseph F. Power, "Love of Benevolence and Liturgy" in *Salesian Studies* III, no. 1 (Winter 1966) and No. 3 (Summer 1966); pp. 27–34 are the most germane.

ist tradition, that the spiritual life is not primarily about understanding, nor solely a matter of enthusiasm. It is a dynamic, integrative process that is brought about through the engagement of the whole person. The heart in Salesian thought is the seat both of intellect and of will. There the affective as well as cognitive capacities of the person are seen to dwell. All Salesian praxis then proceeds from this conceptual point of departure.

Francis de Sales was renowned as a preacher because he proclaimed the gospel in a way that stirred his audiences' very hearts.[7] This did not mean that he simply inflamed the emotions of his listeners or that he stimulated them with challenging ideas. His congregations were moved at the profound level where love of God is activated. He reached into the human heart knowing that that heart opens onto a living divine heart. He asserted that in preaching the Word one's own words must come out of the heart as well as the mouth. One might speak beautifully, even eloquently, but in communicating the living word, "heart speaks to heart, the tongue speaks but to the ears."[8]

Indeed, the Word spoken from and to the heart is generative. For between human and divine a creative union takes place. There can be a marriage of hearts. As the marriage "ripens" and matures the two hearts of the union become more alike, more closely aligned. Gradually the human heart expands, becoming transformed into the heart of God. Such a marriage is fruitful, giving birth to "mystical children," spiritual offspring born of one's own expanded heart. Persons whose hearts are in the heart of God draw others into a like union.

Direction is part of this spiritual parenting. When Francis and Jane write that they are "holding their correspondents in their hearts" they mean a good deal more than that they wish them well. They mean that they are encircling that person in the prayerful ardor that they know to be a creative medium, opening themselves at the very center of their persons to admit another being and allowing that other to gain access to God through them. The power that draws the directee's heart is the very love of God which compels and

---

7. John Ryan has a fine essay on Francis's preaching as a preface to his translation of the saint's own classic statement on that art in *On the Preacher and Preaching. A Letter by Francis de Sales*, trans. John K. Ryan (Chicago: Henry Regnery Co., 1964).

8. *Oeuvres*, XII, 321: cf. Ryan tr., p. 64.

claims the director's heart. That divine love, like a magnet, draws all other hearts that come near. In Salesian direction the point is not to instruct but to appeal to the whole person through their vital center, to make Jesus live by winning the heart through persuasion and gentle encouragement. The Savoyard was a master of this kind of intuitive interaction that drew his directees to him and into the fire of God's love. He invited all his Philotheas to "pray for a director who is after the heart of God."

But it is in the Visitation and in Madame de Chantal's appropriation of Salesian direction that this sensitive appeal to the heart can be most clearly discerned. Visitandine superiors were entrusted with the task of seeing that this true Salesian spirit of direction was retained.

> I beg you, my dear Sister, govern your community with a great expansiveness of heart; give the sisters a holy liberty of spirit and banish from your mind and theirs a servile spirit of constraint. If a sister seems to lack confidence in you, don't, for that reason, show her the least coldness but gain her trust through love and kindness. . . . The more solicitous, open and supportive you are with them, the more you will win their hearts. This is the best way of helping them advance toward the perfection of their vocation.[9]

If all the heart symbolism given articulation in the Salesian world is visualized (and indeed this is what should be done, for Francis himself thought in images[10]), one sees the great tender heart of God undergirding all created life. Access to that heart is through the

---

9. *Sa Vie et ses oeuvres*, VIII, 557: Letter MDCCCLXXII.
10. See Henri Lemaire, *Les images chez St. François de Sales* (Paris: Editions A. G. Nizet, 1973). It was R.L. Wagner who wrote in his preface to Henri Lemaire, *Lexique des oeuvres complètes de François de Sales* (Paris: Nizet, 1962), p. ii, that "Francis thought in images. That means that for him a notion is never pure but that it results from the subtle and often unforseeable interpenetration of two related concepts. In this interplay what in itself was concrete, dense, becomes light; on the other hand, by these contacts abstractions gain substance; they take root in a nourishing soil." An interesting example of the way in which de Sales thought in images is found in the letter he wrote to Jane de Chantal concerning the emblem he envisioned for the Visitation. See *Oeuvres*, XV, 63–64: Letter DCXCIII. Also, see Abruzzese, *The Theology of Hearts*, on imagery in spirituality and the use of emblem books to convey the characteristic teachings of a particular author.

hidden doorways of the hearts of men and women. At this entry-
way, this crossroads between two realms, one finds the heart of Jesus crucified. In the actual as well as symbolic act of love in death
enacted on the cross, the heart of Christ is seen to be on fire, consumed in a holocaust of loving surrender. The flames kindled in that
oblation shoot off sparks which in turn inflame the hearts of women
and men to abandon themselves to a similar consummation of love.
The proper place, then, for a lover's devotion is kneeling at the foot
of the cross.[11]

Francis de Sales's various writings yield a panorama of images
that depict the human/divine drama as a marriage and union of
hearts, but the accounts left us by his friend Jane de Chantal show
the development of that theme specifically in terms of a martyrdom
of love. In a remarkable colloquy, written down by her sister Visitandines on St. Basil's Day in 1632, Madame de Chantal is reported
as saying,

> 'For myself, I believe that there is a martyrdom of love in which
> God preserves the lives of His servants so that they might work
> for His glory. This makes them martyrs and confessors at the
> same time. I know,' she added, 'that this is the martyrdom to
> which the Daughters of the Visitation are called and which God
> will allow them to suffer if they are fortunate enough to wish for
> it. . . . What happens is that divine love thrusts its sword into
> the most intimate and secret parts of the soul and separates us
> from our very selves.'[12]

Here the experience of living Jesus is consummately described
in terms that show Salesian spirituality as hidden in the heart. No
visible following, no heroic gesture mark the identification of the
devotee and her Lord. Rather, living Jesus takes place in the interior
of the person, in the heart. But Jesus, in this passage which became
a seminal statement of the Salesian spirit embodied in the Visitation,
is both the lover and the dying God. Jane de Chantal's own personal
devotion centered about this vision of Jesus.[13] Through the conflu-

---

11. On de Sales's vision of the heart of Jesus, refer to Abruzzese, *Theology of Hearts*, pp.
142–168.

12. *Sa Vie et ses oeuvres*, I, 356–57: *Mémoire Sur la Vie.*

13. Refer to Wendy M. Wright, "Jeanne de Chantal: Two Faces of Christ," in *Medieval
Religious Women*, Vol. II, *Peace Weavers* (Kalamazoo, Mich.: Cistercian Pub., 1987), pp. 353-
64.

ence of her own experiences of grief, loss, and loving attachment and the beloved face of the crucified, Jane was able to discover her own potential for growth, maturity, and wisdom.

The hiddenness of this loving surrender within the heart that Jane lived so eloquently was noted by her contemporaries.

> "She was hidden deep in an abyss of humility where our Lord's eyes looked on her with a special love, a love of election, as one who perfectly understood His words 'come to me . . . for I am meek and humble of heart.' "[14]

This hidden identification with her Lord was a special and subtle facet of Mother de Chantal's spiritual gift.[15] It was a discipline she had learned over many years. A highly introspective personality, given to brilliant analysis of her inner life yet prone to paralyze herself by her own self-scrutiny, Jane had gradually learned the spiritual discipline of confiding all to the hidden action of grace within the heart. She was counseled by Francis, and later counseled her own spiritual daughters, not to think about or talk about self too much. She learned to keep her focus upon her God, keeping even her own inner life hidden within the mysterious transformative presence of God in the heart. The activity of this presence was thus concealed even from herself. She came to mirror the hidden life of Jesus, to live Jesus precisely in the way in which He bound Himself at the deepest core of His person to the Father and gave Himself utterly to the Father's will.

This legacy of the martyrdom of love, which connected the Christian humanist tradition of love with the early Church's spirituality of martyrdom, was given to the community of the Visitation by its founding mother. They realized the living Jesus in the martyrdom of love hidden closely within the heart.

---

14. *Sa Vie et ses oeuvres*, I, 448: *Mémoires*.

15. This insight comes from a talk given by Elisabeth Stopp in June 1986 at the Waldron Visitation convent in Sussex, England. It represents the fruit of her reflection on Jane twenty-five years after she wrote her excellent biography of the saint, *Madame de Chantal*.

Theme VI

"We cannot always offer God great things, but at each instant
we can offer him little things with great love." (Jane de Chantal)

There is in the Salesian spirit a deep appreciation for the significance
of little things. The insistence on hiddenness in the process of spiritual growth corresponds to this appreciation. Dramatic exploits,
acts of great heroism, visible mortification are left to other members
of the Christian family. The Salesian spirit occupies an unobtrusive
kitchen pantry or perhaps a gardener's cottage in the household of
the larger Church.[1]

Yet in the interior realm a clear sense of the radical world-
changing nature of the Christian vocation is present. The heart of
the living Jesus is encountered on the cross. It is the surrendered
heart of a God bowed in naked abjection and pain. This abject dying
Jesus is very much a part of Salesian spirituality. But the arena of
the dying is interior and the opportunities for Christ-like surrender
present themselves daily in the most ordinary of circumstances. Jesus lives among people as gentleness, kindness, mutual regard,
etc.—all the little virtues that mark one as relationally aware.

That the face of Jesus crucified is also in Salesian thought the
face of the gentle humble Jesus is significant. Francis de Sales's favorite biblical quotation about Jesus, the one statement that for him
exemplified who that person was, was "Come to me . . . and learn
from me for I am gentle and lowly of heart."[2] The full import of this
choice of descriptive phrase is gleaned when one looks at the context
in which the quotation occurs. It is embedded in an eschatological
portion of the Matthean narrative in which dire warnings about im-
pending judgment are unleashed. Jesus's own words that follow reveal the nature of the mission and meaning of his own person, a
mission that is hidden to the eyes of the wise and learned and per-

---

1. An interesting point of fact: when de Sales, in 1622, visited Lyons while he was in
the entourage of the king and queen of France, he chose to lodge in the gardener's cottage on
the grounds of the Lyons Visitation rather than to stay in the overcrowded quarters occupied
by the royal suite. It was there that he died.

2. Matthew 11:29–30.

ceived only by those who take upon themselves the identity of Jesus himself, an identity which confounds the "world" by its lowliness and gentleness. Jesus's sonship, his essential identity with the Father, is stressed. Thus the revelation of the nature of divinity itself through the Son—the kingdom image—is seen as taking upon oneself the yoke of the gentle, lowly heart of Jesus. To take the yoke that Jesus offered was thus, in de Sales's mind, to cultivate all within the self that corresponded to this gentle, lowly Savior. Hence, the "little virtues" take on salvific significance.

These very Salesian virtues were to be acquired by following the time-honored ascetic pattern of self-mortification. Always in the Christian tradition death to self—asceticism—is linked to growing likeness to God—the obtaining of virtues. Only the mortifications prized in Salesian thought were not visible and heroic but ordinary and unobtrusive. Patiently enduring the pains of work rather than observing long fasts, practicing charity toward an unlikable neighbor rather than wearing a hair shirt, curbing the immoderate impulses of one's own heart rather than violently assaulting one's sensual flesh—these are the preferred methods of Salesian asceticism.

Indeed, for de Sales, the mortifications one does not choose are in fact superior to those that one might select oneself. For in those unbidden difficulties, self-discoveries and frustrations which call forth humility and patience, there is "more of God's will than our own." God's will—the will of God's good pleasure—is here discovered. And it is in dying to one's own will, even one's own will to achieve a certain idea of perfection, that God's will can come to live and act in each person.

There are innumerable and varying lists of the little virtues found throughout the writings of Monseigneur de Sales and Madame de Chantal.[3] Perhaps here it is sufficient to explore three such qualities that seem to be especially dear to their two hearts and to describe some of the ways in which they attempted to put these into practice. Chief among the Salesian virtues, and the one that belongs distinctively to this tradition, rather than to the wider contemplative heritage, is *douceur*. A difficult term to translate, *douceur* has been

---

3. See Thomas A. McHugh, "The Distinctive Salesian Virtues, Humility and Gentleness," *Salesian Studies*, October 1963, pp. 45–74.

rendered in English as "sweetness," "gentleness," "graciousness," "meekness," and "suavity." None of these translations do it full justice. *Douceur* is a quality of person that corresponds to the light burden offered by the Matthean Jesus to those otherwise heavy-laden. It connotes an almost maternal quality of serving that is swathed in tender concern. Salesian *douceur* also suggests a sense of being grace-filled, graceful in the broadest use of the term. This gracefulness extends from external demeanor—polite manners and convivial disposition—to the very quality of a person's heart—the way in which a person is interiorly ordered and disposed. Here one is reminded of the tradition of *l'honnête homme* popular in the seventeenth century which stressed the harmony, beauty, and grace of the whole person and which de Sales saw as reflecting the beauty and harmony of God.[4] From this point of view, devotion is expressed by the graceful life. By participation and correspondence it is also life in God.

Douceur is ideally to be exhibited in all situations, even the most difficult, and to underlie one's every act. It was a particular hallmark of the character that the Visitation community was to assume.

> In the name of God, my dear daughter, [wrote Jane,] wait for the improvement of these good sisters with great patience, and bear with them gently. Treat their hearts affectionately, making them see their own faults without undue emotion or strong feelings or harshness, but so that through your help they will be encouraged to overcome them and still remain enamored of your maternal graciousness. This is the matchless way to win souls and it is characteristically ours.[5]

But gentleness of heart was not in Salesian thought restricted to the cloister. All were called to live out the kingdom image to which Christ himself called them. "The one who can preserve gentleness (*douceur*) in the midst of sorrows and sufferings and peace in the midst of the multiplicity and busyness of affairs—that person is almost perfect," wrote Francis.[6] Indeed, Francis lived his *douceur* in the midst of one of the most troubled epochs in history. Rent by the

---

4. On this topic see Ruth Murphy, *Saint François de Sales et la civilité chrétienne* (Paris: A.G. Nizet, 1964) and James Langelaan, *Man in Love with God.*

5. *Sa Vie et ses oeuvres*, IV, pp. 555–56.

6. *Oeuvres*, XVII, 260: Letter MCCXXIII, to Mère de Bréchard.

strife of religious and political warfare and torn by the interpersonal and familial vendettas of the aristocracy, Europe of his day was a hotbed of violence. Francis's early mission to the Chablais, his youthful plans to retake the city of Geneva by prayer and fasting, his intervention in public embroilments, his own personal struggle to transform his anger into the peace of Christ: all these attest to the rightfulness of his reputation as peacemaker.[7]

A second little virtue highly prized in Salesian spirituality is humility. Long an ideal in the classic spirituality of Christendom, humility retained its centrality in the thought of Francis and Jane.[8] Humility expressed for them the recognition of the reality of human dependence upon God, the truth of the profound limitations of the individual person and communities of persons, and the acknowledgement of illusory human pride that strives to be like God and so conspires in its own destruction. This profound sense of humility is a contrapuntal accent to the Salesian theme of human liberty. But by no means is it a negation of that insight. For liberty does not imply a state of God-like omnipotence, a we-can-do-it-by-ourselves attitude. Liberty simply bespeaks the gift of choice, the opportunity given by the Creator to love or not to love. Sustaining this intuition, in Salesian thought, is a deeper sense of the sheer gift of life itself and a recognition of the unmerited, unconditional quality of that gift. The immensity of the gift appears most clearly and in proportion to the extent to which one grasps this fact. Humility is thus not "humiliation" in the negative sense that might be perceived as psychologically unhealthy today. It is rather a recognition of one's own littleness and need in relation to the Creator's immense and lavish abundance.

---

7. Evidence of Francis's career as peacemaker is found in E.J. Lajeunie, *Saint François de Sales, L'homme, la pensée, l'action*, Vol. II (Paris: Editions Guy Victor, 1964), pp. 99ff. Jaroslaw Pelikan in *Jesus Through the Centuries: His Place in the History of Culture* (New Haven: Yale University Press, 1985) p. 175, states the "only truly new answer of the 16th and 17th centuries to that dilemma [of Jesus's teachings on war] came first from Erasmus, then from certain Anabaptists, Quakers, and other peace groups of the radical reformation who bore witness to an understanding of the person and message of Jesus by which holy war was not holy and just war was not just." De Sales cannot be claimed to be a Christian pacifist in this sense but he did see himself and devout individuals as called to making Jesus live as Prince of Peace.

8. Humility as the primary human disposition that allows for the entry of God in the soul is central to the thought of Augustine, Benedict, Bernard, Teresa and innumerable other Christian spiritual writers.

INTRODUCTION

With characteristic subtlety and acuity, Francis de Sales wrote in his *Introduction* of types and degrees of humility that he hoped Philothea would come to acquire.[9] He first treats outward humility, teaching that it resides in refusing to pride oneself in rank, honor, or beauty. Deeper interior humility refers to a lively consciousness of the gifts given to one by God coupled with a sense that one has not merited any of these. This humility does not parade itself for that would be to act against its very nature. True humility should lead the devout person to a knowledge of his or her own lowliness— what de Sales called abjection. It is love of abjection that characterizes the most profound degree of humility. Here, in the cherishing of one's own partial and fragile humanity, one meets God. One loves one's abjection because it is precisely in this kenotic attitude, one's utter emptiness of self, that one enters into a profound participation with the crucified Lord. In imitation of the humble God-man who lovingly embraced his own abjection in his passion and death, Salesian humility seeks to let this Jesus truly live.

The Salesian spirit also shows an affection and preference for persons not generally considered by society to be viable subjects for human actualization. It should be remembered that the gentle, lowly Matthean Jesus beloved by the Savoyard announced that the Father's nature in the Son was hidden from the eyes of the wise and powerful and revealed only to the "little ones." Francis de Sales, like Jesus, sought out and associated himself with such socially abject persons.

It has been noted that Francis de Sales felt himself particularly called to the direction of women. He had a special genius for this work. This undoubtedly is in part because he simply felt an affinity for members of the female sex. He was close to his mother and counted among his closest confidants many women.[10] Perhaps at another level, he felt called to minister to women because they were among those deemed inferior by society. The bishop was conscious of the centuries-long literary debate which focused upon the place and capabilities of women.[11] He threw his lot in with those who fa-

---

9. *Oeuvres*, III, 139–160: *Introduction*, III, 4–7.
10. On Francis and women see especially Th. Schueller, *La Femme et le saint: La femme et ses problèmes d'après saint François de Sales* (Paris: Les Editions Ouvrières, 1970).
11. Francis's relationship to the historic controversy over women is discussed in Th. Schueller, *La Femme*, pp. 36–50.

vorably evaluated the "second sex." Yet paradoxically he cherished women for the very qualities that marked them as unexceptional in the world's eyes. He loved the very hiddenness of most women's lives, their self-effacement and lowly status.

So he, with his friend Jane, established a religious congregation not only specifically for women (the Visitation was not to be an off-shoot of or under the tutelage of any male religious order) but for women who were considered, in seventeenth-century France, unfit for religious life. Their institute was founded for widows, the infirm, those of frail constitution, those not attracted to physical austerities: any woman with a genuine call to a retired contemplative life who did not meet the exacting standards for admission to one of the women's religious communities then abounding in France.[12] For this they were roundly criticized. The Savoyard was accused of wasting his time starting a convalescent hospital when he should be building a genuine religious community. But in fact he was witnessing to his belief that it is to the little ones that the kingdom of God is revealed. Because of the humbleness of their lives, Jesus lives in them.

Along with the humble "little people," Francis stressed the "little occasions" that present themselves daily as opportunities to love God and neighbor. In his mind, great occasions for exhibiting one's devotion rarely presented themselves but little occasions were there every day. Checking anger, selfishness, and pride in unexpected and ordinary encounters was a good deal more humbling than waiting for a dramatic episode through which one might display one's fervor. In fact, the constant and ordinary repetition of small loving acts was, in his view, the most efficacious means to humility which, in its turn, was the living out of the Jesus of Matthew's gospel.

Third of the key Salesian virtues is simplicity. Simplicity unlocks a whole treasure chest full of Salesian wisdom that is best exemplified in the life of the community of the Visitation. This institute was established for women and its spiritual formation was directed toward drawing out what were perceived as the strengths of the feminine character and redirecting what were considered its

---

12. Chief among these were the Carmelites who adopted a life of rigorous physical austerity. The reformed members of the Benedictine family were equally prone to adopt severe regulations—witness Angélique Arnauld's reform of Port Royal, on which see F. Ellen Weaver, *The Evolution of the Reform of Port Royal* (Paris: Editions Beauchesne, 1978).

typical weaknesses.[13] A simple lifestyle was practiced; the women were adequately if modestly dressed, fed, and sheltered. They were encouraged to cultivate an interior state of simplicity, a transparency of self that shed the thick veil that self-protection and self-consciousness could draw about them. Visitandines were not to adorn themselves, either outwardly or inwardly. They were to be simple before the world and before God. The subtlety of this insight for a community of women must be mentioned. In the seventeenth century, vanity was perceived to be chief among the spiritual problems of women. Women habitually had a tendency to see themselves through the eyes of others, to, as it were, become objects to themselves by becoming obsessed with maintaining an attractive arrangement of inner or outer features.[14] Simplicity held the key to unlocking this attitude, which kept a woman focused only on her artificially arranged self and away from the true discernment of her whole self and God.

In keeping with this insight, Visitandines were taught a practice of prayer which turned the attention away from the self and onto God. Artless unself-consciousness and a transparent self open to its creator were to be the fruit of this practice. Similarly, each Visitation sister was encouraged to cultivate a simple quiet faith, a trust in God's mercy that did not focus upon difficulties in prayer or upon undue self-concern—what is known in the tradition as scrupulosity.

> Those who are led by this path [Jane wrote] are obligated to a great purity of heart, humility, submission and total dependence on God. They must greatly simplify their spirit in every way, bypassing each reflection on the past, the present, and the future. And instead of looking to what they are doing or will do, they must look to God, forgetting themselves as much as possible in all things in favor of this continual remembrance, uniting their spirits in his goodness in everything that happens to them from moment to moment. This should be done very simply.[15]

---

13. On de Sales's understanding of the feminine character see Wright, *Bond of Perfection*, pp. 133–40. Also, Schueller, *La Femme et le Saint*.

14. For a contemporary reading of the issue of women and vanity which has informed this analysis of the Visitation, consult John Berger, *Ways of Seeing* (Great Britain: British Broadcasting Corporation and Penguin Books, 1972), pp. 45ff.

15. *Réponses de notre Sainte Mère Jeanne-Françoise Frémiot, Baronne de Chantal* (Annecy: Imprimerie Aimé Burdet, 1849), p. 520.

At the root of this simple self held up as the ideal of Salesian perfection is the belief that in such simplicity Jesus truly lives. The naked Jesus, stripped and dying on the cross, is the paradigm for human actualization. It is in identification with this living God that the Visitandine prepares herself to move farther and farther into an experience of utter dependence on God alone.

Francis de Sales's own predilection in prayer was not identical to that experienced by the Visitandine community. But it is typically Salesian in its affinity for little ways. For Francis, the humble, time-honored valleys of discursive meditation, not the heights of contemplative peaks, were preferable for almost everyone. He wrote to Jane early in their relationship when she had consulted a Carmelite prioress about the methods of prayer practiced within the cloister.

> So the good Mother says that there is no need to employ the imagination in order to envision the sacred humanity of the Savior. Not, perhaps, for those who are already far advanced along the mountain of perfection. But for those of us who are still in the valleys, although desirous of mounting, I think it expedient to employ all our faculties, including the imagination. Nonetheless, I have already stressed in another letter that this imagining must be very simple and, like a humble seamstress, thread affections and resolutions onto our spirits.[16]

Thus de Sales made known his preference for the little, ordinary ways of prayer.

Gentleness, peace, humility, simplicity. These are some of the little virtues esteemed by Francis and Jane. By the practice of such virtues in the little occasions that present themselves every day, Jesus, gentle and humble of heart, lives.

---

16. *Oeuvres*, XIII, 162: Letter CCCXXXIX.

Jane de Chantal and
Salesian Spirituality

It has been appropriate, until this point, to treat the two major forms of Salesian spirituality as essentially one, to focus upon the similarities in the thought of Francis de Sales and Jane de Chantal and to draw a broad picture of the larger vision that the two of them shared. Now it appears necessary to begin the task of making distinctions between the spiritual visions of these two religious leaders. This is a task that has yet to be accomplished by scholarly efforts. As has been mentioned, Jane's perspective has generally been treated as essentially a carbon copy of her mentor's.[1] We have already suggested that the concrete circumstances in which they each lived out the Salesian spirit markedly altered the way in which that spirit was manifested. De Sales was a bishop, a man of constant activity immersed in the world of Counter-Reformation Catholicism. In France, this faith was very much identified with the militant spirit of reform and growth that marked the post-Tridentine Church in Europe through the mid-seventeenth century. It was also much identified with the intentions and activity of the French monarchy. His episcopal responsibilities brought Francis into frequent contact with people in all walks of life, from members of the royal household, courtiers in their entourage, and gentlemen and women in all spheres of society, to religious superiors and members of a wide variety of religious orders. He was also a product of the educational ambiance of his time. Trained in law, theology, philosophy and rhetoric, he made full use of all the skills that delineated him as a man of the world. This immersion in society could not fail to have implications for the way de Sales's spirituality became articulated, particularly since he served as a spiritual director for a great variety of persons.

And what of Jane de Chantal? She was called to a life situation quite distinctive from that of her friend. She became the mother su-

---

1. Jane is almost consistently seen, Pygmalion fashion, as Francis's chief handiwork. See Marcelle Georges-Thomas, *Sainte Chantal et la spiritualité salésienne* (Paris: Editions Saint-Paul, 1963).

INTRODUCTION

perior of a women's religious community. Although the original
structure envisioned for the Visitation was somewhat ahead of its
time, it nonetheless was informed by the traditional assumptions
about monastic life. It was taken for granted in the early seventeenth
century, as it had been in much of the medieval world, that the celibate life and especially the monastic contemplative life was the
queen of lifestyles and a special kind of intimacy with and dedication
to God was offered to persons responding to such a calling. Persons
in this life were expected to dedicate themselves to the process of
sanctification in a way not required by those still "in the world."
Emphasis was placed upon the acquisition of religious virtues and
the cultivation of an attitude of obedience to the superiors and rules
of the order. The process of individual sanctification was placed
squarely within the structural and ideological confines of the community. Hence, there was a virtual identification of the rules of
community with the will of God for all who were indeed called to
participate in the life of a religious order. All this stands in the background of Jane de Chantal's articulation of her spiritual vision. Her
milieu was monastic and contemplative in a way that Francis de
Sales's was not.

Her world was also especially feminine in a way that her
friend's was not. Although the bishop was noted for his direction of
women, and Jane was sought as a guide by men as well as members
of her own sex, her primary experience, the environment in which
she attained spiritual growth and the community to which she was
primarily called to minister, was female. The Visitation was unique
among religious groups of the time in being founded especially for
women. Other women's communities were offshoots or under the
jurisdiction of male orders and their practices and spiritualities derived from these masculine origins. The Visitation was created for
women and the spiritual vision which it eventually embodied came
into being through the experience of women living together and attempting to give articulation to the way they experienced and lived
for God. Jane is at the core of this attempt, for while Francis wrote
a rule for the Visitandines and gave spiritual conferences to them
about the spirit of the life to which they were dedicated, the specific
ways this life came to be enacted in its daily reality was much more
informed by Jane.

These two friends were also very different personalities, a point that scholarship has not been loath to press. This fact has sometimes been used to explain the differences sensed in their teachings. From the hindsight of three and a half centuries one is struck with his equilibrium, her ardor, his patience, her anticipation, his gracefulness, her compassion. It is also important to remember that during the formative years of her self-identity before she met Francis and began collaboration on their joint spiritual pursuits, Jane de Chantal knew herself, not as a vowed religious, but as a baroness, as a wife and mother successfully fulfilling the expectations of these social roles and being shaped by the self-knowledge, relational perceptions and interpersonal skills that marriage and motherhood can bring out in a woman. This early background is very much evident in Jane's sensitive direction of her Visitation sisters.[2]

Given all this, one wonders whether there is not something distinctive in the way Jane lived out the Salesian spirit precisely because she was a woman. She, after all, claims her womanly identity not only by biological happenstance but by the fact that for the first half of her life she aligned herself completely with the societally defined roles of wife and mother, and later exercised her maternal gifts as superior of a women's religious community.

Contemporary research on the psychology of gender lends some support to these assertions. It has been suggested that women's and men's psychological perspectives may be quite different—men exhibiting greater concern for autonomy and achievement, women being oriented toward relationships of interdependence. Indeed, women may, as they mature, find the deepening of their own wisdom in a growing recognition of the vast fabric of relationships that sustain and nurture all human life. Women may view reality, adopt moral perspectives and form a self-concept in a manner at variance from that of men, women tending to give pride of place to values of affiliation and care rather than achievement and principles of jus-

---

2. On Jane's maternal charism, see Wright, "St. Jane de Chantal's Guidance of Women," in *Salesian Living Heritage*, Vol. I, no. I (September 1986), 16–28, and Vol. II, no. 1 (September 1987), 10–22 and Sr. Patricia Burns, "La tendresse en Ste. Jeanne de Chantal" in *Annales Salésiennes*, No. 3 (1972), 10–11. Several recent sources explore the issue of motherhood and a woman's way of knowing. References to this are woven throughout Mary Field Belenky et al., *Women's Ways of Knowing: Development of Self, Voice and Mind* (New York: Basic Books, Inc., 1987). Cf. also Sarah Ruddick, "Maternal Thinking" in *Rethinking the Family: Some Feminist Questions*, ed. Barrie Thorne (New York: London, 1982).

tice.[3] This being the case, a woman's spirituality may differ markedly from a man's. This is an issue of some complexity in the study
of the Christian spiritual tradition, for the language and assumptions
set forward by asceticism as normative tend to orient the person
more toward autonomy than toward interrelationship. Furthermore, while the richness of the discourse from that historical tradition (especially as seen in its entirety) does, we believe, contain a
range of expressions that can offer a wide perspective on humankind's encounter with religious truth, that tradition tends to assume
that its language carries the same spiritual meaning for members of
both sexes. It has only recently been questioned whether the primary metaphors for the life of spirit, such as pilgrimage or journey,
being derived as they are from models of development appropriate
to men, are in fact apt metaphors for women's spiritual perceptions.[4]
Similarly it has of late been questioned whether the classic definition
of human sin as rooted in pride and self-assertion is not really a gen-
der-specific definition. Women's "sins" seem to stem from a lack of
sense of self resulting in diffuseness, triviality, and self-depreca-
tion.[5] The implications of such provocative assertions are of interest
in the study of women in the Christian past.

The following will be an exploration—at best tentative in its
conclusions—of several themes found in Salesian spirituality and
the way in which these themes were distinctively expressed by Jane
and Francis. The language they used was often the same, but what
that language signified, as a spiritual and psychological reality, may
vary. We begin to look at Jane independently of Francis, to see her,
both as superior of the Visitation and as a woman with a unique
spiritual life. She was rooted in the spirit we have come to identify
as Salesian, as was her friend Francis. An imitation of him, she was

---

3. See Carol Gilligan, *In a Different Voice* (Cambridge, MA: Harvard University Press,
1982), Jean Baker Miller, *Toward a New Psychology of Women* (Boston: Beacon Press, 1976), and
Belenky, *Women's Ways of Knowing*. For a view of counseling (which would also be applicable
to spiritual direction) employing this perspective, see Miriam Greenspan, *New Approaches to
Woman and Therapy* (New York: McGraw-Hill, 1983).

4. On this see Carol Ochs, *Women and Spirituality* (New Jersey: Rowan & Alanheld,
1983).

5. Valerie Saiving writes of this in "The Human Situation: A Feminine View." Orig-
inally published in *The Journal of Religion* (April 1960), it is reprinted in *Womanspirit Rising: A
Feminist Reader in Religion*, ed. Carol Christ and Judith Plaskow (San Francisco: Harper &
Row, 1979).

not. The attempt will be made briefly to describe three prominent Salesian themes—abandonment to the will of God's good pleasure, the possibility of human perfection and prayer—as they were experienced differently by these two Salesian exponents.

Abandonment to the Will of God's Good Pleasure

As with de Sales, there is an emphasis on abandonment to the will of God's good pleasure in Madame de Chantal's spirituality. We have seen how central the notion of living between the two divine wills was to the Salesian perspective. Human effort must be directed toward the discernment of and conformity to the signified will of God—the divine will to be done. Yet one must be always ready to abandon oneself to the will of God's good pleasure—God's will done—as it presents itself in the factual situations of everyday life. For the bishop this abandonment manifested itself in a variety of ways but tended to be most clearly identified with indifference: about one's spiritual and material welfare as well as the course of human relationships. Jane also cultivated a flexible attitude toward the spiritual and material goods she might or might not receive. When we turn our attention to this woman's prayer we will be able to see how poignantly and courageously she practiced the virtue of indifference. Yet in the realm of relationship, abandonment takes on a distinctive quality in Jane's version of the Salesian spirit. Rooted as she was in family through her experience of marriage and motherhood as well as through her own woman's apprehensions, abandonment to what life held in store for her was a painful process. She lost her husband barely two weeks after the birth of their last child. Of her four children who survived birth three died before her, one as a child, two in young adulthood. Later in life she suffered the loss of virtually all those who were closest to her. Under these circumstances, an acceptance of things "as they are" as a religious category became involved with the acceptance of the process of grief. For Jane found herself intimately woven into a fabric of relationships. As a woman that relational fabric was fundamental to her self-identity and spiritual well-being. Contemporary research in women's psychology has suggested that in general women's self-identity is threatened by separation while male identity is threatened by intimacy.[6] Moreover, affiliation with others, while important for both sexes, plays a different role in the psychology of women and men. Affiliations tend to make women feel deeply satisfied, fulfilled and successful, free to go on to other things.[7] This is not a "problem" but a strength unless the expectations of religion or culture assume that human development necessarily moves toward a subordination of affiliative bonds to other aspects of development and achievement. This would imply that abandonment to the will of God's good pleasure, especially when it involved the acceptance of the loss of others, could evoke a somewhat different response from a woman than from a man. This is not to suggest that men do not grieve deeply when confronted with loss but that the focus in the grieving differs. For Jane, abandonment meant that hard dying to the very persons to whom nature and temperament had bonded her. Because an identity-shattering grief is so much more present in her experience of abandonment, Jane's response to situations of loss is more emotionally charged and fraught with ambiguity than Francis's. Jane's articulated grief centers more upon the severing of the bond between herself and others and the inner conflict this initiates. It is instructive to compare the ways in which they dealt with the deaths of those close to them. The bishop wrote of his own mother's passing:

> I had the courage to give her the last blessing, to close her eyes and mouth and to give her the last kiss of peace at the moment she passed away; after which my heart swelled and I wept over this good mother more than I have done since I was ordained; but it was without spiritual bitterness, thanks be to God.[8]

Francis, it should be noted, was especially dear to his mother and he was perhaps closer to her than to anyone else. He certainly was deeply moved and affected by her death. Compare now Jane's communication to her brother André in 1622 when Francis himself died.

---

6. This is one of Gilligan's fundamental insights. See her *In a Different Voice*.
7. Cf. Miller, *Toward a New Psychology of Women*.
8. *Oeuvres*, XIV, 262: Letter DLXXXI.

You say you want to know what my heart felt on that occasion. Ah, it seems to me that it adored God in the profound silence of its terrible anguish. Truly, I have never felt such an intense grief nor has my spirit ever received so heavy a blow. My sorrow is greater than I could ever express and it seems as though everything serves to increase my weariness and cause me to regret. The only thing that is left to console me is to know that it is my God that has done this, or at least, has permitted this blow to fall. Alas. My heart is too weak to support this heavy burden, how it needs strength. Yes, my God, you put this beautiful soul into the world, now you have taken it back; may your holy name be blessed. I don't know any other song except 'May the name of the Lord be blessed.'

My very dear brother and dear Father, my soul is filled with grief but also full of the peace of God's will which I would never oppose with even the slightest resistance. No, my dear Father, I affirm what it has pleased Him to do—to take from us that great flame that lit up this miserable world and let it shine in his kingdom, as we truly believe. May His name be blessed. God has chastised me as I deserved because I am certainly too insignificant to merit such a great blessing as well as the contentment that I had in seeing my soul held in the hands of such a great man who was truly a man of God.

I believe that God in his supreme goodness does not want me to take any more pleasure in this world and I don't want to take any more either except to hope to have the joy of seeing my dearest Father in the bosom of His everlasting goodness. Yet I still will to remain in exile—yes, my dear brother, I truly do. It's a terribly difficult exile for me, this miserable life. But I want to stay here, as I said, as long as it is God's plan for me. I will let Him do with me as He wishes. Remember me as well as this little family [the Visitation] in your holy sacrifices. They are so sorrowful and suffer with such grace and resignation that I am consoled. We will leave here soon to go back to poor little Annecy. My pain will be redoubled by seeing our sisters there. God be blest in and for everything. Long live His will. Long live His pleasure.[9]

Jane tends to seek for some unfelt consolation, some explanation that will restore the sense of unity she has lost. She focuses over

---

9. *Sa Vie et ses oeuvres*, Tome V, Lettres 2, 90–92.

and over again, from various perspectives, on the severed relationship that now undercuts her very sense of self: she speaks of Francis as gift that has been taken away, of her soul having been held in his hands, of this world now [with his absence] as "miserable," and "exile," as without pleasure. One finds in her a tendency to view the tragedy as consonant with her own unworthiness or as a chastisement or corrective for human shortcomings. She only rests in the existential fact of loss in the company of these other ways of acceptance and abandonment.

It has been typical to view her style of encounter with loss as a sort of imperfect realization of what Francis de Sales realized perfectly in his version of abandonment. This assumes however (as was then normative in Christian spirituality) that less attachment is to be equated with a better or more spiritual state. We suspect that emphasis on autonomy and separate identity fundamental to male psychology is more in evidence in this assumption than is any intrinsic spiritual good. It is also possible to see Jane's mode of coping as characteristically feminine and at the same time spiritually mature. For, as has been suggested, women seek something more complex than autonomy as it is defined for men, a fuller not a lesser ability to encompass relationships to others, simultaneous with the fullest development of self.[10] Her letters show her as willing to deal realistically with the natural process of grief, as able to admit a great deal of her own emotional experience into the articulated process of abandonment, as aware of the importance of relationship in her life, as willing to live with ambiguity and as capable of admitting the poignant human need for explanation that arises at times of inexplicable loss. We see this woman, whose "lack of indifference" is sometimes judged harshly, as having the mature integrity to value and trust her own experience, to acknowledge the value and importance of relationships and the sacred quality of an attachment that nurtures, provides, sustains and protects in cooperation with a God who does likewise.

Jane's perception of abandonment was not contoured solely by the deep interpersonal ties which she cultivated and then was required to surrender. It was also shaped by her own interior encoun-

---

10. Miller, *Toward a New Psychology*, quoted in Joann Wolski-Conn, *Women's Spirituality, Resources for Christian Development* (New Jersey: Paulist Press, 1986), p. 117.

ter with God. Of all the saints in recorded Christian tradition she has the dubious distinction of having undergone one of the longest periods of spiritual desolation or "dark nights." For somewhere in the vicinity of forty years she struggled in prayer with the painful experience of the absence of God, turbulent doubts against the faith, and revulsions against all things religious. The intensity of her struggle was so great during the last decade of her life that she admitted to a longing even for death. To abandon herself to the state in which she found herself therefore involved tremendous courage and embrace of suffering. During her lifetime and afterward in biographical accounts, the common attribution of these spiritual trials was to a purgative process allowed by God to divest a strong personality of its "all-too-human" attachments. She herself thought of herself as called to a total renunciation of self as her unique way to God.

But we question the traditional equation: more spiritual equals less "human," and regard Jane's identity as a woman the key to unlocking her experience of abandonment. Jane's version is a radical and poignantly suffered version of Francis de Sales's own utter detachment and acquiescence to the will of God which he understood to be manifest in the particular circumstances of each life. The difference between their two experiences of abandonment seems to reside in the fact that he found it acceptable, even enlivening, to live with the emotional tension that such a stance could effect. The "not-knowing" encapsulated in his moment of crisis led him into the arena of freedom. For his female counterpart, however, the act of surrender and abandonment to God was coupled with the yearning for completion, for an experienced relationship with the divine. Jane loved God with all the powerful forces of loving commitment that she came to both by way of temperament and by cultivation in marriage and motherhood. Once again, it is all too easy to see her state of abandonment as merely an imperfectly realized version of what her friend so clearly achieved. For Jane, the emotional ambivalence generated by the tension of loving so deeply, desiring a response and not receiving one, was fraught with poignancy. As a woman shaped by marriage and motherhood, she felt the psychic rightness of continually dwelling in the embrace of a fully realized relationship. Yet she met her fate bravely and did not shrink from honestly acknowledging what was occurring within her. Her love then consisted in accepting the fact that God "wished" her to reduce all her desires to one single desire—to renounce all, even her own desire for relationship with Him, into His hands. Jane de Chantal's embrace of her own inner darkness introduces into Salesian spirituality a sense of courage and unswerving loyalty to one's own experience, be it inviting or not, that is uniquely her own.

The Possibility of Human Perfection

One other element latent in Francis's vision and brought into focus by Jane is the idea of perfection. The bishop, a Christian humanist, certainly believed in the possibility of human perfection but his insistence on indifference as a seminal principle in the spiritual life tended to downplay any zealous quest for perfection or inordinate concern for the achievement of a "perfect" spiritual state. With Jane the issue was somewhat different. She, like her companion, sensed the potential of the human soul. And she, like him, accepted the principle that it was preferable to be indifferent to one's spiritual progress than to be overly concerned about it. Yet early on in her own experience the quest for continual perfection became central to her vision of the life lived in true love of God. As early as 1610, when she was still the young mother superior of the Visitation, she experienced a "ravishment" during Mass while on a visit to Burgundy. The chief communication which she received in this heightened state, about which she spoke to only a handful of people during her lifetime, was an acute sense of

> the pleasure that God takes in a pure and perfect soul. Then she was inspired to vow that she would also do whatever was most perfect and agreeable to God.[11]

---

11. *Sa Vie et ses oeuvres*, I, 156f: *Mémoires*, p. 167. Three incidents in Jane's life have traditionally been singled out as expressive of her temperament. Bougaud in his *Histoire de Sainte Chantal et des origines de la Visitation*, 2 Vols. (Paris: Librairie Poussielgue, 1863) particularly has created an image of the saint, based on these occurrences, as the "strong woman"—hard and unyielding in her personality. These are: the branding of the name of Jesus on her breast, the moment when she walked over her son's body (two complimentary modern interpretations of this can be found in Stopp's *Madame de Chantal* and Wright, *Bond of Perfection*), and the making of a vow to always do the most perfect thing. Elisabeth Stopp, in her talk given in June 1986 at the Waldron Visitation in Sussex, England, focused upon the third exemplary moment, pointing out that some have seen Jane's taking this vow as scrupulosity. She sees it

INTRODUCTION

This emphasis on perfection as pleasing to God is echoed in her instructions to the novices of the fledgling Visitation houses. It was certainly not to be identified with the heroic and visible exploits abounding in other religious orders of the day, but was consistently related to the acquisition of the "hidden virtues" and the embrace of a life of great interior simplicity and conformity to the will of God. Yet, to Jane, this simple life was to be realized perfectly.

The theme of perfection was likewise a dominant factor in her own spiritual development. For years after the ravishment in Burgundy she attempted to come to grips with the perfection that she felt called to by God. She had long felt her vocation to be a continual process of loving surrender to God alone. The self-denial this demanded was to cut into the most intimate of her connections and achieved a peak in the year 1616 when she made a retreat and chose detachment as her topic for reflection. At this time, she and Francis de Sales had enjoyed twelve years of a friendship that was explicit in its affection, its mutuality, and its shared zeal for each other's deepening love of God. The impulse behind the retreat was her own desire to render herself more pleasing to God by a more completely realized interior dependence on Him alone. But she found herself unable to focus upon her chosen theme because her friend Francis was ill. She was constantly preoccupied with concerns about his health. Struggling with this fact, she asked permission of him (they were in contact by letter) to prolong her retirement in order to do justice to her theme. It was at this point that they both realized that their very attachment was itself an obstacle to her desired detachment and dependence on God. Francis agreed to the extended retreat and counseled her to give into God's keeping all her concerns and all her relationships, including her relationship with him.

> You must not take any kind of wet nurse but you must leave the one who nonetheless still remains and become like a poor little pitiful creature completely naked before the throne of divine mercy, without ever asking for any act or feeling whatsoever for this creature. At the same time, you must become indifferent to everything that it pleases God to give you, without considering

---

rather as the "hidden heroism" of a very Salesian gesture as a result of which an impetuous and even proud young woman was slowly transformed into a saint through the practice of the little hidden virtues.

INTRODUCTION

if it is I who serve as your nurse. Otherwise, if you took a nurse
to your own liking you would not be going out of yourself but
you would still have your own way which is, however, what you
wish to avoid at all costs.[12]

Jane likewise perceived her dependence on her friend and, in
an exchange of letters both passionate and full of ecstatic pain, the
two friends released each other from their spiritual embrace and,
without renouncing their shared commitments to each other or their
friendship, did set each other free. The freedom was for Jane, of
course, not without its element of wounding and grief. These she
always had to wrestle with, and her spirituality is marked by its
faithfulness to her own ambiguous and complex experience. She
wrote to her friend:

My God, my true Father, how deep the razor has cut. Can I
remain in this feeling long? At least our good God, if he so
pleases, will hold me firm in my resolutions as I wish. Ah, how
your words have given my soul strength. How it consoled and
touched me when you wrote 'What blessings and consolations
my soul has received to see you utterly naked before God.' Oh,
may Jesus grant you to continue to be consoled by this and me
to have this happiness.

Alas, my only Father, I have been reminded today of that
one time when you ordered me to denude myself, I replied 'I
don't know what is left' and you said to me 'Haven't I told you,
my daughter, that I will strip you of everything?' Oh God, how
easy it is to leave what is outside ourselves. But to leave one's
skin, one's flesh, one's bones and penetrate into the deepest part
of the marrow, which is, it seems to me, what we have done, is
a great, difficult, and impossible thing to do save for the grace
of God. To him alone then glory is due and may it be given forever.[13]

The vividly embodied and relational quality of Jane's love is
attested to in this passage as is her keen desire to give herself utterly
and perfectly to God. That "perfect" also meant "detached" Jane
learned from her Christian heritage. This absolute dependence on

---

12. *Oeuvres*, XVII, 215: Letter MCCIII.
13. *Sa Vie et ses oeuvres*, IV, 115–17: Letter LXV.

God alone Jane lived out with tenacity and passion. One is reminded here that Jane's favorite saints were the Christian martyrs, those heroes and heroines of her heritage whose witness was radical and absolute. Like those she admired, there was in Jane a hunger for complete and uncompromised self-giving, a hunger that could never be entirely satisfied. This hunger fed Jane de Chantal's desire for perfection throughout her life. But as has been suggested, her encounter with perfect detachment was also profoundly contoured by her very woman's capacity for relationship. To detach herself from her primary source of spiritual nourishment, Francis, was indeed an act of martyrdom for this woman who had in her early formative years defined herself in and through relationships of love.

Yet one suspects there is in Jane's insistent quest for perfection, especially as it centered on perfect dependence upon God alone, something that reflects her own instinctual woman's wisdom. For part of the maturation that must occur in any woman's spiritual life is an increasing trust of her own experience, her coming into a sense of self and God which does not slavishly depend upon others' definition of what that relationship should be. The feminine "sinful" tendency to live vicariously or parasitically through others (to the detriment of both others and self) must be countered by a courageous attempt to author one's own life-vision and to give oneself completely in a mature surrender to God.[14]

The inner integrity that centers the self on God is not necessarily inconsistent with the recognition of the deep need for human ties that sustains a woman's sense of self. Somehow these two realizations must be artfully balanced. Yet it seems clear that the Christian tradition's version of perfect dependence on God too often reflects a male model of autonomy that is nuanced quite differently from what one begins to see through Jane de Chantal's experience.

With Francis, Jane shared a view of the human person as capable of perfection. But, unlike her friend, Jane's spirituality also exhibits a keen awareness of the imperfection discovered in human beings. Not that the great bishop was unaware of human frailty. Indeed, he was extremely sensitive to individual differences of temperament and gift and adapted his direction to accommodate these,

---

14. On this growing beyond predetermined expectations that marks a woman's spiritual maturation see Joann Wolski-Conn, "Therese of Lisieux from a Feminist Perspective," in her *Woman's Spirituality*, 317–25.

never expecting too much of those given only moderate talents and capacity. Yet the balance in his spirituality leans toward optimism and shows a trust in human and divine resources to bring all things into the fullness of their potential. Jane's perception was less sunny. In part, we suspect this was due to her own ambivalence felt when struggling for perfect detachment—an ideal, as traditionally expressed, perhaps more congruent with male identity. The language of Christianity, while replete with examples of relational values as part of spiritual maturity, does tend to emphasize values of detachment and autonomy when envisioning the heights of spiritual attainment. Jane, courageous in her articulation of her inner life, lived her quest for perfection within the ambiguous context of a spiritual language that held up this sort of detachment as an ideal and of a temperament and life experience that suited her to the cherishing of relational attachments.

But it was not simply the high ideals she set herself that may have contributed to her sense of the reality of human imperfection. Her own inner tribulations, her difficulties with her headstrong son and one determinedly worldly daughter, her sorrow at the suffering generated by the religious wars that plagued her century, all contributed to push her from optimism to a sense of the fragility and limitation of the person. She seems to have had a gift for identifying with others' sufferings. Throughout her married life and widowhood she spent herself lavishly in service to the poor and ill: visiting the incurably sick, nursing those with diseases too loathsome for others to bear, operating a daily bread line for the poor. Jane had a capacity—related in part no doubt to her feminine relational gifts—for feeling others' anguish as her own. Hence, her awareness of suffering and limitation, both others' and her own, was acute. Coupled with her high ideals about the perfection that she believed pleased God, this sense of the human condition lent her spiritual posture a certain poignant and passionate awareness of the necessity for divine grace. She knew how deeply she loved God and had glimpsed how much the divine love inclined to her, yet between the two the ambivalence of evil, of sorrow, of grief and of disappointment loomed. These were the issues around which her spiritual struggle revolved.

INTRODUCTION

Prayer

The location in which this struggle took place was an interior one. Like de Sales, Jane's spirituality definitely focused upon the interior life, especially the heart, as the place of encounter with God. There in the inner realm all asceticism and human transformation was felt to have its proper beginning. Like her friend also, Jane did not espouse the practice of rigid devotional exercises or highly structured interior regimes of any kind. For both of them the basic task of any interior practice was to cultivate a freedom to follow the voice of God that is discerned uniquely in each individual. For Jane de Chantal, that voice had a certain quality with which the interiority of her spiritual life is marked. For her the central fact of her inner being, the way in which she was drawn by God, was a contemplative type of prayer which she referred to as the prayer of "simple attentiveness" or "simple entrustment to God" ("*simple regard*" or "*simple remise en Dieu*"). This prayer consisted in a hidden and quiet waiting, an expectant attention to the presence of God. It was a virtually imageless and wordless type of prayer to which she had been drawn early in her own development. Her practice in this prayer was fostered by her contact with the Carmelites of Dijon when she was a young widow newly under Francis's direction. The prayer practiced in the French Carmel at the time was influenced by the spirit and teachings of Barbe Acarie, who was in part responsible for the Teresian Carmel's introduction onto French soil.

Francis seems to have been generally supportive of Jane's attraction to this simple wordless prayer although he attested to the fact that he was hesitant about the advice Jane received at the Carmel which introduced her to the idea that she should deliberately repress all images and thoughts in prayer. Such teaching would be inconsistent with the interior freedom cultivated by the bishop in his spiritual vision. Yet for Jane this prayer seemed to come quite naturally. It was the prayer that she identified throughout her life as most uniquely her own. It was the prayer which later became the inner charism of the Order of the Visitation and about which she wrote:

> When the time comes to present ourselves before His divine Goodness to speak to Him face to face, which is what we call

84

prayer, simply the presence of our spirit before His and His before ours forms prayer whether or not we have fine thoughts or
feelings. . . . He is touched with the prayer of a soul so simple,
humble and surrendered to His will.[15]

Deeply interior and characterized by its hiddenness, this prayer was
expressive of Jane de Chantal's entire approach to the spiritual life.
This life was for her essentially a mystery shrouded both from the
eyes of others and from herself as well. The living Jesus slowly being
impressed upon her heart was a reality she could herself only
obliquely discern. Her own sense of darkness and of a distance from
God that was so continuous and painful masked for her the actual
activity of God within. To others, it was radiantly obvious. Virtually all accounts depict her late in life as gentle, patient and as surrendered in "an abyss of humility."

The interiority of the widow de Chantal's experience was a
quality shared by her friend Francis. But her spiritual life had a distinctive and hidden quality all of its own. The slow working of God,
unseen and unfelt, rendered Jane utterly simple and transparent.
Through her wordless prayer she brought herself into a divine presence that would shape her into itself. Perhaps her deep longing for
consummated relationship and the facts of both her inner and her
outer losses prepared her for an encounter with God that could not
be contained in words. For there is a realm of both human experience and of the taste of God that partakes more of the spirit of music,
of dance, of poetry than of discursive capacity. There is in icon and
in image a perception of this realm far more accurate than in syllo-
gism or worded definition.[16] And Jane, tenaciously faithful to her
own wisdom, discovered an iconic prayer for herself that became the
vessel through which her unique religious perception could be born.
In her wordless relationship she saw herself as an uncarved statue

---

15. *Sa Vie et ses oeuvres*, I, 447.
16. Susanne Langer in her *Philosophical Sketches* (New York: Mentor, 1962), 79–81 writes:

> There is, however, an important part of reality that is quite inaccessible to the
> formative influence of language: that is the realm of the so-called "inner experi-
> ence," the life of feeling and emotion. . . . Art objectifies the sentence and desire,
> and self-consciousness and world-consciousness, emotions and moods, that are
> generally regarded as irrational because words cannot give us clear ideas of them.

waiting before a sculptor who alone held in imagination the image of what she, as the final work of art, might be.

Within herself Jane indeed waited in this way. Her prayer was the iconic gesture of her total person as it inclined toward its God. There the depths of love, the heights of expectations, the hard facts of loss and grief could be gathered up and offered at the place within herself—that fine point of the soul—where explanation, construct, description and human knowledge fail and something of the immense and mysterious undivided will of God is grasped.

Texts

The text of Francis de Sales's letters translated here is that of his *Oeuvres complètes*, a critical edition begun in 1892 by an English Benedictine, Dom H.B. Mackey, and published over many years by the Sisters of the Visitation of Annecy.[1] The twenty-sixth and final volume of text appeared in 1932, and was followed eventually by a twenty-seventh volume of indices in 1964. Of this edition, Volumes XI through XXI, published from 1900 to 1923, contain Saint Francis's extant correspondence, about 2,100 letters, which has been estimated to be about one-tenth of the letters he actually wrote. A challenge to the authenticity of some of these letters has been refuted by André Ravier and Albert Mirot,[2] with the result that the overall critical value of the Annecy edition has been reaffirmed. The same André Ravier has published a selection of almost 400 letters which, in its notes and appendices, has been very helpful to those preparing the present volume.[3]

The text of the letters of Jane Frances de Chantal is generally that of the Plon edition of her life and works,[4] published in the 1870's, with Volumes IV through VIII containing the letters, again, in total a little over 2,000. At present a critical edition of her letters is being published by Editions du Cerf. Though only the first two volumes have appeared, the editor, Sister Marie-Patricia Burns of the Visitation Monastery of Annecy, has checked the Plon text of the letters selected here against the new critical work, and has also supplied some previously unpublished texts; these valuable contributions will be noted in each case.

---

1. *Oeuvres de Saint François de Sales, Evêque de Genève et Docteur de l'Eglise, Edition Complète*, d'après les autographes et les éditions originales. . . . Publiée . . . par les soins des Religieuses de la Visitation du Ier Monastère d'Annecy, 27 Volumes (Annecy: J. Niérat, *et al.*, 1892–1964).

2. *Saint François de Sales et ses faussaires* (Paris: Picard, 1971).

3. *François de Sales Correspondance: Lettres d'amitié spirituelle* (Paris: Desclée de Brouwer, 1980).

4. *Sainte Jeanne-Françoise Frémyot de Chantal, Sa Vie et ses oeuvres*. Edition authentique publiée par les soins des religieuses du premier monastère de la Visitation Sainte-Marie d'Annecy, 8 Volumes (Paris: Plon, 1874–79).

INTRODUCTION

Given the extent of the correspondence left by each of our authors, it is clear that the present volume represents but a sampling, not only of the total number of letters, but even of those which are primarily concerned with spiritual direction. The selection was made on the basis of which letters seemed most representative of Salesian spirituality, and which have a certain unity and focus, both literary and doctrinal; that is, we have preferred whole letters to quotations from here and there, although we have taken the liberty of omitting certain extraneous or repetitive material, indicating such omissions in the usual way. A third and less important guideline has been that of not redoing letters already available in recent English translation. This explains the absence here, for example, of the sublime correspondence between Jane and Francis during her retreat of 1616,[5] or of certain letters of Francis contained in Elisabeth Stopp's selection.[6]

In both major parts of this volume we have grouped the letters according to the person or class of persons addressed, and, within each group, followed a chronological order. In this way the reader, once introduced to the correspondent by the preliminary heading, may follow the contours and the progress of the direction given to this specific person, albeit on the basis of a very fragmentary record.

With specific regard to the selection of Francis's letters, many others of great interest from the point of view of Francis's own personal life,[7] his role as bishop and preacher, his various diplomatic missions, both religious and civil, and the like, have been omitted simply because they are not letters reflecting a continuing spiritual direction relationship. One consequence of this is that, with one exception, all of Francis's letters in this volume are addressed to women. Francis corresponded with many men, some of them close friends (e.g., Antoine Favre; Jean-Pierre Camus, Bishop of Belley; the Duke of Bellegarde), and these letters contain spiritual advice and responses to specific questions. He may have directed men in a

---

5. See Wendy M. Wright, *Bond of Perfection*, pp. 163–170.

6. *Saint Francis de Sales, Selected Letters* (New York: Harper, 1960).

7. Manfred Tietz has rightly questioned the extent of the autobiographical content of Francis's letters in his *Saint François de Sales' "Traité de l'amour de Dieu" und seine Spanischen Vorläufer* (Wiesbaden: F. Steiner, 1973), pp. 36–40. Though the letters of Francis hardly reflect an outpouring of his soul, A. Ravier has gathered many references to "l'expérience spirituelle de Saint François de Sales à travers ses confidences épistolaires," in *Lettres d'amitié spirituelle*, pp. 745–758.

continuing way, but his extant correspondence does not reflect this. In fact, a criticism made of him during his lifetime suggests the contrary.[8]

Jane de Chantal's letters, on the other hand, reflect a great variety of direction relationships: with men and women, religious and lay, her brother the archbishop, and a military commander who eventually became an Oratorian priest, to say nothing of her own daughter, Françoise. Another important part of her correspondence selected here was addressed to other members of her young community for their own personal direction and the guidance of others. One correspondent who does not figure in the present selection is Francis de Sales himself, and that fact calls for some explanation, especially in view of what has been said about their relationship. While a number of Jane's letters to Francis are extant,[9] all those from the early years of their friendship when she was almost always in Burgundy and he in Savoy, and almost all the letters which prompted and responded to Francis's letters over the years are not extant. Francis had kept them carefully, and after his death they were given to Mother de Chantal, who consciously and personally burned them. Her action, which must be understood in its unique context,[10] remains in many ways mysterious and inexplicable. One may well regret, along with all her devotees since her earliest Visitandine biographer, the irreparable consequences of her decision, without daring to judge it from afar.

The marvel is that we do have as complete a record as we do, both of the friendship of Francis and Jane, and of their respective relationships with their various directees.

Finally, to avoid unnecessary repetition we have generally omitted the following:

• the motto "Live Jesus" at the beginning and "God be praised" at the end of individual letters;

---

8. "You are a bishop, and you spend your whole time with women!" was the charge of an overzealous Paris priest. See Maurice Henry-Coüannier, *Saint Francis de Sales and His Friends*, Trans. Veronica Morrow (Staten Island, N.Y.: Alba House, 1964), p. 352.

9. See Jeanne-Françoise Frémyot de Chantal, *Correspondance*. Edition critique établie et annotée par Soeur Marie-Patricia Burns (Paris: Les Editions du Cerf, 1986—), Vol. I, 1605–1621.

10. See the excellent treatment of Elisabeth Stopp in *Madame de Chantal: Portrait of a Saint* (Westminster, Md: Newman, 1963), pp. 190–94.

INTRODUCTION

- the salutation, except where it helps to suggest the tone of a letter;
- the place where the letter was written, especially when it is Annecy;
- the complimentary close and signature.

Scriptural Citations

In a manner remarkable for a Counter-Reformation bishop, Francis de Sales exuded a familiarity with the stories, the sense, and indeed the text of the Bible. He spontaneously used scriptural examples and phrases, as he said, "not always to explain them, but to explain myself by means of them."[11] If this was true of his published works, it is even more evident in his letters.

Following the Annecy edition, we have endeavored to identify these scriptural quotations, adaptations, and allusions by way of footnote. In the case of direct quotations, the *New American Bible* version is followed as closely as possible, and the footnote simply gives the scriptural citation. Often, however, the quotation will differ somewhat from our modern English versions either because Francis cites from memory, or he adapts the material slightly to fit the context. The abbreviation "cf." ("confer," "compare") indicates such situations. Sometimes Francis relies upon a Vulgate reading which differs from the Greek and Hebrew sources used as the basis for today's English translations. Thus, the reader who consults an English translation may find a text quite at variance from the one Francis used. In this case, the Vulgate version is included in the note.

Chapter and verse citations for the Old Testament follow the numbering of the Hebrew text. The abbreviations for the books of the Bible follow those used in the *New American Bible*.

---

11. *Oeuvres*, III, 2: *Introduction*, "Advice to the Reader."

Francis de Sales

LETTERS

MADEMOISELLE DE SOULFOUR

*Mlle de Soulfour, whose father was an acquaintance of Francis
de Sales through the "Cercle Acarie," was a novice in a religious
community in Paris at the time Francis wrote her the following letters. Young, fervent, with high ideals of perfection, she had difficulty in accepting human frailty in herself and in the nuns with
whom she lived. She had confided her disillusionment and uncer-
tainties to Francis and told him of her wish to enter the more strict
Carmelite Order. While respecting her youthful idealism and her
desire for the absolute, Francis directs the troubled young woman
to a more realistic appreciation of her own limitations and the imperfections of others, and to greater trust in God's providence. She
did enter the Carmelite monastery at the rue Saint-Jacques in Paris
and persevered in her vocation until her death in 1633.*

July 22, 1603[1]

Mademoiselle,

My brother has just brought me one of your letters, a letter that
makes me praise God for the bit of spiritual light He has given you.
And if the clouds have not yet completely disappeared, don't be surprised. Spiritual fevers, like physical fevers, are ordinarily followed
by after-effects which are useful to the one who is recovering, for
several reasons, but especially because these reactions destroy other
infections which had caused the illness.[2] They remind us of our recent illness and make us fear a relapse, which could easily happen if
we allowed ourselves too much freedom. They hold us in check,
warning us to take care of ourselves until we have completely re-
gained our health.

But, my dear daughter, since you have already half escaped

---

1. *Oeuvres*, XII, 202–206: Letter CXC.
2. In an earlier letter (*ibid*. pp. 180–184: Letter CLXXXI) Francis had used the language of spiritual illness and cures to suggest that Mademoiselle de Soulfour was in distress
because of the multiple and lofty desires she had conceived without bringing any of them to
reality. By this time the crisis had passed, but more remained to be drawn from the experience.

from the terrible path which you were following, it seems to me that now you ought to try to get a little rest, and take time to think about the vanity of the human mind and how easily it becomes confused and wrapped up in itself. I'm sure you can readily see how the interior trials you have experienced were caused by the multiplicity of reflections and desires that came about in your great hurry to attain some imaginary perfection. By this I mean that your imagination had formed an ideal of absolute perfection which your will wanted to reach, but, frightened by the huge difficulty, or rather, impossibility of attaining it, remained, as it were, heavy with child, unable to give birth.[3] On this occasion your will multiplied futile desires which, like bumblebees and hornets, devoured the honey in the hive, while the true and good desires remained starved of all consolation. Therefore, slow down, take a few deep breaths, and by reflecting on the dangers you escaped, avert those that might come your way. Treat as suspect all those desires which, in the common opinion of wise persons, cannot be followed up by good effects. Such would be, for example, the desire for a certain kind of Christian perfection that can be imagined but not carried out, one that many people can talk about but that no one puts into practice.

Know that patience is the one virtue which gives greatest assurance of our reaching perfection,[4] and, while we must have patience with others, we must also have it with ourselves. Those who aspire to the pure love of God need to be more patient with themselves than with others. We have to endure our own imperfections in order to attain perfection; I say 'endure patiently' not 'love' or 'embrace': humility is nurtured through such endurance.

In truth, we have to admit that we are weak creatures who scarcely do anything well; but God, who is infinitely kind, is satisfied with our small achievements and is very pleased with the preparation of our heart.[5] And what do I mean by 'the preparation of our heart'? According to Scripture, "God is greater than our heart,"[6] and our heart is greater than the whole world. When our heart, by itself, in its meditation, prepares the service it should ren-

---

3. Cf. 2 Kgs 19:3.
4. Cf. Jas 1:4.
5. Cf. Ps 108:2; Vulgate Ps 107:2: "Paratum cor meum," which becomes the theme of the rest of this letter.
6. 1 Jn 3:20.

der God, that is to say, when it makes plans to serve God, to honor Him, to serve the neighbor, to mortify our exterior and interior senses, and similar good projects, at such times it performs marvels; it prepares and plans its action so that it may reach a high degree of admirable perfection. All this preparation is still not at all in proportion to the grandeur of God—which is infinitely greater than our heart—yet it is ordinarily greater than the world, greater than our strength and our exterior actions.

On the one hand, anyone who reflects on the grandeur of God and the immensity of His goodness and dignity can never go to excess in making grand and glorious preparations of the heart for Him. It prepares for Him a body that is mortified and not rebellious, an attention to prayer that is not distracted, gentle conversation free of rancor, and a humility in which there are no bursts of vanity. All this is very good; these are fine preparations, but there is still more that we must do to serve God as we should. When all this preparation is done, it remains to be seen who will carry it out, for when it comes to putting all this into practice, we fall short and realize that these perfections can be neither so grand nor so absolute in us. We can mortify the flesh, but not so perfectly that it doesn't rebel; in prayer, our attention will be often interrupted by distractions; and so with the other things I have mentioned.

Must we, for that reason, be worried, anxious, pressured, distressed? Certainly not. Is it necessary to think up volumes of desires in order to stimulate ourselves to reach this indication of perfection? Of course not. All we need to do is express simple wishes which witness to our gratitude. I can say, "Well, well, so I can't serve and praise God as fervently as the seraphim!" but I mustn't waste time making wishes as if I were going to reach such exquisite perfection in this world, and say, "I *want* this, I'm going to make every effort to get it, and if I don't, I'm going to be furious!" I don't mean that we shouldn't head in the direction of perfection, but that we mustn't try to get there in a day, that is, a mortal day, for such a desire would upset us, and for no purpose. In order to journey steadily, we must apply ourselves to doing well the stretch of road immediately before us on the first day of the journey, and not waste time wanting to do the last lap of the way while we still have to make it through the first.

I have one thing to tell you, so remember it well: we are sometimes so busy being good angels that we neglect to be good men and women. Our imperfections are going to accompany us to the grave. We can't go anywhere without having our feet on the ground, yet we don't just lie there, sprawled [in the dust]. On the other hand, we mustn't think we can fly, for we are like little chicks who don't have wings yet. We die little by little; so our imperfections must die with us, a little each day. Dear imperfections, they force us to acknowledge our misery, give us practice in humility, selflessness, patience, and watchfulness; yet, notwithstanding, God looks at the preparation of our heart and sees that it is perfect.

I don't know if I am writing you to the point, but it came to my heart to say this to you, since I figured that part of your recent pain came about because you had made such grandiose preparations; then when you discovered that the results were very small and your strength insufficient to put all these desires and projects into practice, you felt a kind of let-down and a measure of impatience and anxiety. These feelings were followed by a lack of self-confidence, weariness, and moments of weakness and depression. If this is what happened, learn from the experience and from now on be very careful.

Let us go by land since the high sea is overwhelming and makes us seasick. Let us stay at our Lord's feet, like Mary Magdalene[7] whose feast we are celebrating, and practice those ordinary virtues suited to our littleness—little peddler, little pack—these are the virtues which are better practiced in going downhill than in climbing, and suit our legs better: patience, forbearance toward our neighbor, service of others, humility, gentleness of heart, affability, tolerance of our own imperfections, and similar little virtues. I do not say that we are not to ascend by prayer, but that we do so one step at a time.

I recommend to you holy simplicity. Look straight in front of you and not at those dangers you see in the distance. As you say, to you they look like armies, but they are only willow branches; and while you are looking at them you may take a false step. Let us be firmly resolved to serve God with our whole heart and life. Beyond that, let us have no care about tomorrow.[8] Let us think only of living today well, and when tomorrow comes, it also will be today and we

---

7. Lk 10:39.
8. Cf. Mt 6:34.

can think about it then. In all this we must have great trust and resignation to God's providence. We must make provision for enough manna for the day, and no more.[9] Let us not doubt that God will provide more for us tomorrow, and the day after tomorrow, and all the days of our pilgrimage.

I heartily agree with Father N.'s advice that you find a director into whose care you may place your soul. You would love to have no other director than our gentle Jesus, but He does not want us to disregard the direction given us by His servants when it is available; when it is lacking, He can make up for all we need; but it is only if you are reduced to such an extremity that you will experience this.

What I wrote you was not by way of keeping you from writing to me and speaking to me of your soul which is very dear to me, but simply to lessen the intensity of the confidence you are placing in me, which, considering my inadequacy and the distance that separates us, cannot be of much use to you, even if I am affectionately devoted to you in Jesus Christ. So write to me in all confidence and have no doubt that I shall answer you faithfully. I have added what you want at the bottom of this letter so that it will be for you only.

Pray hard for me, please. It's unbelievable how busy and overwhelmed I am by this great and difficult charge.[10] You owe me this charity by the very nature of our friendship, and by the fact that, in return, I remember you continually at the altar and in my feeble prayers. Blessed be our Lord. I beg Him to be your heart, your soul, your life. . . .

[1605–1608][11]

Mademoiselle,

Recently I received a letter from you which is very precious to me because it shows that you have confidence in my affection which certainly and without a doubt is all yours. My only regret is that I hardly know how to answer what you ask me concerning the diffi-

---

9. Cf. Ex 16:16–21.

10. The years of Francis's most extensive direction by letter coincided with his first years as bishop, a responsibility entailing an ever increasing busyness to which he often alluded.

11. *Oeuvres*, XIII, 385–388: Letter CDXLI. The date is uncertain, as is the recipient of this letter which, since the earliest editions, has been inscribed "to a young woman." We follow the Annecy editors who, on the basis of internal evidence, proposed de Soulfour as the likely addressee.

culties you are experiencing in prayer. Also, I know that you are in a place and among people where you lack nothing on this subject; but charity, which delights in mutual exchanges, prompts you to seek my opinion, just as you are sharing yours with me. So I shall say a little something to you.

The uneasiness that you experience at prayer, together with your anxiety to find a subject that can captivate and satisfy your mind, is in itself enough to prevent you from finding what you seek. When we are too intent in our search for something, we can look at it a hundred times without seeing it.

Such useless anxiety can only result in weariness of mind which in turn produces this coldness and numbness in your soul. I don't know what remedies you should apply, but I do think you would gain a great deal if you could keep from being so anxious, for that is one of the greatest obstacles to devotion and real virtue. It pretends to incite us to good, but all it does is cool our ardor; it makes us run, only to have us stumble. That's why we have to be on guard against it at all times, especially during prayer.

And to help you be vigilant in this, remind yourself that the graces and benefits of prayer are not like water welling up from the earth, but more like water coming down from heaven; therefore all our efforts cannot produce them, though it is true that we must ready ourselves to receive them with great care, yet humbly and peacefully. We must keep our hearts open and wait for the heavenly dew to fall. Never forget to carry this thought with you to prayer: in prayer we approach God and place ourselves in His presence for two reasons.

The first is to render to God the honor and praise we owe Him, and this can be done without His speaking to us or our speaking to Him. We can fulfill this duty by acknowledging that He is our God and we, His lowly creatures,[12] and by remaining before Him, prostrate in spirit, awaiting His orders. How many courtiers there are who go into the presence of the king over and over again, not to speak to him or listen to him speak, but just to be seen by him and to indicate by their regular appearance that they are his servants! This aim we have in presenting ourselves before God simply to demonstrate and prove our willingness and gratitude to be in His

---

12. Cf. Ps 95:6–7.

service is excellent, very holy and very pure, and, therefore, a mark of great perfection.

The second reason why we present ourselves before God is to speak to Him and to hear Him speak to us through inspirations and the inner stirrings of our heart. Ordinarily, we take great delight in doing this because it is very beneficial for us to speak to such a great Lord; and when He answers us, He pours out much balm and precious ointment, and in this way fills our soul with tremendous consolation.

So, Mademoiselle, my dear daughter (since this is how you want me to address you), one or other of these two benefits can never be absent from your prayer. If we are able to speak to our Lord, let us do so; let us praise Him, pray to Him, listen to Him. If we are unable to speak because our voice fails us, let us, nevertheless, stay in the hall of the King and bow down before Him; He will see us there, will graciously accept our patience, and look with favor on our silence. Another time we will be very surprised when He takes us by the hand, chats with us, and walks with us up and down in His garden of prayer; and even if He never does this, let us be satisfied that it is our duty to be in His entourage and that it is a great grace and a still greater honor that He allows us to be in His presence. In this way, we won't be overeager to speak to Him because this other manner of being near Him is no less useful to us and, in fact, may be more so, although not so much to our taste.

So when you come before the Lord, talk to Him if you can; if you can't, just stay there, let yourself be seen, and don't try too hard to do anything else. This is my advice. I don't know if it will work, but I'm not worried about that, for, as I've told you, you are in a place where much better advice than mine is available to you.

As for your fear that your father may cause you to lose your desire to be a Carmelite because he insists on your waiting so long before carrying out your wish, say to God: "O Lord, all my desire is before You,"[13] and let Him do as He wills. He will manage your father's heart and will shape it to His glory and your profit. Meanwhile, nurture your good desire and keep it alive beneath the ashes of humility and resignation to God's will.

You have my prayers, as you ask, for I could not forget you,

---

13. Ps 38:10.

especially at holy Mass. I trust that in your charity you do not forget me in your prayers either. [. . .]

MADAME BRÛLART

The Lenten sermons Francis de Sales preached in Dijon in 1604 marked the beginning of an exchange of letters of spiritual direction with several women of high birth in Burgundy. Among these were Madame de Chantal and two of her friends: Madame Brûlart and her younger sister, the abbess of Puits d'Orbe. Marie Bourgeois married Nicolas Brûlart, president of the Burgundian Parliament, in 1602. Francis's sermons had inspired the young woman to live her Christian commitment in a more fervent manner, but she needed guidance, especially in leading a devout life in the midst of the responsibilities and privileges of her high position. Because she was energetic, active, and anxious, Francis had to be patient in encouraging her to be calm and to avoid excess.

Annecy, May 3, 1604[14]

Madam,

I cannot write you in one letter what I promised you, for I don't have enough free time to summarize all that I have to tell you on the subject you want me to explain. I will tell it to you a little at a time; besides being convenient for me, this will be advantageous for you too, as it will give you time to mull over my suggestions.

You have a great desire for Christian perfection; this is the most generous desire you could have. Nurture it and help it to grow every day. The means of attaining perfection vary according to the diversity of callings: religious, widows, and married persons—all must seek this perfection, but not all by the same means. For you, Madam, who are married, the means is to unite yourself closely to God and to your neighbor, as well as to all that concerns them.

The principal means of uniting yourself to God are the sacraments and prayer. As to the sacraments, you should not let a month go by without receiving communion; and after a while, depending on the progress you will have made in the service of God and fol-

---

14. *Oeuvres*, XII, 267–271: Letter CCXVII.

lowing the counsel of your spiritual guides, you should communicate more often.[15] But as to confession, I advise you to go even more frequently, especially if you have fallen into some imperfection which troubles your conscience, as often happens at the beginning of the spiritual life. Still, if you cannot conveniently get to confession, then contrition and repentance will do.

As for prayer, you should apply yourself to it frequently, especially to meditation, for which, it seems to me, you are well suited. So every day spend a short hour in prayer in the morning before going out, or else before supper; be careful not to make your prayer either after dinner or after supper, for that would be harmful to your health. To help yourself pray well, you might prepare beforehand the point on which you are to meditate so that, as you begin your prayer, you have your subject matter ready. And for this purpose you may read authors who have written on the life and death of our Lord [. . .]; from these choose the meditation you want to make, read it attentively so as to remember it at the time of prayer when you will have nothing more to do than to recall the points, still following the method which I wrote out for you in the meditation I gave you on Holy Thursday.

Besides that, often pray spontaneously to our Lord, whenever you can, and in whatever setting, always seeing God in your heart and your heart in God. Enjoy Grenada's books on prayer and meditation, for there are none that can teach you better or move you more powerfully than these.[16] I should like you not to let a day go by without giving half an hour or an hour to spiritual reading, for that could be like a sermon for you. These are the principal means of uniting yourself to God.

The ways by which we can unite ourselves to our neighbor are very numerous; but I will mention only a few of them. Since God wants us to love and cherish others, we must see our neighbor in Him. This is the counsel of St. Paul who orders servants to serve

---

15. The frequency with which Christians in the West have received communion has varied through the centuries. See, for example, Joseph Jungmann, *The Mass of the Roman Rite* (New York: Benziger, 1951–55), Vol. 2, pp. 359–367. The Council of Trent had encouraged more frequent communion, but at the time of Francis de Sales, reception of communion by a lay person more than once a month was still somewhat exceptional.

16. Louis of Grenada (1504–1588), a Spanish Dominican often recommended by Francis de Sales, had written a book of meditations which was available in French translation since 1572.

God in their masters and their masters in God.[17] We must practice this love of our neighbor and express it outwardly; and even if at first we seem to do so reluctantly, we must not give up on that account, for this feeling of aversion will, in the end, be conquered by the habit and good dispositions that result from repeated acts. We must bring this intention to our prayer and meditation; having begged God for His love, we must ask Him also to grant us love of others, especially of those persons we have no inclination to love.

I advise you to take the trouble now and then to visit hospitals, to comfort the sick, and to have compassion for their infirmities, letting these touch your heart; and pray for the sick even as you give them whatever help you can. But in all this, be very careful that your husband, your servants, and your relatives be not inconvenienced by overly long visits to church, by too lengthy withdrawals to pray and noticeable neglect of your household responsibilities or, as sometimes happens, by your trying to control the actions of others, or showing too much disdain for gatherings where the rules of devotion are not precisely observed. In all these instances charity must prevail and enlighten us so that we yield to the wishes of our neighbor in whatever is not contrary to the commandments of God.

You must not only be devout and love devotion, but you must render it lovable to everyone. Now you will make it lovable if you render it useful and pleasing. The sick will love your devotion if they receive care and comfort from it; your family will love it if they see you more attentive to their well-being, more gentle in handling affairs, more kind in correcting, and so on; your husband will love it if he sees that as your devotion increases, you become more warm and affectionate toward him; your relatives and friends will love it if they see you more free, supportive of others, and yielding to them in matters that are not contrary to God's will. In short, we must, as far as possible, make our devotion attractive.

I am sending you a little paper I have written about Christian perfection, which I would like you to pass on to Madame du Puits d'Orbe. Receive it in good part, as also this letter, which comes from a heart that is totally devoted to your spiritual good and which has no greater desire than to see the work of God accomplished in you perfectly.

---

17. Eph 6:5–7.

I beg you to remember me in your prayers and communions, and I assure you that I shall always remember you in mine and shall ever be, Madam, your very affectionate servant in Jesus Christ.

Memo on Christian Perfection[18]
(Fragment)

Everyone is obliged to strive for the perfection of Christian life, because our Lord commands that we be perfect and St. Paul says the same.[19] Perfection of Christian life consists in conforming our wills to that of our good God, who is the sovereign standard and norm for all actions. So in order to acquire perfection we must always consider and recognize what God's will is in everything that concerns us, so that we can flee what He wants us to avoid and accomplish what He wants us to do.

There are some matters in which it is clear what God's will is, as in what concerns the commandments or the duties of one's vocation. That is why we must always seek to carry out well what God expects of all Christians, as well as what our own vocation requires of us in particular. Anyone who does not do this much with care can possess nothing but a fraudulent devotion.

There are still other matters about which there is no doubt whether God wills them, such as trials, illnesses and chronic conditions. That is why we should accept them with a good heart, and conform our will to that of God who permits them. Anyone who can arrive at the point of not only supporting them patiently but even of willing them, that person can be said to have acquired a great conformity. Thus, the death of relatives, various losses, illnesses, dryness or distractions in prayer—these give us opportunities to grow in perfection.

But we must go further and see this will not only in great afflictions but even in little reversals and minor inconveniences that we will always meet with in this unhappy life.

In this regard many people make a mistake because they pre-

---

18. *Oeuvres*, XXVI, 185–187. Francis would occasionally draft short memos on basic topics which could circulate among several of his directees. This memo, though not complete, is an interesting example of the genre.

19. Mt 5:48; 2 Cor 13:11 which in the Vulgate read "perfecti estote."

pare themselves only for major afflictions and remain totally without defense, strength or resistance when it comes to small ones. Actually it would be more understandable to be less prepared for major afflictions which happen but rarely, and to be prepared for the little ones which come up every day and at every moment. I will give you an example of what I mean: I prepare myself to suffer death patiently—which can happen to me but once—and I do not prepare myself at all to put up with the inconveniences I encounter from the moods of those I am with, or the pressing spiritual demands which my work brings me and which arise a hundred times a day. And that is what makes me imperfect.

There are many other things I am not obliged to do either by the general commandments of God or by the duties of my own vocation, and with these it is necessary to consider carefully in liberty of spirit what would tend to the greatest glory of God, because that is what God wills. I said "in liberty of spirit" because this should be done without pressure or anxiety, but by a simple glance at the good which our action can produce, such as, for example, to make a short pilgrimage, to go to confession, to visit a sick person, to give a small sum for the love of God. If it is not a matter of great importance, then we should not invest a great concern in it, but after a little thought we must decide. And if afterward the action or the decision doesn't seem good, and it looks as if I had made a mistake, I should in no way blame or bother myself about it, but rather humble myself and laugh at myself.

But if it is a matter of importance, like changing one's profession, making final vows, undertaking a long voyage, or giving a great sum of money to charity—after having thought about it for a while, we must confer with the spiritual persons to whom we look for direction, and go along with their advice with simplicity, for God will assist them to direct us rightly. And if through their fault the decision is not the best in itself, that won't prevent it from being the most useful and meritorious for you, for God will render it fruitful.[20]

---

20. The manuscript breaks off in the middle of the next paragraph. Compare this early text with the *Treatise on the Love of God*, VIII and IX, especially VIII, 14 (*Oeuvres*, V, 105–107).

November 22, 1604[21]

I praise God with all my heart that your letter shows the great determination you have to conquer all difficulties in order to be truly devout in your vocation. Do this and expect great blessings from God; more blessings will result in one hour of such well-ordered devotion than in a hundred days of an exaggerated or mournful piety, the product of your own ideas. Hold fast to your present way and don't let yourself be shaken in your resolve.

You tell me that you have let up somewhat on your practices of devotion while living in the country. Well, you have to restring your bow and begin again with that much more care; but another time you must not let being in the country throw you off course. No, for God is found there as well as in the city. You now have my little note on meditation, so put it into practice with peace and calm.

Please forgive me, dear Madam, for making this letter a little shorter than you would like. It's because the good man who is going to deliver it is in such a hurry to get on his way that he isn't allowing me time to write. I pray our Lord to give you the special help of His Holy Spirit to enable you to serve Him heart and soul, according to His good pleasure. Pray for me, for I need it. I never forget you in my poor prayers. [. . .] May God be ever with you and in your heart. Amen.

[March] 1605[22]

I was very happy with your letter of January 20 because it seems to me that despite all the troubles you describe, you have made progress in the spiritual life and have profited by these troubles. I shall be more brief in answering you than I had intended, as I have less leisure and more work than I realized; nevertheless, I shall say enough to keep you going until I have occasion to write you a longer letter.

You tell me that it bothers you that you are not perfectly open with me, or so it seems to you. And I tell you that even though I don't know what you are doing in my absence—for I am not a prophet—I still believe that even from the few conversations I have

21. *Oeuvres*, XII, 395–396: Letter CCXLII.
22. *Oeuvres*, XIII, 18–22: Letter CCLXXVII.

had with you, there are few secret places in your heart where I do not have access. However little you have opened the doors of your heart to me, I feel that I can look right in it and see all that is hidden there. This is a great advantage for you, since you want to use me for your salvation.

You complain that there is quite an admixture of faults and imperfections in your life in spite of your great desire to attain perfection and the pure love of God. I answer that it is not possible to empty ourselves completely of ourselves. While we are here below, and until such time as God bears us up to heaven, we must always bear with ourselves; and as long as we are bearing with ourselves we won't be bearing much of real value. So we must be patient and not think that we can overcome in a day all the bad habits we have acquired through the poor care we have taken of our spiritual health. God did cure some people instantly, without leaving in them a trace of their former illness, as in the case of Mary Magdalene whom He transformed in an instant from a quagmire of corruption into a clear fountain of perfection; and from that moment, she was never again troubled. On the other hand, this same God left in several of His dear disciples many marks of their evil inclinations for some time after their conversion, all for their greater good: for example, blessed St. Peter who stumbled many times after his initial calling and who on one occasion failed totally and miserably by denying the Lord.[23]

Solomon said the maidservant who suddenly becomes the lady of the house can be very insolent.[24] There is a great danger that the soul which has catered to its own passions and affections over a long period of time might become proud and vain if in a moment it could master them completely. We must, little by little and step by step, acquire that self-mastery which the saints took years to acquire. Please, be patient with everyone, but, first of all, with yourself.

You tell me you do nothing at all in prayer. But what would you want to do that you are not already doing, that is, presenting and re-presenting your nothingness and your misery to God. The most eloquent appeal that beggars make is to show us their sores and their neediness. But sometimes, you tell me, you can't even do that much and just stay there like a shadow or a statue. Well, that in itself

---

23. Mt 26:69–75.
24. Prv 30:21–23.

is no small achievement. In the palaces of princes and kings there are statues that serve only to please the eye of the prince; be satisfied then to serve the same purpose in the presence of God. He will bring the statue to life when He chooses.

Trees bear fruit only because of the presence of the sun, some sooner, some later, some every year, and others every three years, not all of them always yielding equal harvests. We are very fortunate to be able to remain in the presence of God; so let us be content that He will make us bear our fruit sooner or later, every day or only occasionally, according to His good pleasure to which we should be fully resigned.

What a marvelous thing you tell me: "So long as I am serving God, He may put me in whatever sauce He likes; it's all the same to me." But take care to savor this sauce; let it melt in your mouth, and do not gulp it down. Mother Teresa, whom you love so much—I am delighted about this—says somewhere that we often repeat such sayings from habit and from a rather superficial grasp of their meaning.[25] We think we are uttering them from the depths of our soul, but that's not the case at all, as we find out later when we try to put them into practice. You say it's all the same to you, whatever the sauce God puts you in. Come now, you know perfectly well in what sauce He has put you, in what state and condition of life; tell me, is it all the same to you? You are not unaware either that He wants you to satisfy that daily duty about which you write me; still, it is not all the same to you. Oh! how subtly self-love insinuates itself into our feelings, however devout these appear to be!

Here is the most important point: find out what God wants, and when you know, try to carry it out cheerfully or at least courageously; not only that, but we must love this will of God and the obligations it entails, even if it means herding swine the rest of our lives and performing the most menial tasks in the world, because whatever sauce God chooses for us, it should be all the same to us. Therein lies the very bull's eye of perfection, at which we must all aim, and whoever comes nearest to it wins the prize.

But be of good heart, I beg you; little by little train your will to follow God's will, wherever it may lead you; see that your will is strongly roused when your conscience says: God wants this. Grad-

---

25. Teresa of Avila, *The Way of Perfection*, Chapter 38.

ually the resistance you feel so strongly will become weaker and soon disappear altogether. But especially, you must try to stop acting out your inner struggle or, at least, to do so in moderation. There are persons who when angry or annoyed, show their displeasure by simply saying: "What's all this?"; but there are others who speak sharply and show, not only displeasure, but a certain arrogance and spite. What I mean is that you should gradually correct such outbursts, moderating them every day.

As for your desire to see your dear ones make progress in the service of God and in their longing for Christian perfection, I praise this desire of yours tremendously and, since you wish it, shall add my poor prayers to your supplications to God for this intention. But to tell you the truth, I am always afraid that in these desires which are not of the essence of our salvation and perfection, there may be a trace of self-love and self-will; for example, we may indulge so much in these desires which are not really essential that we may not leave enough room in our hearts for those that are: humility, resignation, gentleness of heart, and the like. Or else the intensity of these desires may bring about anxiety and overeagerness, and in the end we do not submit ourselves to God's will as perfectly as we should.

This is what I fear in such desires. That's why I beg you to be very careful to avoid these dangers and to pursue your aim gently and quietly, that is to say, without upsetting those with whom you would like to share your desire for perfection. Do not even tell them what you hope for, because, believe me, this would do more harm than good. By what you say and do you must gently sow seeds which might sway them to your views; without pretending to want to teach them or win them over, gradually plant holy inspirations and reflections in their minds. In this way, especially if you pray about it too, you will do more good than you would in any other way. . . .

June 10, 1605[26]

My dear Sister,

Here I am writing you, not knowing what to say except to tell you to continue joyfully along the heavenly path where God has

---

26. *Oeuvres*, XIII, 53–54: Letter CCLXXXIX.

placed you. I shall bless Him all my life long for the graces He has prepared for you. In exchange for this, you, on your part, should be ready to be totally abandoned to Him and courageously bring your heart to carry out those things which you know He is asking of you, despite all sorts of contradictions that could oppose this.

Do not consider the importance of the things you do, for of themselves they are insignificant; consider only the dignity they have in being willed by God's will, arranged by His providence, and planned according to His wisdom. In a word, if they are pleasing to God and acknowledged to be so, to whom should they be displeasing? Take care, my very dear daughter, to become more pure of heart each day. This purity consists in appraising all things, weighing them on the scales of the sanctuary, which is nothing other than the will of God.[27]

Do not love anything too much, I beg you, not even virtues, which we sometimes lose by our excessive zeal. I don't know if you understand me, but I think you do: I am speaking of your desires and your fervor. It seems to me that white is not the color proper to roses, for red roses are more beautiful and more fragrant; however, white is the distinctive characteristic of lilies. Let us be what we are and be that well, in order to bring honor to the Master Craftsman whose handiwork we are. People laughed at the painter who, intending to paint a horse, came up with a perfect bull; the work was handsome in itself, but not much credit to the artist who had had other plans and succeeded in this one only by chance. Let us be what God wants us to be, provided we are His, and let us not be what we would like to be, contrary to His intention. Even if we were the most perfect creatures under heaven, what good would that do us if we were not as God's will would have us be?

I may have repeated this too much already, but I will not be saying it so often in the future since our Lord Himself has already strengthened you in this matter.

Do me the kindness of letting me know the subject of your meditations for the current year; it would comfort me to know this and to know the results they produce in you. Rejoice in the Lord, my

---

27. This image, derived from Numbers 7, occurs in the *Introduction*, V, 2, and in several letters.

dear sister, and keep your heart in peace. I greet your husband, and am forever your very loving and faithful servant and brother.

[June], 1607[28]

[. . .] I approve of the idea that in your prayer you remain with the beginners' method a little longer, preparing your mind by reading and arranging the points, using your imagination only as needed in order to focus your thoughts. Now I know very well that when we are so fortunate as to find God, it is good to just look at Him and to rest in Him; but, my dear daughter, to expect that we are always going to meet Him so spontaneously, without preparation, would not, I think, be good for us who are still beginners and need to meditate on the virtues of the Crucified Lord one after the other, rather than to admire them collectively, as a whole. Now if after having applied our mind to this humble preparation, God still does not give us any delight or consolation, then we must go on patiently, eating our dry crust and doing our duty without any immediate reward. [. . .]

Persevere in overcoming yourself in the little everyday frustrations that bother you; let your best efforts be directed there. God wishes nothing else of you at present, so don't waste time doing anything else. Don't sow your desires in someone else's garden; just cultivate your own as best you can; don't long to be other than what you are, but desire to be thoroughly what you are. Direct your thoughts to being very good at that and to bearing the crosses, little or great, that you will find there. Believe me, this is the most important and the least understood point in the spiritual life. We all love what is according to our taste; few people like what is according to their duty or to God's liking.

What is the use of building castles in Spain when we have to live in France? This is my old lesson, and you grasp it well; but tell me, my dear, whether you are putting it into practice.

I beg you, moderate your spiritual exercises, and in this regard give a good deal of weight to how your husband feels about them. Just laugh at these silly temptations in which the enemy depicts the world as a place to which you are obliged to return; laugh at these temptations, I say, as at something ridiculous. The only response to

---

28. *Oeuvres*, XIII, 289–292: Letter CD.

give them is that of our Lord, "Get behind me, Satan, you shall not tempt the Lord your God."[29] My dear daughter, we are walking in the footsteps of the saints; let us go on courageously in spite of the difficulties we find there. [. . .]

June 25, 1608[30]

Madam, my very dear sister,
     I have received your letter of May 16. I would be very sorry if the good project for the reform of Puits d'Orbe were to vanish like that![31] Still, if the hope I have of going to Burgundy is not thwarted, I have decided to go to that abbey to see what is going on. I am not a stubborn man and I am willingly persuaded to compromise when something cannot be accomplished in its entirety. [. . .]
     You mention your impatience. Is it really impatience or only natural repugnance? Since you call it impatience I'll take it for such until this fall when I hope to speak to you more fully about this in person. Meanwhile, judging by what I have come to know of you through your letters, more than through the few conversations I have had with you, I must tell you, my very dear sister, in liberty of spirit, that I think you have a heart which is too attached to the means of arriving at your goal. I know very well that your goal is none other than the love of God, and you have to use means and practices to reach it; however, I say that you attach yourself tenaciously to those means which you like, and want to reduce everything to that. That is why you are upset when anything gets in your way or distracts you.
     The remedy would be to try to convince yourself—to fill your mind with this conviction—that God wants you to serve Him just as you are, both by practices that are suited to your state in life, and by the actions that go with it. Once you are convinced of this, you must bring yourself to a tender affection for your state in life and for everything about it, out of love for Him who wills it so.
     You see, my dear sister, it's not enough to give this a thought in passing; you must give it first place in your heart, recalling it often, thinking it over seriously, welcoming and enjoying the truth

---

29. Cf. Mt 4:7, 10.
30. *Oeuvres*, XIV, 39–41: Letter CDLXII.
31. See the heading introducing the next correspondent, the Abbess of Puits d'Orbe.

of it. Take my word for it, all that is contrary to this advice is nothing but self-love. [. . .]

The various conditions in which you find yourself at prayer and outside of prayer, sometimes feeling strong, sometimes weak, at times looking at the world with delight, at other times with disgust—all this is something God is allowing you to live through humbly and gently. This is how you can see what you are of and by yourself and what you are with the help of God; in no way should this discourage you. [. . .]

May the holy love of God ever live and rule in our hearts. Amen.

[early September, 1613][32]

A month ago, dear sister, I had an attack of fever that lasted almost until now; during that time I received three letters from you. One, especially, was most consoling to me, as I found in it indications of the total confidence you have placed in me, telling me, as you did, what has been happening with and troubling your soul. It's true, I may not understand fully what you tell me, and I could be mistaken; nevertheless, it seems to me that I understand you well enough to answer you.

You see, my dear sister, it often happens that just when we think we're finished with old enemies over whom we were once victorious, we find them approaching from another direction where we least expected to see them.

Even that unique man of wisdom, Solomon—who had performed such marvels in his youth, and who was so self-assured by his enduring virtues and by a confidence built up over the years—just when he seemed to be safe from attack was caught off guard by an enemy from whom he would ordinarily have had least to fear.[33] All this is by way of teaching us two important lessons: one is that we should always mistrust ourselves, go on our way with holy fear, continually seek help from heaven, and live in humble devotion; the other is that our enemies may be repulsed but cannot be eliminated. They sometimes leave us in peace, only to attack us more forcefully later.

---

32. Oeuvres, XVI, 62–65: Letter CMX.
33. Cf. 1 Kgs 11.

But, my very dear sister, you must not yield to discouragement on this account. Be peacefully vigilant and take the time, as well as the care, to heal your dear soul of the harm it may have received from these attacks; humble yourself profoundly before our Lord and don't be in the least astonished at your weakness. If we didn't suffer attacks and didn't feel miserable, then we would have reason for astonishment.

These little upsets, dear sister, bring us back to reality, make us reflect on our frailty, and cause us to have recourse more quickly to our Protector. St. Peter was walking very confidently on the waves; yet, when the wind arose and the waves seemed about to engulf him, he cried out "Lord, save me!" and our Lord, taking hold of his hand said "Man of little faith, why do you doubt?"[34] It's when we are disturbed by our passions, when we feel the winds and the storm of temptation, that we call upon our Savior, for He allows us to be upset only in order to incite us to call out to Him more fervently. Finally, don't be angry, or at least don't be agitated over the fact that you've been agitated; don't be disturbed at having been disturbed; don't be upset at the fact that these annoying emotions have upset you. But very gently put your heart back into the hands of our Lord, begging Him to heal it. For your part, do all you can by renewing your resolution, by appropriate reading, and by doing whatever else can help bring about this healing. If you do this, you will gain much from your loss, and will end up healthier for having been ill.

My dearest daughter, since your pregnancy prevents you from making your usual long mental prayer, make your prayer short and fervent. Make up for the loss by frequently lifting your heart to God; often read from some good spiritual book, but only a little at a time; when you go for a walk, often turn your thoughts to God; pray often and briefly; offer your listlessness and weariness to our crucified Lord. After your delivery, quietly resume your usual devotions, and discipline yourself to use the subject matter presented in some spiritual book, so that when it is time to go to prayer you are not at a loss, like the person who, when it is time for dinner, has nothing ready. If sometimes you don't have a book to turn to, med-

---

34. Cf. Mt 14:29-31.

itate on a mystery rich in meaning, like the death and passion [of our Lord], or whatever first comes to your mind. [. . .]

ROSE BOURGEOIS

The situation of Madame Brûlart's sister was quite different. Because she was the younger daughter, her father had placed her in the abbey of Puits d'Orbe where she was elected abbess for life. The religious observance there was seriously relaxed. Some of the nuns desired a reform, but the abbess herself did not give the proper example of poverty, fervor, or fidelity to their cloistered life. After hearing Francis de Sales preach during Lent in 1604, however, she was inspired to reform her own life first, then that of her abbey.

Francis instructed Rose, the neophyte, on how to make progress in the devout life; he guided Rose, the abbess, in her efforts to undertake the reform of her monastery; and he empathized with Rose, the woman, who endured much physical suffering because of a diseased leg that never healed. Despite all the excruciating medical and surgical treatment she underwent after 1604, she remained a cripple the rest of her life. Her physical infirmity had a debilitating effect on her activities and morale. Francis, in his letters, encourages her to accept this suffering which she has not chosen and to use it as a means of achieving closer union with her crucified Savior.

Sales, April 15–18, 1605[35]

My very dear Sister,

Here is the most important phrase which makes me totally yours: God wills it so. Of this I have absolutely no doubt. There is no better reason in the whole world than this one.

You will already have heard the news of my recovery, which is so complete that I preached the whole Lenten series. My illness never seemed very serious to me; but the doctors, who thought I had been poisoned, so frightened those who love me, that it seemed to them I was going to slip away from them. [. . .]

Not only your messenger, but your dear father himself has told me how much you have been suffering and how much he has suf-

---

35. *Oeuvres*, XIII, 25–35: Letter CCLXXX.

fered with you. May our Lord be blessed for this. This is the safest, most royal road to heaven for you; and, from what I understand, you will be on it for some time, since, according to what your father wrote me, you are still under the care of the physicians and surgeons. I certainly feel great compassion for you in your sufferings and often recommend these to our Lord, that He may make them useful for you and that when you come through them all, it can be said of you as it was said of the good man Job: In all these things he never sinned, but hoped in his God.[36]

Courage, my dear sister, my daughter! Look at your Spouse, your King, see how He was crowned with thorns and so racked on the cross that all His bones could be numbered.[37] Consider how the crown of the bride ought not be of softer stuff than that of the Bridegroom, and that if His flesh was so lacerated that all His bones could be counted, it is only right that one of yours be seen. "As the rose among the thorns, so is my beloved among the maidens."[38] It is the natural place for that flower to be; it is also the most fitting place for the Bridegroom. Accept this cross a thousand times a day; kiss it gladly for the love of Him who sends it to you out of love and as a rich present. Often picture your crucified Savior there in front of you, and think which of the two of you is suffering more for the other; you will find your pain much less. How happy you will be eternally if you endure for God this lesser evil which He sends you!

You will not be deceiving yourself if you imagine that I am near you in these tribulations; I am there in heart and affection and feel great consolation in often speaking to your Spouse of your sufferings and labors.[39] But, my dear daughter, trust and be strong. "If you believe, you will see the glory of God."[40]

What do you think a bed of suffering is? It is nothing else than the school of humility where we learn all about our misery and weakness, and how vain, delicate, and weak we are. And so, beloved daughter, it is on that bed that you will discover your imperfections. Why there, I ask, more than elsewhere, save that any-

---

36. Cf. Jb 1:22; 13:15.
37. Cf. Ps 22:18.
38. Cf. Song 2:2. The flower named is actually the lily, but Francis has adapted the text to his correspondent's name.
39. Cf. Ps 142:3.
40. Cf. Jn 11:40.

where else they remain hidden within the soul, whereas in suffering, they become visible. The turbulence of the sea affects every type of person, even those who think themselves quite well, for, after sailing a while, they discover, through the seasickness brought on by the violent tossing of the waves, that they are not as invulnerable as they thought. One of the great benefits of suffering is that we come to see the depths of our own nothingness, and that the debris of our bad inclinations floats to the top. But are we to be disturbed on that account, dear daughter? Certainly not. It is then that we have to cleanse and purify our heart still more, and take greater advantage than ever of the sacrament of confession.

This major concern and the other worries which have beset you and left you in pain do not surprise me, since there is nothing worse. So do not be anxious, my dearest daughter. Are we to let ourselves be swept away by the current and the whirlwind? Let the enemy rage at the gate; let him knock, pound, scream, howl; let him do his worst. We know for certain that he cannot enter our soul except by the door of our consent. So let us keep that door shut tight, often checking that it is really well closed; and let us not worry about the rest, for there is nothing to fear.

You ask me to write you something concerning peace of soul and humility: I would do so gladly, my very dear daughter, but I don't know if I can in the little time I have for writing to you. However, here are three or four words on the subject, dearest daughter. It is God who inspired you to ask me at one and the same time about peace of soul and humility, for in truth we cannot have the one without the other.

Nothing can disturb us but self-love and the importance we give ourselves. If we are without feelings of tenderness and compassion in our heart, have no delight or devotion in prayer and no interior sweetness in meditation, we fall into sadness; if we have difficulty in doing things well or if something gets in the way of our plans, at once we are anxious to overcome it and fret about getting rid of it. Why all this? Undoubtedly because we love our consolations, our comfort, our convenience. We would like our prayer to be steeped in orange-flower water, and ourselves to become virtuous by eating candy; we do not look at our gentle Jesus who, prostrate on the ground, sweats blood and water in agony[41] because of the deadly conflict He experiences inwardly between the affections of the inferior part of His soul and the resolutions of the superior part.

Self-love, then, is one of the sources of our disturbance; the other is the importance we give ourselves. Why is it that when we happen to commit some imperfection or sin, we are so surprised, upset, and impatient? Without doubt, it is because we thought we were something special, resolute, and steady, and therefore, when we discover that in reality we are nothing of the kind and have fallen flat on our face, we are disappointed, and consequently we are vexed, offended, and upset. If we really knew ourselves well, instead of being astonished at finding ourselves on the ground, we would marvel that we ever manage to remain standing up. That's the other source of our disquiet: we want nothing but consolation and are taken aback when we see and experience our misery, our nothingness, and our weakness.

Let us do three things, my dearest daughter, and we shall have peace: let us have a very pure intention of seeking, in all things, the honor and glory of God; let us do the little we can toward this end, according to the advice of our spiritual father; and let us leave to God the care of all the rest. Why does anyone who has God for the object of his intentions and who is doing the best he can, let himself be disturbed? Why is he troubled? What has he to fear? No, no, God is not so frightening to those He loves. He is content with little because He knows very well that we don't have much. And you, my dear daughter, know that our Lord is called Prince of Peace in the Scriptures,[42] and that, wherever He is absolute master, He holds everything in peace. It's true, however, that before bringing peace to any situation, He brings the sword there first,[43] separating the heart and soul from their most cherished, familiar, and ordinary attachments, such as inordinate self-love, self-sufficiency, self-complacency and similar feelings. Now, when our Lord separates us from these attachments we are so fond of, it's as if He were flaying our hearts alive. We suffer acutely and almost inevitably we resist

41. Mk 14:35; Lk 22:44.
42. Is 9:5.
43. Cf. Mt 10:34–36.

with our whole being because we feel this separation most keenly. Yet all this inner resistance is not without peace, when in the end, though overwhelmed by our distress, we remain resigned to the will of our Lord. We keep our own will nailed to His divine good pleasure and in no way abandon our responsibilities and tasks; rather, we carry them out courageously. Our Lord gave us an example of this in the Garden. Although He was overwhelmed by interior and exterior anguish, He was completely and calmly surrendered to His Father and His divine will, saying, "Let not My will, but Yours be done."[44] Despite His agony, He went three times to his disciples and admonished them.[45] To be at peace in the midst of warfare, to live serenely amid trials, this, indeed, is to be "Prince of Peace."

From all this I want you to draw the following conclusions. The first, that very often we think we have lost peace because we are afflicted, and yet, we have not lost it at all; we can be sure of this if in spite of our affliction, we continue to renounce ourselves, remain totally dependent on the good pleasure of God, and do not fail to perform whatever duties we have. The second is that we must necessarily suffer interior pain when God tears off the last bit of skin from the "old man" in order to refashion him after "the new man" created according to God.[46] It follows that we should not be disturbed about this or think it means that we are in disfavor with our Lord. The third is that no thoughts which cause us disquiet and agitation come from God who is Prince of Peace; they are, rather, temptations of the enemy, and therefore we must reject them and take no notice of them.

In all things and everywhere we must live peacefully. If troubles, either interior or exterior, come upon us, we should receive them peacefully. If joy comes our way, we must receive it peacefully, without getting all excited about it. If there is some evil to avoid, let us avoid it peacefully, without anxiety; for otherwise, in running away from evil, we could fall and give the enemy time to do us in. Is there some good to be done? Let us do it peacefully. "Thus is my bitterness transformed into peace," said the penitent.[47]

As for humility, I hardly want to talk about it except to suggest

---

44. Cf. Lk 22:42.
45. Mt 26:40–45.
46. Cf. Eph 4:22–24.
47. Is 38:17.

that your dear sister [de Chantal] show you what I have written her on the subject. Read carefully what Mother Teresa has to say about it in *The Way of Perfection*. Humility makes it possible for us to be untroubled about our own faults by reminding us of those of others; for why should we be more perfect than anyone else? In the same way, why should the shortcomings of others bother us when we recall our own? Why should we find it strange that others have faults when we ourselves have plenty? Humility makes our hearts gentle toward the perfect and the imperfect: toward the perfect, out of respect; toward the imperfect, out of compassion. Humility helps us to receive afflictions serenely, knowing that we deserve them, and to receive blessings with reverence, knowing that they are undeserved. Where the exterior is concerned, I would approve of your making some act of humility each day, either in words or in deed. I mean, in words that come from the heart, as, for example, humbling yourself to someone in a lower position than yours; and in deed, by doing some lowly work or service, either for the house or for some particular person.

Do not be distressed about having to stay in bed and not being able to meditate, for to endure the scourging of our Lord is no less a good than to meditate. No, it is undoubtedly better to be on the cross with the Lord than to be only looking at Him. But I know very well that there, on your sick bed, you cast your heart a thousand times a day into the hands of God, and that's enough. Be very obedient to your doctors, and when they forbid you certain practices, whether fasting, mental or vocal prayer, or even the Office, or anything beyond short, spontaneous prayers, I beg you as earnestly as I can, and because of the respect and love you have for me, to be most obedient, for God has so ordained this.[48] When you are well and strong again, resume your journey quietly, and you will see that with God's help we will make great progress. We will go beyond the reaches of the world, beyond its limits and boundaries.

My dear daughter, you write me that in every respect you are the "little sister," but you're mistaken—I expect greater accomplishments from you than from anyone else. Believe me, please, that I have nothing more at heart than your advancement before God, and

---

48. Cf. Sir 38:1: "Hold the physician in honor, for he is essential to you, and God it was who established his profession."

if my blood could further this, you would soon see in what rank I hold you. [. . .]

There was no need for you to make excuses to me about the openness of your letter; for if it weren't that my imperfections and weaknesses might bother you, my own heart would like to be wide open before you. Have confidence in me and be assured that I have no greater desire than to see in you a spirit of charity that is thoroughly spontaneous and free. Why do I say this? Because it seems to me that you are somewhat afraid of offending me: I am by no means thin-skinned and sensitive in this matter, especially when it comes from those with whom I have a friendship rooted in Mount Calvary, near the Cross of our Lord.

I am writing to that daughter of yours to whom you asked me to write, and I am doing so as appropriately as I can, considering her difficulty. How well St. Bernard expresses it when he says that the care of souls is not for the strong, for they can stand on their own two feet; rather, it is for the weak and faint-hearted who have to be carried and supported on the shoulders of charity, which is all-strong. This poor little one is of the latter type: pining away, depressed about the problems that stem from her various weaknesses and which seem to overwhelm her. We must help her as much as we can and leave the rest to God.

I should never finish writing this letter to you if I followed my inclination, which is full of love. But enough; Mass calls me. There I shall present our Lord to His Father for you, my dearest daughter, and all your house, in order to obtain from Him the Holy Spirit who directs all your action and affections to His glory and your own salvation. I beg Him to keep you from useless sadness and worry, and to take His rest in your heart so that your heart may rest in Him. Amen.

MADAME DE CHANTAL

Since the life and person of Jeanne Françoise Frémyot de Chantal have been sketched in the Introduction to this volume, it only remains to point out here a few characteristics present to some degree in all of Francis's letters, which reach fullest expression in this the greatest of his correspondences, reflecting the greatest of his friendships. For if it is true that for de Sales, letters of spiritual direction tend to be letters of spiritual friendship, then one may expect to find—above all and eminently here—the following facets of spiritual friendship: warm expressions of personal caring and concern focused on the spiritual welfare of the friend, but extending to her total well-being and indeed her entire family; reflections on the friendship relationship itself as a gift of God which grows and develops without ceasing to be gift; discussion of how the friendship can be nourished and sustained through God-given times of meeting and through continuing correspondence; recognition of the increasing mutuality of the relationship; recognition of the cross of suffering in one another's lives—supporting the other in inevitable trials, without interfering in a purifying process or attenuating the demands of the cross.

All these themes are clearly present even in this small sample drawn from a total of over four hundred letters which Francis wrote to Jane.

May 3, 1604[49]

Madam,

This letter will assure you again and all the more that I shall very carefully keep the promise I made of writing you as often as I can. The greater the physical distance between us, the closer I feel is our interior bond. I shall never stop praying God to perfect His work in you,[50] that is, to further your excellent desire and plan to attain the fullness of Christian life, a desire which you should cherish and nurture tenderly in your heart; consider it a work of the Holy Spirit and a spark of His divine flame.

I once saw a tree in Rome which had been planted by St. Dominic; people go to see and venerate it out of love for him who planted it. In the same way, having seen the tree of your desire for holiness that our Lord planted in your soul, I cherish it tenderly and take more pleasure in thinking about it now than I did while I was with

---

49. *Oeuvres*, XII, 263–267: Letter CCXVI. Its abrupt beginning reflects this letter's origins shortly after Jane and Francis first met in Dijon. It followed on the heels of a note Francis has sent while en route back to Annecy: "God, so it seems to me, has given me to you; of that I am more convinced every hour. That is all I can tell you; recommend me to your good angel." *Oeuvres*, XII, 262: Letter CCXV.

50. Cf. Phil 1:6.

you. I beg you to do the same and to say with me: "May God make you grow, O beautiful tree planted by Him; and you, divine and heavenly seed, may God grant that you yield your fruit in due season,[51] and when you have produced it may He protect you from the wind that makes fruit fall to the ground where it will be eaten."

Madam, this desire of yours should be like orange trees along the seacoast of Genoa which almost all year long are covered with fruit, blossoms and leaves all at the same time. Every day presents occasions for your desire to ripen, so you should bear fruit constantly; yet, you should never stop hoping for further opportunities to advance. Such longings are the blossoms on the tree of your desire; the leaves are the frequent admissions of your weakness, which keeps both your good works and your desires in a healthy condition. You may look upon all this as one of the pillars of your tabernacle.

The other pillar is the love of your widowhood, a love that is holy and desirable for as many reasons as there are stars in the sky, and without which, widowhood is worthless and deceptive. St. Paul commands us to honor widows who are truly widows;[52] but those who do not like their widowhood are widows in appearance only, for their hearts are still married. They are not the ones of whom it is said: "Blessing, I will bless the widow";[53] and elsewhere "God is the judge, the protector, and defender of widows."[54] Praise God who has given you this precious, holy love; help it to grow more and more each day, and your own consolation will increase proportionately, since the whole structure of your happiness rests on these two pillars. At least once a month take a good look to see if one or the other of them might have become loosened; make use of some devout meditation similar to the one of which I am enclosing a copy and which has been helpful to other souls in my care. Nevertheless, do not tie yourself down to this particular meditation, for this is not my reason for sending it. I am sending it simply to give you an idea of the direction your monthly self-examination ought to take in order to be more beneficial to you. If you prefer to use this meditation, it will not be completely useless. But, I say, use it only if you really prefer it,

51. Cf. Ps 1:3.
52. 1 Tm 5:3.
53. Ps 132:15, following the Vulgate Ps 131:15.
54. Pss 68:6; 146:9.

for in everything and at all times I want you to have a holy liberty of spirit in the means you take to attain perfection. As long as the two pillars of your tabernacle are in good condition and stable, it doesn't matter very much how you do this.

Be on your guard against scruples, and rely entirely on what I told you in person, for I spoke in the Lord. Keep yourself constantly in God's presence in the manner you already know. Avoid anxiety and worries, for nothing so impedes our progress toward perfection. Place your heart in our Lord's wounds gently, and not by force; have the utmost confidence that in His mercy and kindness He will not forsake you; yet, for all that, do not relax your hold on His holy cross.

Next to love of our Lord, I commend to you love of His Bride, the Church, that dear, gentle dove which alone can rear fledglings for her Bridegroom. Praise God a hundred times a day that you are a "daughter of the Church," following the example of Mother Teresa who found great consolation in repeating these words often at the hour of her death. Cast your glance frequently on the Bridegroom and the Bride, and say to the Bridegroom: "You are the Spouse of such a beautiful Bride!" and to the Bride: "You are the Spouse of a divine Bridegroom!" Have great compassion for all pastors and preachers in the Church; notice how they are scattered over the whole face of the earth, for there is no corner of the world where you would not find at least a few of them. Pray God for them so that they may obtain the salvation of souls at the same time that they are saving themselves. In this regard I beg you never to forget me, since God has given me such a strong determination never to forget you either.

I am sending you a paper I have written about the perfection of life for all Christians.[55] I didn't write it for you, but for a number of other persons; still, you can see if there is anything in it for you. Write to me, I beg you, as often as you can and with complete trust; in my great concern for your advancement, I shall be distressed if I do not know how things are going with you.

Recommend me to our Lord, for there is no one on earth who needs prayer more than I. I beg Him to grant an abundance of His holy love to you and all who are dear to you.

---

55. See the memo on Christian perfection, *supra*, pp. 101f.

I am ever, and beg you to look upon me as, your most sincere and devoted servant in Jesus Christ.

June 24, 1604[56]

Madam,

The other letter I wrote will help you reassure the good father to whom you wanted to be able to show it. I put in it many things in order to forestall any suspicion he might have that I had written with some purpose in mind; yet, I wrote it in truth and sincerity, as I must always do, but not with the freedom with which I am writing this one where I want to speak to you heart to heart.

I quite agree—along with those who tried to give you scruples about it—that it is advisable to have but one spiritual father whose authority in all things and at all times should be preferred to one's own will, and even to the advice of other persons; but in no way should this preclude other relationships and communication, nor our following the advice and counsel given by others.

One evening, shortly before I received your letters, I picked up a book about Mother Teresa,[57] as a way of relaxing my mind after the day's work, and I discovered that she had made a vow of special obedience to Father Gratian, of her Order, to do during the rest of her life whatever he might require of her that would not be contrary to God or to the obedience she owed her ordinary superiors of the Church or of her Order. Besides that, she always had some special great confidant with whom she discussed things and whose advice and counsel she followed faithfully and practiced in whatever would not go against the obedience she had vowed. This worked out well, as she herself testifies in several places in her writings. This is just to tell you that union with one's spiritual father does not preclude communicating with someone else, provided that the promised obedience keeps the first and preferential place.

Think no more about this, I beg you, and do not worry about where to rank me, for all this is only a temptation and a useless subtlety. What difference does it make if you know whether or not you

---

56. *Oeuvres*, XII, 282–288: Letter CCXXIII. The first line refers to another letter Francis had sent ten days earlier. (*Ibid.*, pp. 277–281: Letter CCXXI.)

57. Most likely a Latin life of St. Teresa by Ribera or Ribadeneira (1527–1611), a Spanish Jesuit.

can consider me your spiritual father, as long as you know how my soul is disposed toward yours, and I know how yours is toward mine? I know you have complete confidence in my affection; I have no doubt about this and delight in the thought. I want you to know and to believe that I have an intense and very special desire to serve you with all my strength. It would be impossible for me to explain either the quality or the greatness of this desire that I have to be at your spiritual service, but I can tell you that I believe it is from God, and for that reason, I cherish it and every day see it growing and increasing remarkably. If it were appropriate, I would say more, and say it in all truth, but I had better stop here. Dear Madam, you can see clearly enough to what extent you may call on me and trust me. Make the most of my affection and of all that God has given me for the service of your soul. I am all yours; give no more thought to the role or to the rank I hold in being yours. God has given me to you; so consider me as yours in Him, and call me whatever you like; it makes no difference.

Further, in order to cut short all the rebuttals which may be taking shape in your mind, I must tell you that I have never understood that there was any bond between us carrying with it any obligation but that of charity and true Christian friendship, what St. Paul calls "the bond of perfection";[58] and truly, that is just what it is, for it is indissoluble and never weakens. All other bonds are temporal, even that of a vow of obedience which can be broken through death or other circumstances; but the bond of love grows and gets ever stronger with time. It cannot be cut down by death, which, like a scythe, mows down everything but charity. "Love is strong as death and firm as hell,"[59] says Solomon. So there, dear sister (allow me to call you by this name, which is the one used by the apostles and the first Christians to express the intimate love they had for one another), this is our bond, these are our chains which, the more they are tightened and press against us, the more they bring us joy and freedom. Their strength is gentleness; their violence, mildness; nothing is more pliable than that; nothing, stronger. Think of me as very closely bound to you, and don't try to understand more about

---

58. Col 3:14, following the Vulgate: "vinculum perfectionis."
59. Cf. Song 8:6.

it than that this bond is not opposed to any other bond either of a vow or of marriage. Be totally at peace on that score. Obey your first director freely, and call on me in charity and sincerity.

I want to answer another point in your letter. You were afraid of having fallen into some kind of duplicity by communicating your thoughts to me and seeking my advice. I am happy to see that you have such a dislike of shrewdness and duplicity, for there is hardly any vice which is more contrary to the good health and activity of the mind. Nevertheless, it was not duplicity, for if there was some fault which caused you to have scruples about opening your heart to me and seeking instruction from me, you have sufficiently atoned for it since then, and have no further obligation to speak to anyone about it. Nevertheless, I praise your frankness and am happy that you have told me about this, as well as all the rest; but you must hold fast to the resolution I gave you: what is told in the secrecy of the sacrament of Penance is so sacred that it should never be spoken of outside. And if anyone should ask you if you have said what you have in fact said under the holy seal of confession, you can say "no" forthrightly and without fear of duplicity; don't let that pose any difficulty. Anyway, God be praised: I would rather have you be ingenuous than lacking in candor. So, once again, stand firm and consider as unsaid and totally secret whatever is covered with the sacramental veil. Meanwhile, have no scruple, for you have committed no offense in speaking of it, though it would have been better not to have done so, out of a reverence for the sacrament which should be so great that nothing spoken there is mentioned outside. I remember clearly the first time you spoke to me about this.

You say that I may have the pleasure of seeing you around September. I shall be delighted to see you, and also Mme. Brûlart and Mlle de Villars.[60] Knowing that you are coming, I shall try to give you as much time as I can, and shall pray God in a special way so that whatever help I give all of you may be as great as my affection for you. I have taken up my pen a dozen times to write these two pages and it seems as if the enemy has been sending me distractions and concerns in order to prevent my writing you. Interpret favorably the length of this letter, for I have tried to escape from the ar-

---

60. Jeanne Humbert, wife of Phillipe de Villers (or Villars), was another friend Francis had met during the Lent of 1604 in Dijon. Cf. *Oeuvres*, XIII, 23, note 1.

guments and scruples that arise easily enough in women's minds. Be on your guard against this, I beg you, and have courage.

When exterior or interior troubles overtake you, take your two resolutions into your arms, and like a mother who rescues her child from danger, put them in our Lord's wounds, asking Him to protect both you and them; then wait there in that sacred shelter until the storm has passed.[61] You will meet with opposition and bitterness; the contractions and pangs of spiritual childbirth are not less than those on the physical order. You have experienced both. I have often been encouraged in the midst of my little difficulties by these words of our gentle Savior: "When a woman gives birth she is in great distress, but after the birth she forgets the suffering of the past because a child is born to her."[62] I think these words will comfort you too if you ponder them and repeat them often. Our souls should give birth, not outside themselves, but within, to the dearest, most charming and handsome male child that one could wish for. It is Jesus whom we must form and bring to birth in ourselves;[63] you are pregnant with Him, my dear sister, and praised be God who is His Father. I speak this way because I know your ardent desires; but have courage, for one must suffer much to bring Him to birth. Besides, the Child is well worth whatever we endure in order to bring Him to birth and to be His mother.

I am talking too much; I shall stop here, begging this heavenly Child to make you worthy of His graces and favors and to grant that we may die for Him, or, at least, in Him. Madam, pray to Him for me who am so imperfect and burdened with myself and others; this burden would be intolerable if He who has already carried me and all my sins on the cross[64] were not carrying me to heaven. Be that as it may, I never say holy Mass without you and all those closest to you; I never receive communion without you, and finally, I am as much yours as you could ever wish me to be. Guard against anxiety, depression, and scruples. You would never in the world want to offend God; that is reason enough to live joyously.

My dear mother considers herself and all her children to be at your service; she thanks you very humbly for your kindness. My

---

61. Cf. Song 2:14; 1 Kgs 19:9–13.
62. Cf. Jn 16:21 which Francis adapts to his own purpose.
63. Cf. Gal 4:19.
64. Cf 1 Pt 2:24.

brother [Canon Jean-François de Sales] is most grateful for your remembrance of him and returns your kind thought by remembering you continually at the altar. He is away as I write this. I would like to know the names and ages of your children, for I hold them as my own in the Lord.

About the women you mentioned—I wouldn't dare urge them to make the trip for that would not be fitting; but, nevertheless, I do hope it takes place and I delight in looking forward to it.

Madam, I am your very humble and devoted servant in our Lord.

Sales, October 14, 1604[65]

Madam,

I have a very great desire to make myself clearly understood in this letter; please God, I will find the means to match my desire! I am sure that you will be encouraged by my response to part of what you asked me about, especially the part about the two doubts which the enemy is suggesting to you concerning your choice of me as your spiritual director. So I am going to tell you what I can, in order to put into a few words what I think you need to consider in this matter.

First of all, the choice you have made gives every indication of being a good and legitimate one; so, please, have no further doubt about this. Indications such as these: the strong impulse of your heart which carried you to this decision almost by force, yet with joy and contentment; the time I took to deliberate before agreeing to your wish; the fact that neither you nor I relied on ourselves but sought the opinion of your confessor who is a good, learned and prudent man; the fact that we allowed time for your first enthusiasm to subside in case it had been misplaced, and we prayed about this, not for one or two days only, but for several months; without a doubt, all these are infallible signs that we acted according to God's will.

Impulses that come from the evil spirit or from the human mind are very different: they are frightening, vehement, vacillating. The

---

65. *Oeuvres*, XII, 352–370: Letter CCXXXIV. The meeting alluded to in the previous letter actually took place, not in Annecy, but at St. Claude, a pilgrimage town located roughly midway between Dijon and Annecy. Francis and Jane were able to talk at length. Still, a short time later Jane wrote that she was being tried by doubts concerning both her choice of him as director and some unspecified matters of faith. This is Francis's response.

first thing they whisper to the agitated soul is not to listen to any advice, or if it does, to listen only to the advice of persons of little or no experience. These impulses urge us to hurry up and close a deal before having discussed the terms, and they are satisfied with a short prayer which serves as a pretext in deciding most important questions.

Our case was not at all like this. Neither you nor I made the final decision in this matter; it was made by a third person who had no reason to consider anything but God's will. The fact that I hesitated at first—and this was because of the deliberation I was bound to make—ought to put your mind completely at rest. You may be sure it was not from any disinclination to serve you spiritually (my inclination to do so is great beyond words), but in a decision of such moment I didn't want to follow either your desire or my inclination, but only God and His providence. So please stop right there and don't go on arguing with the enemy about it; tell him boldly that it was God who wanted it and who has done it.[66] It was God who placed you under that first direction, profitable for you at the time; it is God who has brought you under my direction and He will make it fruitful and useful to you, even though the instrument is unworthy.

As to your second point, my very dear sister, be assured that, as I was just saying from the very beginning when you consulted with me about your interior, God gave me a tremendous love for your soul. As you became more and more open with me, a marvelous obligation arose for my soul to love yours more and more; that's why I was prompted to write you that God had given me to you. I didn't believe that anything could be added to the affection I felt for you, especially when I was praying for you. But now, my dear daughter, a new quality has been added—I don't know what to call it. All I can say is that its effect is a great inner delight which I feel whenever I wish you perfect love of God and other spiritual blessings. I am adding nothing to the truth, and I speak in the presence of the "God of my heart"[67] and yours. Every affection differs in some particular way from every other affection; that which I have for you has a certain something about it which brings me great con-

---

66. Cf. Pss 115:3; 135:6.
67. Cf. Ps 73:26 = Vulgate Ps 72:26: "Deus cordis mei."

solation and, when all is said, is extremely good for me. Hold that for the truest truth and have no more doubt about it. I didn't intend to say so much, but one word leads to another, and I think you will know what I mean.

To me it's an amazing fact, my daughter, that holy Church, in imitation of her Spouse, teaches us to pray, not for ourselves only, but always for ourselves and our fellow Christians. "Give us . . ." she says, "grant us . . ." and similar all-inclusive terms. It had never occurred to me when praying in this general way to think about any person in particular; but since leaving Dijon, whenever I say "we" I think of particular individuals who have recommended themselves to my prayers; ordinarily you are the one who comes to mind first, and when not first (which is rarely the case), then last, so that I have more time to think of you. What more can I say than that? But for the honor of God, do not speak about this to anyone, for I am saying a little too much, though I say it in total honesty and purity. This should be enough to help you answer all those temptations in the future, or at least to give you the courage to laugh at the enemy and spit in his face! I'll tell you the rest some day, either in this life or the next.

In your third point you ask me what remedies there are for the suffering caused you by the temptations the devil suggests to you against the faith and the Church. At least, that's what I understand to be the difficulty. I shall tell you what God inspires me to say. In this kind of temptation we must take the same stance that we take against temptations of the flesh, not arguing at all, but doing as the Israelite children did with the bones of the Paschal Lamb, not trying to break them but simply throwing them into the fire.[68] In no way must we answer or even pretend to hear what the enemy is saying, no matter how hard he pounds on the door. We mustn't even say "Who is it?" "That's true," you tell me, "but he is so annoying and is making such a loud racket that those inside can't even hear each other speak." It's all the same; be patient, speak by means of signs: we must prostrate ourselves before God and stay there at His feet; He will understand very well from this humble gesture that you are His and that you want His help even though you are unable to speak. But especially, stay inside; don't so much as open the door

---

68. Cf. Ex 12:10.

either to see who is there or to chase this pest away. Finally he will grow tired of shouting and will leave you in peace. "It's about time!" you will tell me.

[. . .] So, courage then! Things will improve soon. So long as the enemy doesn't get in, the rest doesn't matter. Still, it's a very good sign that he is raging and beating at the door; it's a sign that he doesn't yet have what he's after. If he had it, he would no longer carry on this way. He would come in and stay. Remember this so as never to get caught up in scruples.

And here is another remedy for you. The temptations against faith go directly to the understanding to draw it to argue, and to get caught up in all these things. Do you know what you should do while the enemy wastes his time trying to scale the walls of your intellect? Slip out the gate of your will and take the offensive against him. That is, when a temptation against faith starts raising questions in your mind such as, "How can this be? But what if this? What if that . . . ?", instead of debating the enemy with arguments, let your affective side attack him with full force, and even let your thoughts be reinforced by your voice, crying out "You traitor, you wretch! You left the Church of the angels, and you are trying to get me to leave that of the saints! Disloyal, unfaithful, perfidious one! You gave the apple of perdition to the first woman[69] and now you want me to bite it too! 'Get behind me, Satan! It is written: you shall not tempt the Lord your God.'[70] No, I will not argue with you. When Eve tried to dispute with you, she was lost; she argued and was seduced. Live Jesus in whom I believe, live the Church to which I cling!" Say these and similar impassioned words. You must speak also to Jesus Christ and to the Holy Spirit in whatever way He inspires you, and even pray as well to the Church: "O Mother of the children of God, may I never be separated from you; I want to live and die in you."

I don't know if I'm making myself clear. What I'm trying to say is that we have to strike back with the heart and not with our reason, with intense feelings and not with arguments. It's true that at such times of temptation our poor will is without feeling. So much the better. Its blows will strike the enemy that much harder. And when

---

69. Gn 3:1–6.
70. Cf. Mt 4:10, 7.

he discovers that instead of delaying your progress, he is giving you the opportunity of expressing countless virtuous affections, particularly that of affirming your faith, he will finally leave you alone.

As a third remedy, it would be good once in a while to take fifty or sixty strokes of the discipline, or only thirty, depending on what you can take. It's surprising how effective this measure has been for someone I know. Undoubtedly that's because the physical sensation distracts from interior suffering and calls forth the mercy of God. Moreover, when the devil sees that his partner, the flesh, is being subdued, he gets afraid and runs away. But this third remedy must be taken in moderation, depending on the good it achieves, as you will know after trying it out for a few days.

When all is said and done, these temptations are simply trials like any other, and you must calm yourself, for as Scripture reminds us: "Blessed is he who undergoes temptation; for having been proved, he will receive the crown of glory."[71] I have seen few people make progress without experiencing trials, so you must be patient. After the squall, God will send the calm. But make use especially of the first two remedies I have suggested.

As for your fourth point [. . .][72]

But if you really like the prayers you are used to saying, please don't drop them; and if you happen to leave out some of what I am telling you to do, have no scruples about it, for here is the general rule of our obedience written in capital letters:

"DO ALL THROUGH LOVE, NOTHING THROUGH CONSTRAINT;
   LOVE OBEDIENCE MORE THAN YOU FEAR DISOBEDIENCE."

I want you to have the spirit of liberty, not the kind that excludes obedience (this is freedom of the flesh), but the liberty that excludes constraint, scruples and anxiety. If you really love obedience and docility, I'd like to think that when some legitimate or charitable cause takes you away from your religious exercises, this would be for you another form of obedience and that your love would make up for whatever you have to omit in your religious practice.

---

71. Cf. Jas 1:12.
72. Much of this "fourth point" is devoted to daily prayers and practices similar to those proposed in the *Introduction to the Devout Life*, Part II.

I want you to get a French translation of all the prayers you will be saying; not that I want you to say them in French, for they are more devotional for you in Latin, but I want you to understand them better. The same goes for the Litanies of the Name of Jesus, of Our Lady, and the other prayers. But do all this without anxiety and in a spirit of gentleness and love.

Your meditations will focus on the life and death of our Lord. I approve of your using the *Exercises* of Tauler, the *Meditations* of Saint Bonaventure, and those of Capiglia, for in the end, it is always the life of our Lord presented there, as it is in His Gospels.[73] But you must simplify all this in the manner I have written out for you. Meditations on the four Last Ends will be good for you, on condition that you always close your meditation with an act of confidence in God, never thinking about death and hell on the one hand, without picturing the Cross on the other, so that after having been moved to fear by the first consideration, you will have recourse to the other through confidence. Your period of meditation should not exceed three quarters of an hour. I like spiritual canticles, but sung with feeling.

As for brother ass, I approve of a Friday fast and a frugal supper on Saturdays. It's a good idea to hold him down during the week, not so much by cutting down on the quantity of food he is given (moderation must be observed), but by cutting back on the variety of foods you put before him. Nevertheless, I recommend that you treat him once in a while by giving him oats, as Saint Francis did, to make him go faster. That's where taking the discipline comes in, for it has a marvelous power of quickening the spirit by stinging the flesh; but use it only twice a week.

Do not go to communion less frequently than you've been doing, unless your confessor tells you to. It is a special comfort for me on feast days to know that we go to communion together.

Now for your fifth point. True, I have a particular affection for Celse-Bénigne and your other children. Since God has put into your

---

73. Of the titles mentioned the first two are spurious works attributed to Johann Tauler (1294–1361) and Saint Bonaventure (1221–1274); the third, by Andrew Capiglia, a Spanish Carthusian, had been translated into French in 1601. Note that Francis was unable to refer his directees to the Gospel texts since no approved Catholic translation was available to them; hence the referral to meditation books as another means of praying with the life and death of Christ.

heart a desire to see them totally devoted to His service, you must bring them up with this in mind, gently encouraging them to think along these lines. Find the *Confessions* of Saint Augustine and read carefully Book VIII and what follows. There you will see Saint Monica, a widow like yourself, and her care for her son Augustine; you will find other things too that will encourage you.

As for Celse-Bénigne, you will have to inspire him with generous motives and plant in his little soul a noble and courageous ambition to serve God; and you will have to minimize the idea of purely human glory, but do this very gradually; as he grows up, with God's help, we shall think of specific ways of doing this. Meanwhile take care that he and his sisters sleep alone, as far as possible, or with persons whom you can trust as completely as you would yourself. I can't tell you how important this is: experience teaches me this every day.

If Françoise wants to be a nun of her own accord, fine;[74] otherwise, I do not approve of her being influenced by any recommendations, but only, as in the case of other young girls, by gentle inspirations. As much as possible, we must touch the hearts of others as do the angels, delicately and without coercion. Still, I think it's a good idea that you send her to be educated at the monastery of Puits d'Orbe where I hope true devotion will flourish again very soon. I would like you to cooperate toward this end. Try to remove traces of vanity from the hearts of your daughters; vanity seems almost innate to their sex.[75] I know you have the *Letters* of Saint Jerome in French; read the one he wrote about Pacatula and the others about the education of girls.[76] You will find them refreshing. But do all this in moderation. "Gentle inspirations" sums all I have to say on the subject.

I see that you owe someone two thousand crowns. As soon as you can, get this paid, and be very careful not to withhold from others anything you owe them. Give alms in little ways, but very humbly. I like the practice of visiting the sick, the elderly—women especially—and very young children. I like the practice of visiting the poor, especially poor women—humbly and with kindness.

---

74. In fact, Françoise was not so inclined. See Jane's letters to her, below.
75. See Wendy M. Wright, *Bond of Perfection* (New York: Paulist, 1985), pp. 135–138.
76. See *Select Letters of St. Jerome* with an English translation by F.A. Wright (Cambridge, Mass.: Harvard, 1980), letters CXXVIII, XXII, and CVII.

As to your sixth point, I agree that you should divide your time between your father and your father-in-law, and that you try to obtain the good of their souls (the way the angels do, as I said above). It doesn't matter if you spend more time in Dijon; after all, that is where your first duty lies. Try to be more humbly attentive to both fathers, and work gently toward their salvation. I think it would probably be better for you to spend the winter in Dijon.

I am writing to your father. Since he asked me to write him something that would benefit his soul, I have done so in all simplicity, maybe too much so. My advice to him is two-fold: first, he should review his life as a whole in order to make a general confession—this is something that any man of honor should do before he dies; second, he should try, little by little, to detach himself from worldly ties. Then I suggest to him ways of going about this. I present all this as my opinion, quite clearly and gently, giving him to understand that he must not suddenly break off all his worldly connections, but that he should loosen and untie them. He will show you the letter, I'm sure; help him to understand it and to put my suggestions into practice.

You owe him the great charity of accompanying him as he journeys toward a happy end of life. No human respect should stand in the way of your doing this with humble affection, for he is the first "neighbor" the Lord obliges you to love; and the first thing you should love in him is his soul; and in his soul, his conscience; in his conscience, his honesty; and in his honesty, his concern for his eternal salvation. The same goes for your father-in-law.

Perhaps your father, who doesn't really know me yet, will misinterpret the liberty I have taken; so help him get to know me, for when he does, I'm sure that more than anything else about me, it's that very liberty that he will love. I have written a five-page letter to the Archbishop of Bourges[77] in which I describe for him a method of preaching, and along with that, I tell him quite freely what I think about certain responsibilities in an archbishop's life. In his case, I have no fear of being misunderstood. So, what more could you want? Your father, brother, uncle, children—all are infinitely dear to me.

---

77. Madame de Chantal's brother, André. The letter (*Oeuvres*, XII, 299–325: Letter CCXXIX) has been translated by John K. Ryan as *On the Preacher and Preaching* (Chicago: Regnery, 1964).

In answer to your seventh point, about the spirit of liberty, I shall tell you what I think it is. Every good person is free of committing mortal sins and has no willing attachment to them. Such freedom is necessary for salvation, but that's not what I'm talking about here. The freedom I'm referring to is the "freedom of the children of God"[78] who know they are loved. And what is that? It's the detachment of a Christian heart from all things so that it is free to follow the known will of God. You will readily understand what I'm trying to say if God gives me the grace to explain to you the characteristics and effects of this freedom, and the occasions when it is practiced.

We pray to God above all, that His name may be hallowed, that His kingdom come, that His will be done on earth as it is in heaven.[79] All this is nothing other than the spirit of freedom; for, provided that the name of God is hallowed, that His kingdom is coming in us, that His will is being done, a free spirit has no other concern.

First characteristic: The heart that enjoys this freedom is not attached to consolations, but accepts affliction with as much docility as nature can manage. I'm not saying that the person doesn't like or long for these consolations, but just that her heart isn't bound to them. Second characteristic: A person who has this spirit is not emotionally bound to her spiritual exercises; so, if she can't do them because of illness or some emergency, she doesn't get upset. Again I'm not saying that she doesn't like them, but that she is not attached to them. Third, she hardly ever loses her joy, for no deprivation can sadden a person whose heart is attached to nothing. This isn't to say that she can't lose her joy, but if she does, it's never for very long.

The effects of this freedom are a great inner serenity, a great gentleness and willingness to yield in everything that isn't sin or an occasion of sin; it's a flexible disposition, able gracefully to do the virtuous or charitable thing. For example: try interrupting the meditations of someone who is very attached to her spiritual exercises and you will see her upset, flustered, taken aback. A person who has this true freedom will leave her prayer, unruffled, gracious toward the person who has unexpectedly disturbed her, for to her

---

78. Rom 8:21.
79. Cf. Mt 6:9–10.

it's all the same—serving God by meditating or serving Him by responding to her neighbor. Both are the will of God, but helping the neighbor is necessary at that particular moment. We have occasion to practice this freedom whenever things don't go the way we'd like them to; for anyone who is not attached to her own ways will not get impatient when things go otherwise.

This freedom has two opposite vices: instability and constraint or, in the extreme, dissoluteness and slavishness. Instability is a kind of excessive freedom which makes us want to change our practices or our state in life for no good reason or without knowing if to do so is God's will. The least pretext is enough to make us change a practice, a plan, a rule; for the flimsiest excuse we give up a rule or a good custom. Before we know it, our heart is scattered and loses its way; it becomes like an orchard open on all sides, where the fruit is not for the owner but for all who pass by.[80]

Constraint or slavishness is a certain lack of freedom that causes the soul to be unduly anxious or angry when it cannot carry out what it had intended to do, even though it could now do something better. For example: suppose I have decided to make my daily meditation in the morning. If I am unstable, then for the slightest excuse I will put it off until evening, e.g., a dog kept me awake, or I have a letter to write (though there is no urgency about it). On the other hand, if I have a spirit of constraint or slavishness I wouldn't give up my meditation even if a sick person had great need of my help at that very moment or if I had some pressing obligation which should not be postponed; and so on.

I still want to give you two or three examples of this freedom to help you understand what I'm not explaining very well. But, first of all, I must point out two rules which must be observed if we are not to fail in this matter. First, we should never neglect our exercises and the common norms of virtue unless to do so appears to be God's will. Now the will of God is indicated in two ways: through necessity or charity. Example: I would like to preach the Lenten sermons in a small town in my diocese. But if I get sick or break a leg, there's no point in feeling sorry or worried about not preaching, for I can be sure that God wants me to serve Him by suffering and not by preaching. However, if I'm not sick and an occasion comes along to

---

80. Cf. Ps 80:13.

go preach in another place where people might become Huguenots if I didn't go, this would be the will of God, signifying clearly enough that I should very simply change my plans.

The second rule is that when we use our freedom for charity's sake it must be without scandal or injustice. Example: I am certain I could be more useful somewhere far from my diocese. I must not use my freedom to follow through with this, for I would give scandal and act unjustly since my obligation is here. Therefore, it's a false use of freedom for married women to absent themselves from their husbands without a legitmate reason, under pretext of devotion or charity. Our freedom must never take us away from our vocation. On the contrary, it should make us content each with our own calling, knowing that it is God's will that we remain in it. [81]

Now let's look at Cardinal Borromeo who will be canonized in a few days. [82] He was one of the most precise, rigid, austere men you could imagine; he lived on bread and water; he was so austere that after he became Archbishop, in twenty-four years he went to his brothers' homes only twice when they were ill, and only twice did he go in his own garden. And yet, this strict man who often dined with his Swiss neighbors (he did this in the hope of having a good influence on them) had no problem drinking a couple of toasts with them at every meal, over and above what he drank to quench his thirst. Here you have an example of holy freedom in the most austere man of our times. An undisciplined person would have drunk too much; one who is very constrained would have been afraid of committing a mortal sin; a person with a true spirit of freedom does it out of love.

Bishop Spiridion, a bishop of long ago, took in a pilgrim almost dead from hunger. It was during Lent and there was nothing to eat in his place but salt meat. He had some of it cooked and offered it to the pilgrim who refused to take it, hungry though he was. Spiridion, who wasn't at all hungry, out of charity ate some first in order to remove, by his example, any scruples the pilgrim might have. That's the loving freedom of a holy man.

Father Ignatius of Loyola, who will also soon be canonized, [83]

---

81. Cf. 1 Cor 7:20, 24.
82. Actually the deaths of two Popes, Clement VIII and Leo XI, delayed the canonization until 1610.
83. This canonization actually took place March 12, 1622.

ate meat on Wednesday of Holy Week simply on the order of his physician who thought it would be good for some minor ailment he had. A constrained spirit would have had to be coaxed for three days before doing this.

But now I want to show you a "sun" that shines more brilliantly than any of these: a really open, detached spirit who holds on to the will of God alone. I've often wondered who was the most mortified of all the saints I know, and after much reflection, I decided it was Saint John the Baptist. He went into the desert at the age of five, and was aware that our Savior was born in a place very close by, maybe two or three days' journey away. God only knows how much his heart, which had been moved to love his Savior from the time he was still in his mother's womb, would have wanted to enjoy the Lord's sweet presence! Yet, he spent twenty-five years in the desert, without once coming to see Him; then leaving the desert, he went about catechizing without going to visit the Lord, but waited for the Lord to come to him. Afterward, having baptized Him, he didn't follow Him but stayed behind to do his appointed work.[84] What mortification! To be so close to his Savior and not see Him! To have Him so near and not enjoy His presence! Isn't this having one's spirit completely detached, bound to nothing, not even to God, in order to do His will and serve Him; to leave God for God, and to not love God so as to love Him better? This example overwhelms me with its grandeur.

I forgot to mention that God's will is known, not only by the call of necessity and charity, but also by obedience; so true is this that a person who receives a command should believe that this is the will of God. I hope this isn't too much. My mind is running ahead faster than I would like, carried away by my eagerness to serve you.

In response to your eighth point, remember the feast day of King Saint Louis, the day on which you took the crown of the kingdom from your own heart to lay it at the feet of Jesus, your King; the day on which you renewed your youth like the eagle's,[85] plunging into the sea of penance; the day that heralded the eternal day of your soul. Remember that to your great resolution of belonging totally to God—body, heart, and soul—I said "Amen" in the name of

---

84. Mt 3:1–17; Lk 3:1–22.
85. Cf. Ps 103:5.

the whole Church, our Mother; at the same time, the Blessed Virgin and all the angels and saints made heaven resound with their great "Amen" and "Alleluia." Remember that all the past is as nothing and that every day you must say with David: only now have I begun to really love my God.[86] Do much for God, and do nothing without love: refer everything to this love; eat and drink with it in mind.[87]

Have devotion to Saint Louis and admire his great constancy. He became king when he was twelve years old, had nine children, was continually at war against either rebels or enemies of the faith, and was king for more than forty years. At the end of it all, after his death, the holy priest who had been his confessor all through his life testified that King Louis had never fallen into mortal sin. Twice he had made voyages overseas; both times he lost his army, and on the last trip he died of the plague. After having devoted much time to visiting, nursing, and healing the plague-stricken men of his army, he himself died, cheerful and calm, a verse from David on his lips. I give you this saint as your special patron for the year; keep him before your eyes, along with the others I named above. Next year, please God, I will give you another saint, after you have profited much in the school of this one.

As to your ninth point, I want you to believe two things about me: first, that God wants you to avail yourself of me, so do not hesitate; and, second, that in what concerns your salvation, God will give me the light I need to serve you. As for my will to serve you, He has already given it to me to such a degree that it couldn't be stronger. I have received the copy of your vows, which I will carefully treasure, looking upon it as a fit instrument of our union, which is totally rooted in God and which will last for all eternity, by the mercy of Him who is its author.

[. . .] In one passage in your letter, you seem to consider it settled that some day we shall be seeing each other again. Please God, my very dear sister, we shall. But for my part, I see nothing ahead to warrant my hoping to find time to get there. I told you the reason in confidence at Saint-Claude. I'm tied up here, hand and foot; and you, dear sister, don't the difficulties of your last journey frighten you? Well, between now and Easter we'll see what God

---

86. Ps 77:11; Vulgate 76:11: "et dixi nunc coepi."
87. Cf. 1 Cor 10:31.

wants from us; may His holy will ever be ours. I ask you to praise God with me for the effects of the trip to Saint-Claude. I can't tell you about them, but they are great. At your first opportunity, write me the story of the gate of Saint-Claude, and please believe that I'm not asking you this out of curiosity.[88]

My mother could not have been more taken with you. I was happy to see that you willingly call Madame du Puits d'Orbe "sister." She has a greatness of soul, if she receives the right help, and God will use her to the glory of His name. Help her and visit her by letter. God will be pleased with you for this.

It looks to me as if I'll never finish this letter which I've written only with the intention of answering you. Still, I really must finish it now, asking for your prayers which are a great help. How I need them! I never pray without including you in my petitions; I never greet my own angels without greeting yours. Do the same for me, and get Celse-Bénigne to pray for me also. I always pray for him and all your little family. You may be sure that I never forget them in my Mass, nor their deceased father, your husband.

May God be your very heart, mind and soul, my dearest sister. I am, in His merciful love,

your very devoted servant

[. . .] Pray once in a while for the conversion of my poor Geneva.

June 8, 1606[89]

So then, my dear daughter, it will be a year from now, please God, that we shall see each other, but that without fail, either around Pentecost or Corpus Christi. Not having to wonder about any other meeting, we can prepare ourselves for that one well in advance. What shall we do in the meantime? We shall resign ourselves totally and without reserve to our Lord's will, surrendering into His

---

88. The story involved a dream Jane had had before she met Francis, and a voice which said, "you will never find the peace of God's children except through the gate of St. Claude." The decisive meeting just prior to this letter took place, as was noted, in the town of St. Claude. On the dream and its interpretation see Elisabeth Stopp, *Madame de Chantal: Portrait of a Saint* (Westminster, Md.: Newman, 1963), pp. 63–65.

89. *Oeuvres*, XIII, 181–192: Letter CCCLI. In the interval between the long letter just presented and this one Francis wrote Mme de Chantal twenty-six letters that are extant; and Jane, in addition to the correspondence, had journeyed to visit Francis at the Château of Sales in May 1605. At this writing, then, it is over a year since they have seen each other, and after several failed efforts, a date has been agreed upon.

hands all our consolations, both spiritual and temporal. Purely and simply, we shall entrust to His providence the life and death of all those who belong to us, letting Him arrange according to His good pleasure who is to outlive the others; for we are confident that, provided His sovereign goodness be with us, in us, and for us, we have all we need and more.

You want me to pray that I outlive you? Really, may God do with me as He pleases, whether sooner or later; that is certainly among the things I try to be resigned to. But now you tell me that you are not yet detached in this matter. My God, what are you saying, my very dear daughter? Could I possibly be a hindrance for you—I who have no greater desire for you than to see you living in the total and perfect liberty of heart of the children of God?[90] But I understand you well, my dear daughter, and know that is not what you mean; you mean that you think my longevity is for God's glory, and for that reason you feel yourself wishing it. So it is to our Lord's glory that you are attached, not to his creatures. I know this very well, and I thank and praise His divine majesty for it.

But do you know what I am going to promise you? To take better care of my health from now on—even though I have always taken better care of myself than I actually deserve; and thanks be to God, I am feeling quite well now, since I've totally cut out staying up late and the excessive writing that I used to do at that hour. And I've been eating more sensibly too. But believe me, these decisions owe a lot to your desire; because I care intensely about what pleases you and makes you happy, though with a certain liberty and sincerity of heart that makes this caring resemble a dew which falls on my heart softly and silently. And if you want me to tell you all, my caring for you didn't used to act so smoothly at the beginning when God gave it to me (it is without doubt his gift) as it does now that it is very strong and seems to be growing ever stronger, though still smooth and calm. That's too much said on a topic I wasn't even going to mention! [. . .]

I've been thinking about what you wrote me concerning the advice Father X had given you about not using your imagination or your understanding in prayer, and the similar advice regarding

90. Cf. Rom 8:21.

144

imagination that Mother Marie de la Trinité gave you.[91] On this latter point if your imagination is very vivid and you spend a lot of time this way, you undoubtedly needed this correction; but if you use your imagination briefly and simply, only as a means of helping your mind be attentive and bringing it back to the subject of your meditation, I don't think that there's as yet any need to give up all use of it. You must neither linger over your images, nor totally disregard them. Neither should you imagine in too much detail, for instance, wondering about the color of our Lady's hair, the shape of her face, and details of that sort; but simply and in a general way, imagine her longing for her Son, or the like, and only briefly.

I say the same about not using the understanding. If without forcing itself your will moves right along with its affections, there is no need to linger over considerations. But, because that doesn't ordinarily happen to less than perfect people like us, we may still have to make use of considerations for a while yet.

From all this, I would summarize that you should abstain from long periods of prayer (for I don't consider three-quarters or half an hour long), and from very detailed and long, drawn-out imaginings; for the latter should be simple and short, serving only as transitions from distractions to recollection. The same goes for the use of the understanding, for this too should serve only to move the affections; the affections then move us to resolutions, resolutions to action, and action to the accomplishment of God's will, in which our soul should dissolve and be transformed. This is all I can tell you about it. If I told you anything to the contrary, or if you understood me otherwise, it should, no doubt, be revised.

I approve of your Friday abstinence, but done without vow or too much constraint. I approve even more that you busy your hands with spinning, for instance, whenever you have nothing more important to do, and that your handiwork be used for altar linens or given to the poor, but not that this be adhered to so strictly that if you happen to make something for yourself or for one of your relatives, you should feel obliged to give an equivalent sum to the poor.

---

91. Marie (née d'Hannivel) de la Trinité was a young Carmelite then in Dijon, and the Annecy editors suggest the priest in question was likely Jacques Gallemand, who was active with Bérulle and others in bringing the Carmelites into France. Cf. *Oeuvres*, XIII, 183 and XII, 118.

In all things a holy liberty and freedom must reign and we must have no other law or coercion than that of love. When love moves us to make something for our relatives, we must not reprimand it as if it had done something wrong, nor require it to make amends, as you suggest. Whether love invites us to make something for the poor or for the rich, it does all things well and is equally pleasing to our Lord. I think that if you really understand me, you will see that I speak the truth and that I am fighting for a good cause when I defend a holy and charitable liberty of spirit, which, as you know, I hold in highest esteem provided, of course, that it is true liberty and far removed from laxity and from libertarianism, which is only a parody of liberty.

After that I laughed, and laughed heartily, when I read you planned to give me some of your serge for my own use and then expected me to give whatever it was worth to the poor. I'm really not making fun of the suggestion because I can see that it springs from a good and clear intention, even if the resulting stream is a bit troubled. May God make me such that all I use is referred to His service and that my life is so totally His that what is used to maintain it may be said to serve His divine majesty.

I'm laughing, my daughter, but my laughter is mixed with a keen awareness of the difference that exists between what I am and what some people think I am. [. . .]

These desires you have to see yourself removed from all these worldly diversions must, as you say, be good since they are not upsetting you at all. But be patient; we shall talk about this next year, if God keeps us here on earth. That will be time enough. Also, I don't want to answer you now about your desires to leave your homeland and to enter a novitiate of women who aspire to become religious. All this, my dear daughter, is too important to discuss on paper. There will be plenty of time to do so later. Meanwhile you will wield your distaff, not with big, loaded spindles which your fingers couldn't handle, but with small ones that you can manage: humility, patience, abjection, gentleness of heart, resignation, simplicity, charity to the sick poor, forbearance with difficult persons, and similar imitations of the Lord which can easily be wound on your little spindle. Then you will spin in the company of St. Monica, St. Paula, St. Elizabeth, St. Lydwine, and several others who are at the feet of your glorious Abbess, who herself was able to ply any kind of spindle but preferred smaller ones.[92] I think she did this in order to set us an example.

[. . .] I'll be leaving here in ten days to continue my visitation and will be spending five whole months in our high mountains where kind folk are awaiting my visit with affection. I shall take care of myself as much as possible, for love of myself (whom I love only too much) and also for love of you who want me to be careful and who will have a share in anything good that takes place here, just as you share, in a general way, in all that is done in my diocese, according to the ability that I have by virtue of my position to communicate it to you.

My brother, the Canon,[93] wanted to write to you, but I don't know if he will. The poor fellow is not well and he is dragging himself around as best he can, with more good will than actual strength. He will be able to recuperate somewhat at his mother's while I leap from rock to rock on our mountains. [. . .]

Goodbye, my dear daughter. Let us always belong to God, unreservedly and without interruption. May He ever live and reign in our hearts. Amen. [. . .]

February 11, 1607[94]

I was ten whole weeks without a word from you, my dear, my very dear daughter, and your last letters were written early last November. But one good thing is that my patience had almost given out and I think it would have given out entirely if I hadn't remembered that I must preserve it in order to be free to preach it to others. But at last, my dearest daughter, yesterday a bundle arrived, like a fleet from India, full of letters and spiritual songs.[95] Oh, how welcome it was and how I loved it! There was a letter dated November 22, another, December 30 of last year, and the third, written early this year. If all the letters I wrote you during that time were put in one packet, they would be more numerous than that, for as much as I could, I always wrote via Lyons and Dijon. I say this to ease my

---

92. The Abbess is, of course, the Virgin Mary. Cf. *supra*, Introduction.
93. Jean-François de Sales.
94. *Oeuvres*, XIII, 260–267: Letter CCCLXXXV.
95. In a postscript to his letter of June 6, 1906, Francis asked Jane to send him some spiritual songs available in Dijon.

conscience, which would bother me greatly if it were not responsive to the heart of a specially loved daughter.

I am going to write you many things, about this and that topic, following the content of your letters. You do very well to entrust to the hands of divine Providence your wish to leave the world so that this desire does not preoccupy you needlessly, as it undoubtedly would if you allowed it to run things according to its own fancy.

I shall give the matter serious thought and will offer several Masses, asking for the light of the Holy Spirit in order to make the right decision, for you see, my dear daughter, this is a decisive step and should be weighed in the scales of the sanctuary.[96] Let us pray God to make His will known to us and to dispose our will to want nothing except by and through His, then let us remain at peace, without hurry or agitation in our hearts. The next time we see each other, God will, if He wishes, be merciful to us.

[. . .] I see that all the seasons of the year converge in your soul: at times you experience all the dryness, distraction, disgust, and boredom of winter; at other times, all the dew and fragrance of the little flowers of Maytime; and again, the warmth of a desire to please God. All that remains is autumn, and you say that you do not see much of its fruit. Yet it often happens that in threshing the wheat and pressing the grapes we discover more than the harvest or vintage promised. You would like it to be always spring or summer; but no, my dear daughter, we have to experience interior as well as exterior changes. Only in heaven will everything be springtime as to beauty, autumn as to enjoyment, and summer as to love. There will be no winter there; but here below we need winter so that we may practice self-denial and the countless small but beautiful virtues that can be practiced during a barren season. Let us go on our little way; so long as we mean well and hold to our resolve, we can only be on the right track.

No, my very dear daughter, it is not necessary to be always and at every moment attentive to all the virtues in order to practice them; that would twist and encumber your thoughts and feelings too much. Humility and charity are the master ropes; all the others are attached to them. We need only hold on to these two: one is at the very bottom and the other at the very top. The preservation of the

---

96. Cf. *supra*, note 27.

whole building depends on its foundation and its roof. We do not encounter much difficulty in practicing other virtues if we keep our heart bound to the practice of these two. They are the mother virtues, and the others follow them the way little chicks follow the mother hen. [. . .]

I praise God that you wish to settle your lawsuits. Since my return from visiting the diocese, I have been so pressured and busy settling differences between litigating parties that my house has been full of clients who, on the whole, by the grace of God, have gone home in peace. I must admit, however, that it has taken much of my time. But there is no remedy for it; we must yield to the need of our neighbor.

I am happy to hear of the healing of that good person who had been caught up in illicit love or false friendship. Such maladies are like mild fevers: after they pass, we are left in a state of good health.

I shall go now to the altar and speak to our Lord about our affairs. I shall write the rest afterward.

No, you are not going against obedience by not raising your heart to God as often or by not following the recommendations I gave you as precisely as you would like. They were recommendations for you, but not commands; when we give orders, we use terms that make our meaning very clear. Do you know what our recommendations require? They require to be loved and not scorned—that is quite sufficient—but in no way do they bind. Courage, my sister, my daughter; enkindle your heart during this Lent.

[. . .] What more can I tell you? I have just come from teaching a catechism lesson where I played the comedian with the children and made the audience laugh a bit by making fun of masks and balls. I was in high spirits, and a big audience encouraged me by its applause to continue to play with the children. They said the role suited me well, and I believe it! Would that God might make me really childlike in innocence and simplicity! But am I not a true simpleton to be telling you all this? It can't be helped; I let you see my heart such as it is and in its various moods so that, as the apostle says, you may not think more of me than what I really am.[97]

Live joyously and courageously, my dear daughter. We must

---

97. Cf. 2 Cor 12:6.

not doubt that Jesus Christ is ours. "Yes," a little girl once answered me, "He belongs to me more than I belong to Him, and more than I belong to myself."

[. . .] Goodbye, my very dear, my truly very dear sister and daughter. May Jesus always be in our hearts and live and rule there for all eternity; may His holy name and that of His glorious mother be ever blessed. Amen. Live Jesus, and may the world perish if it does not wish to live for Jesus. Amen.

January 16, 1610[98]

[. . .] In regard to your coming here, do not hurry because of my anticipated trip to Paris, because, having heard nothing more about that beyond what I showed you, I doubt if it will take place; also it seems to me that to take your three little daughters on a trip during Lent would be rather difficult; besides, your nephew told me that your father and your brother had settled on the time immediately after Easter. Your heart may be saying by now, "Look how this man keeps on postponing!" O my daughter, believe that I am waiting for your day of joy with as much longing as you are; but I am forced to act this way for reasons it is not expedient that I write you about. So wait, my very dear sister, "Wait," I say, using words of Scripture, "while you wait."[99] Now to wait while we wait means not to worry while waiting, for many persons do not really wait while waiting, but are anxious and restless.

So we'll be all right, dear daughter, with God's help. All the little complications and hidden contradictions that come up unexpectedly to disturb my peace actually fill me with an even more serene peace and, it seems to me, are a sign that my soul will soon be settled in God. This really is the greatest and, I believe, the only ambition and passion of my heart. When I say my heart I mean my whole heart, including the person to whom God has united me indissolubly.

While I am on the subject of my soul, I want to give you some good news about it: I am doing and shall continue doing for it all

---

98. *Oeuvres*, XXI, 89–98: Letters DXL and DCCCXXXVIII. What had been treated as two separate letters since the first publication of letters (1626) appeared in a single manuscript which surfaced in Lisbon in 1911 and was printed as such in the supplementary volume of letters.

99. Cf. Ps 40:1; Vulgate 39:2: "expectans expectavi Dominum."

that you asked me to do—have no doubt about this. Thank you for your concern for its welfare, which is undivided from the welfare of your own soul (if we can even use the terms "yours" and "mine" when speaking on this subject). And I'll tell you something else: I am a little happier than usual with my soul in that I no longer see anything in it which keeps it attached to this world, and I find it more in tune with eternal values. How happy I should be if I were as deeply and closely united to God as I am distanced and alienated from the world! And how delighted you would be, my daughter! But I'm speaking of my inner dispositions and my feelings; as for the exterior and, what is worse, my actions, these are full of all kinds of contrary flaws, for "I fail to carry out the good things I want to do."[100] Yet I know very well, without pretense and without swerving, that I really want to do them. But, my daughter, how can it be that even with such good will, I still see so many imperfections growing in me? Surely, these come neither from my will nor by my will, although they appear to form part of it. It seems to me that they are like mistletoe which grows and appears on a tree though it is not part of it—on it but not of it. Why am I telling you all this? It's because my heart always expands and pours itself out spontaneously when it is near yours.

Your way of praying is good. Just be very faithful about staying near God, gently and quietly attentive to Him in your heart, sleeping in the arms of His providence, peacefully accepting His holy will; for all this pleases Him.

[. . .] I'd like to say more about your prayer, for I reread your letter late last night. Go on doing as you described. Be careful not to intellectualize, because this can be harmful, not only in general, but especially at prayer. Approach the beloved object of your prayer with your affections quite simply and as gently as you can. Naturally, every now and then, your intellect will make an effort to apply itself; don't waste time trying to guard against this, for that would only be a distraction. When you notice this happening, be content simply to return to acts of the will.

Staying in God's presence and placing ourselves in God's presence are, to my mind, two different things. In order to place ourselves in His presence we have to withdraw our soul from every

100. Cf. Rom 7:15.

151

other object and make it attentive to that presence at this very moment, as I have explained in the book.[101] But once we are there, we remain there, as long as either our intellect or our will is active in regard to God. We look either at Him or at something else for love of Him; or, not looking at anything at all, we speak to Him; or again, without either looking at Him or speaking to Him, we just stay there where He has placed us, like a statue in its niche. And if while we are there, we also have some sense that we belong to God and that He is our All, then we must certainly thank Him for this.

If a statue that had been placed in a niche in some room had the ability to speak and were asked "Why are you there?" it would answer, "Because my master, the sculptor, has put me here." "Why don't you move about?" "Because he wants me to be perfectly still." "What use are you there? What do you gain by staying like this?" "I'm not here for my own benefit, but to serve and obey the will of my master." "But you don't see him." "No, but he sees me and is pleased that I am here where he has put me." "But wouldn't you like to be able to move about and to get closer to him?" "No, not unless he ordered me to." "Isn't there anything at all that you want then?" "No, because I am where my master put me, and all my happiness lies in pleasing him."[102]

Dear daughter, what a good way of praying, and what a fine way of staying in God's presence: doing what He wants and accepting what pleases Him! It seems to me that Mary Magdalene was a statue in her niche when, without saying a word, without moving, and perhaps even without looking at Him, she sat at our Lord's feet and listened to what He was saying. When He spoke, she listened; whenever He paused, she stopped listening; but always, she was right there.[103] A little child who is at its mother's breast when she has fallen asleep is really where it belongs and wants to be, even though neither of them makes a sound.

O my daughter, how I enjoy talking with you about these things! How happy we are when we want to love our Lord! Let's really love Him, my daughter, and let's not start examining in detail what we are doing for love of Him, as long as we know that we never want to do anything except for love of Him. For my part, I think

---

101. I.e., *Oeuvres*, III, 73–76: *Introduction to the Devout Life*, II, 2.
102. Cf. *Oeuvres*, IV, 339–343: *Treatise on the Love of God*, VI, 11.
103. Lk 10:39. Cf. *Oeuvres*, IV, 332: *Treatise*, VI, 8.

we remain in God's presence even while we are asleep, because we fall asleep in His sight, as He pleases, and according to His will, and He puts us down on our bed like a statue in its niche; when we wake up, we find Him still there, close by. He has not moved, nor have we; evidently, we have stayed in His presence, but with our eyes closed in sleep.[104]

Well, your baron is here, telling me to hurry up. Good night, my dear sister, my daughter. You will have news of me as often as I can write. Believe me that the very first note I wrote you was absolutely true—that God had given me to you.[105] I am more convinced of this in my heart every day. May this great God ever be our All.

I send greetings to my dear little sister[106] and all your household. [. . .] Stand fast, dear daughter, and do not doubt: God holds us in His hand and will never abandon us. Glory be to Him for ever and ever. Amen.

Live Jesus and His most holy mother! Amen. And praise be to our good father, Saint Joseph! May God bless you with countless blessings.

Chambéry, March 28, 1612[107]

Well, now, my very dear and only daughter, it is about time I answer your long letter—if I can. Unfortunately, my very dear, most truly very dear daughter, I must answer it in haste for I have very little leisure, and if the sermon which I have to give shortly had not pretty well taken shape in my mind, I wouldn't be writing you anything but the little note enclosed.

Now let us talk about the interior trials of which you have written me. It is clearly a total absence of feeling that keeps you from enjoying not only consolation and inspirations, but even faith, hope and charity. You do possess them, however, and very much so, only you do not derive any enjoyment from them. You are like a child

---

104. Cf. *Oeuvres*, IV, 342: *Treatise*, VI, 11.

105. Cf. *supra*, note 49.

106. Marie-Aimée, Madame de Chantal's oldest daughter, who had recently married Francis's brother Bernard, was a favorite of the bishop.

107. *Oeuvres*, XV, 197–199: Letter DCCLXIV. Our last sample of this unique and extensive correspondence was written more than two years (and sixty letters) later. Madam is now Mother de Chantal of the first Visitation community in Annecy, and Francis is away preaching the Lenten series in Chambéry.

whose guardian does not allow him to spend all his fortune, and so, although the money belongs to him, he cannot touch it, nor does he seem to possess anything but his very life. As St. Paul says, "though he is master of all his possessions, his condition is no different from that of a slave."[108] And so, my dearest daughter, God does not want you to have control over your faith, your hope, and your charity, nor to have use of them, except just enough to live on and to draw from in times of absolute necessity.

My dearest daughter, how fortunate we are to be thus constrained and held back by our heavenly Guardian! All we have to do, undoubtedly, is nothing more than what we are already doing, which is to adore the lovable providence of God and to throw ourselves into His arms and into His keeping. "No, Lord, I want no more delight from my faith, my hope, or my charity than to be able to say in very truth, though without taste or feeling, that I would rather die than give up my faith, my hope and my charity. Lord, if it is Your good pleasure that I take no delight in practicing the virtues which Your grace has granted me, I accept this most willingly, even though it goes against what my will feels."

It is the peak of holy resignation to be content with naked, dry, unfelt acts made only by the higher will, as it would be the highest level of abstinence to be satisfied with eating, not simply without enjoyment or savor, but with distaste and aversion.

You have described your suffering very well and need do nothing more than what you are already doing to remedy your situation. Assure our Lord, even aloud or sometimes in song, that you are willing to endure a living death and be nourished as though you were dead, that is, without taste or feeling or awareness. In short, our Savior wants us to be so entirely His that we have nothing left and may be totally and unreservedly surrendered to the mercy of His providence.

Therefore, my dearest daughter, remain thus in the darkness of the Passion. I say "in the darkness" for I leave you to ponder this: when our Lady and St. John stood at the foot of the Cross in the strange and frightening darkness that surrounded them, they no longer heard nor saw our Lord and felt only bitterness and distress; and although they had faith, this too was in darkness, for it was nec-

---

108. Cf. Gal 4:1.

essary that they should share in our Savior's sense of abandonment. How fortunate we are to be the slaves of this great God who became a slave for our sake![109]

But it is time now for my sermon. Goodbye, my dearest mother, my daughter in our Savior. Long live His divine goodness! I have the greatest concern for the progress of our heart, for which I surrender all my other joys into the hands of His supreme and fatherly providence.

Good night once again, my very dear daughter. May Jesus, our gentle Jesus, only heart of our heart, bless us with his holy love. Amen.

MADAME DE LIMOJON

Jeanne-Louise de Genton, daughter of the nobleman, François de Genton, married Jean de Limojon in 1598. The couple lived not far from the Château de Sales, in the town of LaRoche where it is very likely that Madame de Limojon had the opportunity of hearing sermons of Francis de Sales on various occasions. He was her spiritual director at the time this letter was written.

Annecy, June 28, 1605[110]

Madam,

I had no reason to refuse Monsieur Mondon's request since not only does it promise to be carried out in a fine, charitable way, but also because it gives me the opportunity of receiving letters from you, letters full of good news.

Yes, truly, ever so gently we must continue to cut out of our lives all that is superfluous and worldly. Don't you see that no one prunes vines by hacking them with an axe but by cutting them very carefully with a pruning hook, one shoot at a time?

I saw a piece of sculpture once that an artist had worked at for ten years before it was completed; during all that time with chisel and burin he never stopped chipping away at everything that was in the way of exact proportions. No, there is no doubt about it, we

---

109. Cf. Phil 2:7.
110. *Oeuvres*, XIII, 58–60: Letter CCXCI.

cannot possibly arrive in a day where we aspire to be. We have to take this step today; tomorrow, another; and thus, step by step, achieve self-mastery, which is no small victory.

I beg you, keep up confidently and sincerely this holy pursuit on which depends all the consolation you will have at the hour of your death, all true peace in this present life, and every assurance of the next life. I know this is a huge undertaking, but still it is not as great as the reward. There is nothing that a generous person cannot do with the help of the Creator.[111] And how happy you will be if in the midst of the world you keep Jesus Christ in your heart! I beg Him to live and rule there eternally.

Keep in mind the main lesson He left us—in *three* words so that we would never forget it and could repeat it a hundred times a day: "Learn of me," He said, "that I am gentle and humble of heart."[112] That says it all: to have a heart gentle toward one's neighbor and humble toward God. At every moment give this heart, the very heart of your heart, to our Savior. You will see that as this divine, delicate Lover takes His place in your heart, the world with its vanities and superfluities will leave.

I have said this to you in person, madam, and now I write it: I don't want a devotion that is bizarre, confused, neurotic, strained, and sad, but rather, a gentle, attractive, peaceful piety; in a word, a piety that is quite spontaneous and wins the love of God, first of all, and after that, the love of others. I've already written too much for this time, considering the little leisure that I have.

Only I must respond to what you ask me about how you should write to me from now on. Do you want to know how? Write to me freely, sincerely and simply. I have nothing else to say about that except that you should not write "bishop" or any other formality in your letters; it is sufficient to put "father," and there is a reason for that. I am not someone who stands on ceremony, but I am someone who loves and honors you with my whole heart for many reasons, above all because I hope that our Lord wishes to have you as His very own. Be His, madam, be His, I beg you. Note well and remember what I have said to you: at every minute offer and give your heart to God, long for Him, make your devotion pleasing, especially

---

111. Cf. Phil 4:13.
112. Mt 11:29.

to your husband, and live in the joy of having chosen this kind of life.

I pray God to hold you always by the hand; do likewise for me and say a few prayers at the foot of the Cross for my soul which is entirely devoted to serving you and all who are most dear to you.

I am, madam, your very affectionate and most humble servant in our Lord.

MADAME DE LA FLÉCHÈRE

Francis himself gave high praise to Madame de la Fléchère when he wrote of her: "After Madame de Chantal, I do not know if I have ever encountered in a woman a stronger soul, a more reasonable mind, or a more sincere humility."[113] *Indeed, Madeleine de la Fléchère resembled her close friend, Madame de Chantal, in talent and temperament, as well as in having known marriage, motherhood, and then the lot of a widow. One of her daughters entered the Visitation of Annecy and some years later Madeleine offered her own house for the foundation of another Visitation monastery. She died there in 1632 after having been permitted to pronounce religious vows on her deathbed.*

Francis had become acquainted with the family de la Fléchère in 1608, when he was giving the Lenten sermons in Rumilly, a small town not far from Annecy, and in fact used to stay in their house. Especially during the next two years many letters were exchanged, and most of Francis's letters are extant. In fact in number of letters surviving, if not in total length, or spiritual depth, this correspondence is comparable to that which Francis addressed to Madame de Chantal.

April 8, 1608[114]

Madam,

I was particularly pleased with your first letter and see it as a good beginning to the spiritual communication that you and I should have for the advancement of the kingdom of God in our

---

113. *Oeuvres*, XVII, 143: Letter MCLXIV.
114. *Oeuvres*, XIV, 1–3: Letter CDXLIV.

hearts. May this same God inspire me to say what will be best for your direction.

It isn't possible for you to be so soon mistress of your soul and have it so totally in hand right away. Be satisfied if now and then you gain some advantage over the tendencies you fight against. We have to put up with others, but first of all, with ourselves, and patiently accept being less than perfect. Good heavens, dear daughter, what makes us think we can enter into a state of interior rest without going through normal setbacks and struggles?

Observe carefully the points I have mentioned to you. First thing in the morning, prepare your heart to be at peace; then take great care throughout the day to call it back to that peace frequently, and, as it were, to again take your heart in your hand. If you happen to do something that you regret, be neither astonished nor upset, but, having acknowledged your failing, humble yourself quietly before God and try to regain your gentle composure. Say to your soul: "There, we have made a mistake, but let's go on now and be more careful." Every time you fall, do the same.

When you are inwardly peaceful, don't miss the opportunity to perform as many acts of gentleness as you can—and as frequently as you can—no matter how small these acts may seem; for, as our Lord says: "To the person who is faithful in little things, greater ones will be given."[115]

But most important, my dear daughter, don't lose heart, be patient, wait, do all you can to develop a spirit of compassion. I have no doubt that God is holding you by the hand; if He allows you to stumble, it is only to let you know that if He were not holding your hand, you would fall. This is how He gets you to take a tighter hold of His hand.

A Dieu, madam—be completely, absolutely, irrevocably His.

May 19, 1608[116]

[. . .] I remember how you told me that all the things you had to do weighed heavily upon you, and I told you that this was a good opportunity for you to acquire true and solid virtue. Having to attend to so many things is a continual martyrdom; for just as flies are

---

115. Cf. Lk 16:10; Mt 25:21, 23.
116. *Oeuvres*, XIV, 21–23: Letter CDLV.

158

more bothersome and irritating to summer travelers than the traveling itself, so the variety and multiplicity of things you have to do is harder to bear than the actual weight of them.

You need patience, and God will give it to you, I'm sure, if you earnestly ask Him for it and if you strive to practice it faithfully. Prepare yourself to do so every morning, especially by applying some point of your meditation to this, making up your mind to be patient throughout the day whenever you find yourself slipping.

Don't lose any opportunity, however small, of being gentle toward everyone. Don't rely on your own efforts to succeed in your various undertakings, but only on God's help. Then rest in His care of you, confident that He will do what is best for you, provided that you, for your part, work diligently but gently. I say "gently" because a tense diligence is harmful both to our heart and to our task and is not really diligence, but rather overeagerness and anxiety.

Soon we shall be in eternity and then we shall see how insignificant our worldly preoccupations were and how little it mattered whether some things got done or not; however, right now we rush about as if they were all-important. When we were little children how eagerly we used to gather pieces of broken tile, little sticks, and mud with which to build houses and other tiny buildings, and if someone knocked them over, how heartbroken we were and how we cried! But now we understand that these things really didn't amount to much. One day it will be like this for us in heaven when we shall see that some of the things we clung to on earth were only childish attachments.

I'm not suggesting that we shouldn't care about these little games and trifling details of life, for God wants us to practice on them in this world; but I would like to see us not so strained and frantic in our concern about them. Let's play our childish games since we are children; but at the same time, let's not take them too seriously. And if someone wrecks our little houses or projects, let's not get too upset, because when night falls and we have to go indoors—I'm speaking of our death—all those little houses will be useless; we shall have to go into our Father's house. Do faithfully all the things you have to do, but be aware that what matters most is your salvation and the fulfillment of that salvation through true devotion.

Be patient with everyone, but above all with yourself; I mean, don't be disturbed about your imperfections, and always have the courage to pick yourself up after a fall. I'm very glad to hear that you make a fresh start each day. There's no better way of growing toward perfection in the spiritual life than to be always starting over again and never thinking that we have done enough.

Recommend me to God's mercy. I beg Him, through that same mercy, to fill you with His love. Amen.

October 28, 1608[117]

My very dear daughter and friend,

You will see the letter I have written to the Cistercian General and to your own sister.[118] The only other thing I'd like to say to you in the little leisure I have is that I greatly approve of the kind of indifference you are showing, as much in the situation at the de Bons Abbey as in all other matters since it stems from your consideration of the will of God. I have no use for people who have no likes or dislikes, and who, no matter what happens, remain unmoved; they are this way either from a lack of energy and of heart, or through an unconcern for the difference between good and evil. But those whose indifference is the result of being totally surrendered to God ought to be most grateful, for this is a great gift. I could explain this better if I were speaking to you; however, I think you understand what I am trying to say.

Undoubtedly, it is a temptation to waste time at prayer wondering what you have yet to tell me about the state of your soul; prayer is not the time for that. Nevertheless, don't fight these thoughts; instead, very slowly turn your mind away from them by a simple return to the object of your prayer.

I shall write you a more leisurely letter at the first opportunity, but right now I must leave to make the visitation of a parish, and there are lots of people around.

May God dwell in the center of your heart, my dear daughter, and may He set it aflame with His love.

---

117. *Oeuvres*, XIV, 81–82: Letter CDLXXXVIII.
118. The Cistercian Abbey at Bons in the neighboring district of Bugey was in scandalous need of reform. Mme de la Fléchère, whose own sister was a religious of that Abbey, had apparently taken some action favoring reform, but must have expressed doubt whether this was in keeping with "indifference."

January 20, 1609[119]

Of course you would be able to explain yourself better and more freely in person than by letter; yet, until such time as God grants us this opportunity, we have to use the means at hand. You see, you cannot experience drowsiness, apathy, and dullness of the senses without feeling a kind of physical sadness; but so long as in your will and your heart of hearts you are seriously resolved to belong totally to God, you have nothing to fear, for these are flaws of nature and more weaknesses than sins or spiritual failings. Nevertheless, you should stir yourself to courage and spiritual activity, as soon as you are able.

Death is grim, of course, my dear daughter, but the life beyond, which God in His mercy will give us, is most desirable. Truly, in no way must we lose heart because, even though we are weak, our weakness is not nearly as great as God's mercy toward those who want to love Him and place all their hope in Him.[120] When blessed Cardinal Borromeo was dying,[121] he had someone bring him an image of our Lord after His death; this was in order to soften the dread of his own death by uniting it to that of his Savior. Such contemplation of Him who is our life[122] is the best remedy against the fear we have of our own death; we should never think about the one without also thinking of the other.

O dear daughter, don't be examining yourself to see if what you are doing is little or much, good or bad, provided that it is not sinful and that, in all good faith, you are trying to do it for God. As much as possible, do well what you have to do, and once it is done, think no more about it but turn your attention to what has to be done next. Walk very simply along the way our Lord shows you and don't worry. We must hate our faults, but we should do so calmly and peacefully, without fuss or anxiety. We must be patient at the sight of these faults and learn from the humiliation which they bring about. Unless you do this, your imperfections, of which you are acutely conscious, will disturb you even more and thus grow stronger, for nothing is more favorable to the growth of

---

119. *Oeuvres*, XIV, 119–121: Letter DXII.
120. Cf. Pss 33:18; 37:40.
121. Charles Borromeo (1538–1584), Archbishop of Milan.
122. Cf. Col 3:4.

these "weeds" than our anxiety and overeagerness to get rid of them.

There is a real temptation to become dissatisfied with the world and depressed about it when we have of necessity to be in it. God's providence is wiser than we. We imagine we would feel better if we were on another ship; that may be, but only if we change ourselves! I am the sworn enemy of all those useless, dangerous, unwise desires, for even if what we desire is good, the desiring itself is pointless since God does not want that kind of good for us, but another, toward which He expects us to strive. He wishes to speak to us from the thorny bush, as He did to Moses,[123] and we would like Him to speak to us in the gentle breeze, as He did to Elijah.[124]

May His Goodness watch over you, my dearest daughter, but be steadfast, courageous, and rejoice in the fact that He has given you the grace to want to be entirely His. I am, in this Goodness, all yours.

MADAME DE CORNILLON

Gasparde, one of Francis de Sales's younger sisters and sixth child of his parents, married Melchior de Cornillon in 1595. The couple had many children and, it seems, many and varied difficulties as well. Francis brought comfort and support to his "most beloved" little sister in these trials and was, moreover, her spiritual director. The tone of his letters to her—tender, yet firm—gives some indication of how it is possible to achieve deep spiritual growth in the midst of a full and difficult life.

[August 6, 1610][125]

My dearest sister,

I am writing to say good-night and to assure you that I never stop wishing you and my dear brother-in-law countless blessings

---

123. Ex 3:2.
124. 1 Kgs 19:12.
125. *Oeuvres*, XIV, 338–339: Letter DCXIV. The date of this letter is inferred from the content; the sixth of August is the feast of the Transfiguration. The year is less certain, though it could not have been earlier than 1610.

from heaven, especially that of always being transfigured in our Lord. How beautiful is His face, how kind and amazingly gentle His eyes, and how good it is to be near Him on the glorious mountain![126] It is there, my dear sister, my daughter, that we must place all our affections, and not on this earth where there is only vain beauty and beautiful vanity.

So, thanks to our Savior, we are climbing Mount Tabor, since we are firmly resolved to serve Him well and to love His divine Goodness. We must encourage one another in holy hope. Let us climb always, my dear sister, let us climb, without growing weary, toward this heavenly vision of our Savior. Little by little, let us leave behind us affections for the low things of earth and aspire to the happiness that has been prepared for us.

I beg you, my dear sister, to pray earnestly to our Lord for me, that from now on He will keep me in the pathways of His will so that I may serve Him sincerely and faithfully. You see, dearest sister, I want either to die or to love God—death or love—because a life devoid of this love would be absolutely worse than death. My dear sister, how happy we shall be if we love this divine Goodness that has prepared such favors and blessings for us! Let us all belong to God, my daughter, in the midst of so much busyness brought on by the diversity of worldly things. Where could we give better witness to our fidelity than in the midst of things going wrong? Ah, dearest daughter, my sister, solitude has its assaults, the world its busyness; in either place we must be courageous, since in either place divine help is available to those who trust in God and who humbly and gently beg for His fatherly assistance.

I'm sure you are advancing always along the way of your good resolutions. Don't be upset by these little attacks of anxiety and sadness that are brought on by the multiplicity of your household cares. No, my dear daughter, for this gives you the opportunity of practicing the dearest and best virtues that our Lord recommended to us.[127] Take my word for it, true virtue is not produced by outward repose, any more than healthy fish are raised in the stagnant waters of swamps.

---

126. Cf. Mt 17:4.
127. Cf. Mt 11:29, Francis's favorite scripture passage, the source of his love for gentleness and humility.

LETTERS OF SPIRITUAL DIRECTION

PÉRONNE-MARIE DE CHÂTEL

In July 1610 Sister Péronne-Marie joined Mother de Chantal and her first two companions in the nascent Visitation congregation. Her gifts of nature and grace made her a kind of "model" of the Visitandine envisioned by Francis de Sales: she was blessed with a happy disposition, a lively, simple, spontaneous spirit, and a heart ready and eager for the spiritual formation she would receive from the two founders. Her unusual gifts of prayer, however, did not preclude her experiencing discouragement, scruples, and even moments of very human impatience and irritation with some of her tasks. She often needed the assurance and loving encouragement that only Mother de Chantal and Francis de Sales could give her in her struggles.

Annecy, October 28, 1614[128]

Certainly, my dearest daughter, you give me great pleasure by calling me father, for my heart is full of fatherly affection for yours which I see is still rather timid in the face of the ordinary, slight contradictions that come its way. But I continue to love it, for although at times it feels as if it is about to be discouraged over the little reproofs it receives, yet this poor heart of yours never has actually lost its courage; that's because God has held it in His strong hand and, according to His mercy, He has never abandoned His unhappy little creature. Dearest daughter, He never will abandon you, for even if you are troubled and in anguish over these absurd temptations to sadness and bitterness, still, you never want to leave God or our Lady or our congregation which belongs to them or our Rules which are His will.

Truly, you are right, my poor dear Péronne-Marie, when you say there are in you two men, or, rather, two women.[129] One is a certain Péronne who, like her godfather St. Peter long ago,[130] is a bit touchy, resentful and ready to flare up if anyone crosses her; this is the Péronne who is a daughter of Eve and therefore bad-tempered. The other is a certain Péronne-Marie who fully intends to belong

---

128. *Oeuvres*, XVI, 241–243: Letter MVI.
129. Cf. Gn 25:22–23.
130. Péronne is a woman's name derived from Peter.

totally to God, and who, in order to be all His, wants to be most simply humble and humbly gentle toward everyone; this is the one who would like to imitate St. Peter who was so good after our Lord had converted him; this is the Péronne-Marie who is a daughter of the glorious Virgin Mary and therefore of good disposition. These two daughters of different mothers fight each other and the good-for-nothing one is so mean that the good one has a hard time defending herself; afterward the poor dear thinks she has been beaten and that the wicked one is stronger than she. Not at all, my poor dear Péronne-Marie; the wicked one is not stronger than you, but she is more brazen, perverse, unpredictable, and stubborn; and when you go off crying she is very happy because that's just so much time wasted, and she is satisfied to make you lose time when she is unable to make you lose eternity.

My dear daughter, stir up your courage, arm yourself with the patience we should have toward ourselves. Often rouse your heart so that it may be rather on guard against a surprise attack; watch out for this other self; wherever you go, you'd do well to be aware of her, for this mean girl goes with you everywhere, and if you aren't thinking about her she will think up something against you. But when she happens to attack you suddenly, even if she causes you to totter and stumble, don't be upset; instead, call out to our Lord and our Lady. They will reach out a blessed helping hand to you, and if they allow you to go on suffering for a while, it will only be in order to have you cry out again more loudly for their help.

Don't be ashamed of all this, my dear daughter, any more than St. Paul who confesses that there were two men in him—one rebellious toward God, and the other obedient.[131] Be utterly simple and don't be disturbed; humble yourself without discouragement and encourage yourself without presumption. Keep in mind that our Lord and our Lady who put you in charge of the domestic duties know perfectly well and can see that all the busyness bothers you, yet they never stop loving you so long as you are humble and trusting. Dear daughter, don't be ashamed of being a little grimy and dusty; it's better to be covered with dust than with sores, and provided you humble yourself, all will be well.

---

131. Rom 7:15–23.

Pray much for me, my dear and most beloved daughter, and may God be your love and protection forever. Amen.

MADAME DE GRANIEU

Daughter of a King's Counsellor, Laurence de Ferrus had married François de Granieu in 1595. They lived in Grenoble and were among the many who came to appreciate Francis de Sales when he preached there in Advent 1616 and Lent 1617. In fact during those visits he resided in their home.

By that time Madame de Granieu was already advanced in a prayer life which had begun even before her marriage, and she was blessed in having a husband who not only affirmed her in this respect but who was himself a devout Christian, and known as such.

Their friendship with Francis, which was sustained and nourished by Madame's correspondence, was such that Francis could not refuse a favor she asked: as indicated in the one letter selected, he agreed to have portraits painted of Madame de Chantal and of himself. The latter is known as the Turin portrait, since the original is preserved at the Visitation monastery of Turin.

Annecy, June 8, 1618[132]

Since I have this opportunity of writing to you, I will tell you, my dear daughter, that our mother[133] speaks the truth: I am extremely overwhelmed, not so much by events as by difficulties which I cannot avoid. Nevertheless, dear daughter, I certainly would not want you, because of that, to stop writing to me whenever you wish, for your letters are refreshing and most delightful. But you must be indulgent with me, excusing me when I am somewhat slow in answering. I can assure you that it is only through necessity that I would put off writing, for my spirit enjoys conversing with yours.

I could never refuse you anything, my very dear daughter; and so the two portraits you want will be painted. How I wish the image

---

132. *Oeuvres*, XVIII, 237–240: Letter MCDXLI.

133. In April 1618 Mother de Chantal had founded a Visitation convent in Grenoble, where she stayed on for six weeks.

of our heavenly Father were preserved in my soul in a true likeness![134] My dear daughter, you would do me a great favor if you
prayed that this likeness be restored in me.

Your kind of prayer is very good, indeed much better than if
you made many reflections and used many words, for these are only
meant to arouse our affections; if God is pleased to give us affections
without the reflections and words, this is a great grace. The secret
of secrets in prayer is to follow our attraction in simplicity of heart.
Take the trouble to read, or to have read to you if it is too much for
your eyes, the seventh book of the *Treatise on the Love of God;* you will
find there all you need to know about prayer.

I remember that one day when you told me in confession how
you prayed, I said that it was a very good way and that although
you ought to prepare a point for meditation, if God drew you to a
particular affection as soon as you came into His presence, then you
were not to hold on to the point, but follow the affection; the more
simple and peaceful it is, the better, for then it will bind your soul
more closely to its object. Once you have resolved to follow your
affection, dearest daughter, don't waste time during prayer trying
to understand exactly what you are doing or how you are praying;
for the best prayer is that which keeps us so occupied with God that
we don't think about ourselves or about what we are doing. In short,
we must go to prayer simply, in good faith, and artlessly, wanting
to be close to God so as to love Him, to unite ourselves to Him. True
love has scarcely any method.

Be at peace, my dearest daughter, and walk faithfully along the
path which God has marked out for you. Take care to bring contentment to him to whom God has espoused you; like a honey bee,
while you are carefully making the honey of devotion, at the same
time make the wax of your household affairs; for if honey is sweet
to the taste of our Lord who ate butter and honey while on earth,
wax also honors Him since it used to make the candles which give
light to those around us.

God, who has taken you by the hand and set you on the way
of His glory, will be your guide, my dear daughter.[135] I shall never
stop begging Him to do so, for, believe me, my very dear daughter,

---

134. Cf. Gn 1:26–27.
135. Cf. Ps 73:23–24; 139:10.

I cherish your heart and soul tenderly and with a most fatherly love. May God render you ever more His. Amen. Live Jesus!

ANGÉLIQUE ARNAULD, ABBESS OF PORT ROYAL

Angélique Arnauld is perhaps the most widely known of Francis's directees—known in history for events and associations which occurred well after her friendship with Francis de Sales. Their contacts began in April 1619, when Francis, staying in Paris, was invited to Maubuisson, a sister foundation of Port Royal, and the second monastery which Angélique, at the time only twenty-seven, was beginning to reform. An immediate and mutual rapport arose between them. It was nourished by visits of Francis the following June and August, and by letters exchanged over the next three years. Such was her attraction for Francis's spirituality and Mother de Chantal's direction that Angélique applied to Rome for permission to transfer to the Visitation. This possibility, encouraged by Jane but never positively endorsed by Francis, was blocked by the Roman authorities. In Francis's letters to Angélique we find his accustomed warmth, insight, firmness and patience—along with some subtle indications that this friend was not understanding him as well as most. Her later association with M. de Saint-Cyran and the Jansenists led her in a very different direction than that suggested by these letters.

Paris, May 25, 1619[136]

No, I beg you, never be afraid that you will annoy me with your letters; for I tell you truthfully, they will always give me great pleasure, as long as God grants me at the same time the grace of keeping my heart in His love, or at least gives me the desire to have it there. I say this once and for all.

It is undoubtedly true, my dear sister, that if I hadn't come to this city, it would have been difficult for you to discuss your spiritual concerns with me; but since it has pleased divine Providence that I should be here, there is no problem with your taking advantage of this opportunity, if you think it appropriate.

---

136. *Oeuvres*, XVIII, 378–380: Letter MDXIX.

And don't believe for a minute that I thought you were seeking me out as a prominent personality, for, while such a thought is quite in keeping with my sinfulness, it never occurs to me in such situations. On the contrary, there's hardly anything more helpful in leading me to humility; I am amazed that so many men and women, servants of our Lord, place so much confidence in anyone as imperfect as I. This gives me great courage to become what others think I am, and I hope that God, in giving me the holy friendship of his children, will also give me his most holy friendship, according to his mercy and after he has enabled me to do penance in proportion to my sin. It is almost wrong for me to be saying all this to you.

So it is the evil spirit, himself forever deprived of God's love, who wants to keep us from enjoying the fruits of love—of that love which the Holy Spirit wants us to experience so that by communicating with one another in holy matters we might have a means of growing in God's will.

It is difficult, my very dear sister, to find well-rounded spiritual guides who can be equally discerning in all matters; nor is it necessary to have someone like that in order to be well guided. It seems to me there is no harm in gathering from several flowers the honey that can't be found in one alone. "Yes, but," you will tell me, "meanwhile very cleverly I tend to favor my inclinations and moods." My dear sister, I don't see any great danger of this since you don't want to follow your inclinations unless they have been approved; and although you started out by looking for advisors who would go along with you, you did find some who were good, prudent and learned; therefore, you can't go wrong in following their counsel—even if it *is* just what you want to hear—provided that you share very simply your concerns and the difficulties you have. It is enough, my very dear sister, to follow their advice; it is neither necessary nor expedient to wish it to be contrary to our inclinations, but only to want it to be in conformity with God's law and doctrine. Personally, I don't think we should ask for suffering as did our Lord, for we aren't able to handle it as He did. It is quite enough if we endure it patiently. That's why we don't always have to go contrary to our inclinations when they aren't evil and when, in fact, upon examination, they are found to be good.

There is no great harm in taking part in worldly conversations when we do so with the intention of bringing something worthwhile to them, and we mustn't be scrupulous when we examine ourselves about these conversations. It is morally impossible to walk the fine line of moderation all the time. But, my dearest sister, I wouldn't want you to miss your prayer time of at least half an hour, except for pressing occasions or when physical ailments prevent it.

For the rest, I shall do one of two things: either I shall write you a longer letter before I leave, or I shall go to see you on the day I have indicated to this kind messenger. And I assure you, nothing will prevent my having the pleasure of going to see you except the difficulty of getting there; and I shall stay as long as you wish, for truly I want you to be satisfied. God has given me a special affection for your heart which I pray He will bless abundantly.

Therefore, we will talk at leisure about the direction of your life and about whatever you want to bring up; and I won't excuse myself in anything unless I don't have the light required to answer you. I shall be, unreservedly and with all my heart, your very humble brother and devoted servant in our Lord.

Paris, September 12, 1619[137]

At last, I shall be leaving tomorrow morning, my very dear daughter, since such is the will of Him for whom we exist, we live and we move.[138] May this great and eternal God be praised for the mercy He shows us! Your consolation brings peace to my heart which is so closely united to Yours that whatever is received in one is shared totally by the other, for it seems to me they are in perfect communion; and, if I may be permitted to speak in terms used in the early Church, we are "of one heart and one mind."[139] [. . .]

I hope that God will strengthen you more and more; and when you become afraid that your present attention and fervor may not last, respond once and for all to that thought, or rather to that temptation to sadness, that those who trust in God will never be confounded,[140] and that in spiritual as well as physical and temporal matters, you have "cast your care upon the Lord and He will support you."[141] Let us serve God well today; He will provide for to-

---

137. *Oeuvres*, XIX, 14–17: Letter MDL.
138. Cf. Acts 17:28.
139. Acts 4:32.
140. Cf. Sir 2:10.
141. Ps 55:22.

morrow. Each day has its own burden to bear; do not worry about tomorrow,[142] for the same God who reigns today will reign tomorrow. And if in His goodness He had thought, or even known, that you needed more readily available assistance than what I can give you from such a distance, He would have given it to you. He will always give it to you when there is need to make up for my deficiency. Remain at peace, my very dear daughter. God works from near and afar, and calls distant things to the service of those who serve Him[143]—"absent in body, present in spirit," says the Apostle.[144]

I hope I will be able to understand clearly what you will tell me about your prayer, although I don't want you to be curious in observing your method of praying. It will be enough if quite simply you let me know the more noticeable changes as you recall them after you have made your prayer. I think it would be a good idea to jot down your thoughts when you have a chance, so as to send them on to me afterward, whenever you want to, without being afraid of boring me, for you will never bore me.

Beware, my very dear daughter, of the word "fool," and remember the saying of our Lord, "Whoever shall say to his brother 'Raca' (which is a word that doesn't mean anything, but simply shows indignation) "will be answerable to the Sanhedrin";[145] that is to say, deliberation will be taken about how he is to be punished. Little by little, bring your quick mind around to being patient, gentle, humble, and affable in the midst of the pettiness, childishness and feminine imperfections of the sisters who are tender with themselves and obsessed with bothering their superiors. Don't pride yourself on the affection of human fathers, but on that of the heavenly Father who has loved you and given His life for you.[146]

Sleep well. Gradually you will get back to six hours [of sleep], since this is what you want. To eat little, work hard, have lots of concerns on our mind, and then to refuse to give our body sleep is to try to get much work out of a poor, emaciated horse without letting him graze. [. . .]

---

142. Mt 6:34.
143. Cf. Rom 4:17.
144. 1 Cor 5:3.
145. Mt 5:22.
146. Cf. Eph 5:2.

My dear daughter, I tell you goodbye, and beg you to believe that my heart will never be separated from yours—this is impossible—what God unites cannot be separated. Keep your courage high, lifted up in that eternal Providence who has called you by your name,[147] and carries you imprinted[148] on his fatherly breast in such a motherly way. In the greatness of this confidence and courage, practice carefully humility and mildness. So be it.

I am very specially yours, my very dear daughter. Remain in God. Amen.

I am leaving in great haste because the queen has asked to see me before I return.

What is not God must count for little in our estimation. May He be your protection. Amen.

October or November, 1619[149]

[. . .] I can see clearly this "ant hill" of inclinations which self-love feeds and spreads in your heart, my very dear daughter, and I am well aware that your subtle, delicate, and creative mind contributes toward this; still, my dear daughter, these are after all only inclinations, and since you experience them as intrusions and your heart complains about them, it doesn't look as if you are consenting to them at all, at least not deliberately so. No, my very dear daughter, since your dear soul has conceived a great God-given desire to belong to Him alone, don't be so quick to believe that you are consenting to these contrary movements. Your heart may be somewhat shaken by these passions, but I think it rarely sins by consenting to them.

"Oh, unhappy man that I am," said the great apostle, "who will deliver me from the body of this death?"[150] He felt as if an army, made up of his moods, aversions, habits, and natural inclinations, had conspired to bring about his spiritual death; and because he feared them, he showed that he despised them; and because he despised them, he could not endure them without pain; and his pain made him cry out this way and then answer his own cry by asserting

---

147. Is 43:1.
148. Cf. Is 49:16.
149. *Oeuvres*, XIX, 50–53: Letter MDLXIV.
150. Rom 7:24, following the Vulgate.

that the grace of God through Jesus Christ[151] will defend him, not from fear, or terror, or alarm, nor from the fight, but from defeat, and from being overcome.

My daughter, to be in this world and not to feel these stirrings of passion—these two things are incompatible. Our glorious Saint Bernard said it is heresy to claim that we can persist in the same state here on earth, inasmuch as the Holy Spirit, speaking of human beings through Job, has declared that we are never in the same state.[152] This is in reply to what you tell me about the fickleness and inconstancy of your soul, for I firmly believe that it is continually blown about by the winds of its passions and therefore is always unsteady. But I believe just as firmly that the grace of God and the resolution He has inspired in you live continually at the fine point of your soul where the standard of the Cross is always raised on high, and where faith, hope, and charity ever proclaim loudly: LIVE JESUS!

You see, my daughter, these tendencies to pride, vanity, and self-love creep in everywhere, and, whether we are aware of them or not, insinuate themselves into almost all our actions, although they are not the motivation of these actions. One day Saint Bernard, feeling their annoying presence while he was preaching, said, "Depart from me, Satan! I didn't begin because of you and I will not end because of you!"[153]

I have only one thing to say to you, my very dear daughter; you tell me that you feed your pride by certain affectations in your conversations and letters. In conversations, it is true, affectation slips in at times so subtly that we hardly notice it; and yet if we do, we must quickly change our style of speaking. But in letters, really, this is rather, even very, intolerable, for we can see far better what we are doing, and if we perceive a particularly affected passage, we must punish the hand that wrote it by making it write another letter in a different manner.

For the rest, my dear daughter, I don't doubt that in all this twisting and turning in your heart some venial faults do slip in here and there; yet, because they are only fleeting, they do not deprive

---

151. *Ibid.*
152. Jb 14:2. Cf. Bernard of Clairvaux, Letter CCLIV to Guarinus.
153. Cf. Mt 4:10. The Annecy editors were not able to find any basis in the works or biographies of Bernard for this story often told about him.

you of the fruit of your resolutions but only of the consolation you would feel in not committing these failures—if the human condition permitted this.

So now, be fair: neither excuse nor accuse your poor soul except after mature consideration, for fear that if you excuse it for no reason, you render it insolent, and if you accuse it too readily, you weaken its courage and render it timid. Walk simply and you will walk confidently.[154]

I must add an important word at the bottom of this page: don't burden your weak body with any austerity beyond what the Rule prescribes; preserve your physical strength to help you serve God through spiritual practices. Often these have to be given up because we have indiscreetly overburdened the body which should be a partner of the soul in our service of God.

Write to me whenever you wish, without ceremony or fear; do not let respect stand in the way of the love that God wants us to have for each other, and according to which I am invariably and forever. . . .

February 4, 1620[155]

O my dear daughter, what can I say to you on the occasion of this death?[156] Our dear Mother at the Visitation told me about it; at the same time she writes me that she had seen your mother and your sister Catherine brave, determined, and full of courage, and that, moreover, the bishop of Belley had received letters from you which testify to your own steadiness on this occasion. I had no doubt, my dearest daughter, that God was taking care of your heart at this time and that if He were wounding it with one hand, he was applying His healing balm with the other. He strikes and heals,[157] He puts to death and brings life,[158] and so long as we can raise our eyes and see God's Providence, grief cannot overwhelm us.

But that's enough, my very dear daughter; God and your good

154. Cf. Prv 10:9.

155. *Oeuvres*, XIX, 122–127: Letter MDCIV.

156. Antoine Arnauld, the father of Angélique, died December 29, 1619. Mother de Chantal, then in Paris founding the first Visitation community of that city, had written to Francis about the death and also about the family and their mutual friend, Jean-Pierre Camus, Bishop of Belley, later the author of *The Spirit of St. Francis de Sales*.

157. Cf. Jb 5:18.

158. 1 Sm 2:6.

angel having comforted you, I have nothing more to add. Your "most bitter bitterness is transformed into peace."[159] What need is there to say more? In the measure that God draws to Himself, piece by piece, the treasure our heart possesses here below, that is, what we love, He draws our heart as well;[160] and since, as St. Francis said, I no longer have a father on earth, I can say more spontaneously "Our Father who art in heaven."[161] Courage, my dearest daughter, all is ours and we are God's.[162]

I have offered Mass for this soul, and every day at the celebration of Mass remember him very specially before God. [. . .]

Now I shall answer your last two letters, dated November 19 and December 14. It's true that I am extraordinarily busy, but your letters are not business—they are refreshment and solace to my soul. Let this be said once for all.

It's a great thing that exteriorly you are more observant of the Rule. God formed, first of all, the exterior of man, then "breathed into him the breath of life" and this exterior "became a living being."[163] Humiliations, says our Lord, very often precede and open the way to humility; continue in this exterior observance which is easier, and little by little the interior will adapt itself.

Yes, my daughter, I can see you are entangled in these thoughts of vanity; the creativity and subtlety of your mind combine to lend a hand to these suggestions; but why do you let them bother you? When the birds came down upon the sacrifice of Abraham, what did he do? He drove them away with a branch which he kept waving over the holocaust.[164] My daughter, simply saying a few words like our Lord's on the Cross will drive away these thoughts, or at least will remove whatever is bothersome about them. O Lord, pardon this daughter of the old Adam, for she knows not what she does.[165] Woman, behold your Father on the Cross. You must sing very softly: "He has deposed the mighty from their thrones, and has raised the lowly to high places."[166] I repeat that this way of dis-

---

159. Is 38:17; cf. Vulgate: "Ecce in pace amaritudo mea amarissima."
160. Cf. Mt 6:21.
161. Mt 6:9.
162. Cf. 1 Cor 3:22–23.
163. Gn 2:7.
164. Gn 15:9–11.
165. Cf. Lk 23:34.
166. Lk 1:52.

missing troublesome thoughts must be done very quietly, simply, with the words spoken through love and not for the sake of winning a battle.

Accustom yourself to speak rather gently, to walk slowly, to do everything quietly and in moderation; you will see that in three or four years you will have regulated this hasty impetuosity. And remember to act and speak in this gentle manner on those occasions where you are not pushed by your impetuosity and where there is no apparent reason to fear it, as, for example, when you are going to bed, getting up, sitting down, eating [. . .]; in short, don't excuse yourself [from this practice] at any time or anywhere. Now I know perfectly well that you will slip a thousand times a day over all this, and that your very active temperament will always behave impulsively; but that should be no problem, provided that such impulsive movements are not deliberate or willed, and that every time you become aware of them you make an effort to calm them.

Be very careful about whatever may offend your neighbor and do not reveal anything secret that could be to his disadvantage; if you happen to do so, repair the injury as far as you can immediately. Although these slight movements of envy are not serious, they are useful since they make you see clearly your self-love, and they prompt you to do the opposite.

But, my daughter, isn't it a grace that this trait of self-love exists in her whom I have so often recommended to you and who in truth is as dear to me as my own soul?[167] For what is more delicate than this little aversion she has to being called "daughter" by that dear Mother? Ask her, I beg you, if she isn't also averse to my calling her "my daughter" and if she would rather I called her "mother"? What effort it must have cost her to tell me about this bit of nonsense! I really don't know what it cost her, but I wouldn't for anything in the world have it unsaid because it has given her the occasion to practice so much resignation and such confidence toward me.

She is even more pleasing to me when she forbids me to speak of this to the dear Mother. O my daughter, tell her that these little communications of her soul to mine enter into a place they will never leave without the express permission of her who puts them there.

---

167. On occasion Francis would soften an admonition by referring to his correspondent as to a third person. In this case he chides Angélique who was miffed that Jane de Chantal was calling her "daughter."

Besides, my dearest daughter, I don't know what this daughter has done to me, but I find her weaknesses, which she naively describes to me, so obvious that nothing could be clearer. So tell her to write to me always very simply; even though she never showed me the letters she wrote to her sisters when I was with her, she would have no difficulty in doing so if I were there now because she knows me much better than she did and knows that I am not given to making fun of others.

As to prayer, my very dear daughter, I think it's good that you read a little in your Theotimus[168] in order to focus your mind, and that from time to time when you find yourself distracted you speak quietly to our Lord. But come now, don't be surprised at distractions such as "if I were a saint," "if I were speaking to the Pope," and the like, for the very silliness of such thoughts makes them more completely distractions and there is no other remedy for them than gently to bring back the heart to its object.

I think I have answered everything, my dear daughter. [. . .]

May God ever be our all. Amen. I am totally yours in Him, in a way that only His Providence can make you understand. "May the grace, peace, and consolation of the Holy Spirit be with you."[169] Amen.

MADAME DE VILLESAVIN

Isabelle Blondeau de Villesavin first met Francis de Sales in Dijon in 1604 when he was preaching the Lenten sermons in that city. Through the years they became very close friends and corresponded very frequently. Of their voluminous correspondence, however, only four letters have been preserved. Madame de Villesavin left Paris in May 1619, when she accompanied her husband, a member of the court of King Louis XIII, to Angoulême. Although Francis remained in Paris at this time, he knew that he himself would be leaving the city shortly and had no idea if they would ever see each

---

168. Having been chided for addressing the *Introduction* to a (fictional) woman, Philothea, Francis directed the *Treatise* to an equally fictional man, Theotimus, with apologies to the good sense of the readers. (See *Oeuvres*, IV, 12–13: Preface to the *Treatise*.) Both names mean "one who loves God," and both soon became alternate titles for the books.

169. Cf. 1 Cor 1:3 and Acts 9:31.

other again. (Actually, they did meet a few months later, in September when the bishop was going through Tours.)

Very wealthy, living in the most fashionable social milieu of the times, Madame de Villesavin nevertheless lived an intensely spiritual life given to prayer, practices of austerity and the promotion of charitable works in Paris. In every way she was the "Philothea" described in the Introduction to the Devout Life. She died at a very advanced age in 1687.

Paris, July-August, 1619[170]

Don't ever believe, my dearest daughter, that great distances can separate those whom God has united by the bonds of His love. The children of this world are all separated one from another because their hearts are in different places; but the children of God whose hearts are where their treasure is[171] and who all have the same treasure—which is the same God—are consequently always bound and united together. In light of this, it shouldn't matter to us that necessity keeps you out of town and that very soon I will have to leave town to return to my duties. We shall often meet before our blessed crucifix if we observe carefully the promises we have made to each other; it is only there that our conversations are worthwhile.

Even so, my dear daughter, I shall start by telling you that you must do everything you can to strengthen your mind against those useless thoughts which habitually upset and torment you. In order to do this, you must, first of all, so regulate your prayer exercises that their length does not weary you nor irritate those with whom you live: a half or quarter hour, even less, is enough for the morning preparation, three quarters of an hour or an hour for Mass; and in the course of the day, frequent liftings of the heart to God which can be done in a second; the examination of conscience in the evening before going to bed; and of course, the ordinary grace before and after meals, which can be times to reunite your heart with God. In a word, I would like you to be "Philothea" through and through, and nothing more; that is, I would like you to be what I have described in the *Introduction*, which was written for you and others like you.

---

170. *Oeuvres*, XVIII, 415–417: Letter MDXXXIX.
171. Cf. Lk 12:34.

In your conversations, dearest daughter, be peaceful, no matter what is being said or done; if it is something good, praise God for it; if it isn't, you can serve God by turning your heart away from it without acting either shocked or upset. Since you can't do anything about it and don't have the authority to stop the evil talk of those who are indulging in it, these persons would say worse things if you seemed to be trying to stop them. In this way, you will remain completely innocent in the midst of hissing serpents, and, like a sweet strawberry, you will receive no venom from contact with venomous tongues.

I don't understand how you can allow this immoderate sadness into your heart, since you are God's daughter, and were placed a long time ago in the heart of His mercy and consecrated to His love. You should lighten your own burden by dismissing these sad, gloomy thoughts which the enemy suggests for the sole purpose of wearing you down and annoying you. Take great care to practice the humble gentleness that you owe to your dear husband and everyone else, for it is the virtue of virtues which our Lord has so often recommended to us.[172] If you happen to fail in it, don't be disturbed, but with the greatest confidence, pick yourself up and continue to walk peacefully and calmly as before.

I am sending you a little method for uniting yourself to our Lord in the morning and throughout the day.

For now, my dearest daughter, this is what I thought good to say for your comfort. The only thing left to add is to ask you, please, not to stand on ceremony with me, for I have neither the time nor the wish to do so with you. Write to me whenever you like, quite freely, for I shall always be happy to receive news of your soul which I greatly cherish. [. . .]

A GENTLEMAN

The choice of this letter is an exception to some of the criteria enunciated in the Introduction above, notably because the gentleman to whom it was sent cannot be identified, let alone be counted among Francis's directees. Nevertheless, it is included here in order

---

172. Mt 11:29.

to illustrate—in a style and tone appropriate to a correspondent he did not know well—the same personal and pastoral caring which Francis expressed to his close friends. In this case, his caring prompted a rare autobiographical allusion, as Francis empathizes with his depressed correspondent out of his own struggles in Paris years before.

[no date][173]

Sir, I am very sorry to hear how much you have suffered during this serious and irritating illness from which, I trust, you are now recovering. I would have been even more distressed to hear this had I not already been assured from all sides that, thanks be to God, you were not critically ill and that you were regaining your strength and were on your way to being completely healed.

What is of greater concern to me now is that everyone says that besides your physical illness, you are suffering from deep depression. I can imagine how much this will slow down your return to perfect health and breed the very opposite condition. Now, sir, my heart is very sad to hear this, and since I have such deep, inexpressible affection for you, I also feel great compassion for your family.

Please tell me, sir, what reason have you for remaining in this dark mood which is so harmful to you? I'm afraid your mind is still troubled by some fear of a sudden death and the judgment of God. That is, alas, a unique kind of anguish! My own soul, which once endured it for six weeks, is in a position to feel compassion for those who experience it. So, sir, I must have a little heart to heart chat with you and tell you that anyone who has a true desire to serve our Lord and flee from sin should not torment himself with the thought of death or divine judgment; for while both the one and the other are to be feared, nevertheless, the fear must not be that terrible kind of natural fear which weakens and dampens the ardor and determination of the spirit, but rather a fear that is so full of confidence in the goodness of God that in the end it grows calm.

And, sir, when we experience difficulties in avoiding sin, or when we have misgivings or fear that when faced with temptation we may not be able to resist, this is not the time to start questioning whether or not we are strong enough to entrust ourselves to God.

---

173. *Oeuvres*, XXI, 11–14: Letter MCMLXXIV.

Oh no, sir, for the mistrust of our strength is not a lack of resolve, but a true recognition of our weakness. It is better to distrust our capacity to resist temptation than to be sure that we are strong enough to do so, so long as what we don't count on from our own strength we do count on from the grace of God. This is how it happens that many persons who very confidently promised to do marvels for God, failed when under fire, whereas many who greatly mistrusted their own strength and were afraid they would fail accomplished wonders when the time came, because the great awareness of their own weakness forced them to seek God's help to watch, pray and be humble, so as not to fall into temptation.[174]

I say that even if we felt we might have neither the strength nor the courage to resist temptation should it befall us now, as long as we desired to resist it and hoped that if it did come our way, God would rescue us and we would seek His help, then we must not be sad. Neither do we always have to *feel* strong and courageous; it is enough to hope that we will have strength and courage when and where we need them. We don't have to have a sign that these virtues will be ours; it is enough if we hope that God will help us. Samson who was called the "strong one" never felt the supernatural strength with which God assisted him, except now and then; and for that reason it is said that when he faced lions or enemies, he was empowered by the Spirit of God to kill them.[175] Now God, who does nothing in vain, does not give us either strength or courage when we don't need them, but only when we do. He never fails us. Consequently, we must always hope that He will help us if we entreat Him to do so. We should always use these words of David, "Why are you sad, my soul, and why do you trouble me? Hope in the Lord,"[176] and this prayer which he spoke: "When my strength fails, Lord, do not abandon me."[177]

So now, since you want to belong entirely to God, why be afraid of your weakness—on which, in any case, you shouldn't be relying. You do hope in God, don't you? And will anyone who hopes in Him ever be put to shame? No, sir, never.[178] I beg you,

---

174. Cf. Mt 26:41.
175. Jgs 14:6, 19; 15:14.
176. Cf. Ps 42:6, 12; 43:5.
177. Cf. Ps 71:9.
178. Cf. Sir 2:10.

sir, calm all the objections that might be taking shape in your mind and to which you need give no other answer than that you want to be faithful at all times, that you hope God will see to it that you are, without your trying to figure out if He will or not; for such attempts are deceiving. Many persons are brave when they cannot see the enemy, but not so brave when they are in his presence; on the contrary, many are afraid before the skirmish, but the actual danger fills them with courage. We must not be afraid of fear. So much for that, sir.

When all is said, God knows all that I would do and suffer in order to see you completely free of fear. I am your very humble and unworthy servant.

Jane de Chantal

LETTERS

Noël Brulart (1577–1640) came seeking Jane's direction from a background as brother of a chancellor of France, knight of Malta, favorite of Henri IV and Marie de Medici and court-appointed ambassador to Spain and Rome. After a period of worldly vanity this French aristocrat, known also in Jane's letters as the Commandeur de Sillery, underwent a conversion which was then nourished by his association with Vincent de Paul and several of the Visitation superiors in Paris who put him in contact with Jane. He was to become one of the Order's chief benefactors and friends. Their correspondence begins in 1632 and ends with the death of the Commandeur in 1640. The formal "Monsieur" of the first letter soon changes to "my very dear brother" and finally, after his ordination to the priesthood, to "dearest Father." From the beginning of his new life, Noël Brulart used his great wealth for the good of the Church, particularly religious communities such as the Visitation.

One senses in her correspondence Jane's awareness and awe at this man's obvious goodness and emerging sanctity, her gentle support of all that is best in him and something of her own humility when called upon for advice by a man in whom she recognizes the activity of God. Yet she does not hesitate to direct him in the austere ways of Salesian detachment, especially when he is forced because of his increased religious fervor, which has somewhat undermined his health, to restrict his devotions and charitable works. She counsels him that the height of perfection comes when we want what God wishes for us. And in this case, the Commandeur's weak constitution is understood as given by God. This gentle acquiescence she also advises when a cherished charitable project comes to nothing. She emphasizes that one must be content to be idle and powerless before God as well as content to act with devotion and facility. In this contentment consists the loving surrender of the heart to its maker.

The spirituality ascertainable in these letters is at once recog-

nizably Salesian yet less distinctively different from Francis de Sales's spiritual orientation than that seen in the letters to the Visitation sisters, where the concerns are more definitely communal and feminine. The artfulness with which she imperceptibly guides the Commandeur toward what she perceives, by way of him, as the authentic will of God, is evident. There is nothing imposed upon her correspondent, no elaborate program to follow or set of rules to abide by. She offers as direction merely an expert ear, an affection based on a mutual zeal for perfection and the gentle discernment of a friend. Evident is the emphasis on loving surrender to God's will as it is discovered in the events of everyday life.

Live + Jesus!

[Annecy] February 1632[1]

Sir,

You have written me with marks of honor far beyond what I deserve. Even the title of Mother is more respectful than suitable coming from you, Sir, whose birth and dignity make it my privilege to be your very humble servant. But I see plainly by the gracious, candid tone of your letter that you are writing, not according to your rank in the world, but as a true servant of God and lover of the pure, simple spirit of our blessed Founder. This unpretentiousness is apparent throughout your letter. I am amazed to see the extent to which you, Sir, living in the world and busy with public affairs, have acquired that spirit. For this I praise God and beg Him to grant it to you in its fullness, for I regard the spirit with which our blessed Father was graced to be one of the most priceless gifts of God's mercy. I must confess frankly, Sir, that, considering the grace God had given me and the genuine kindness with which our true Father communicated with me, I should possess this treasure and be as enriched by it as you believe me to be.

But unfortunately, I must admit, to my shame, that my weakness has been so great that I seem to have been content to admire and desire the excellence which I recognize in this great Saint without seriously applying myself, as one would have to do, to acquiring the solid virtues he taught me. For that reason, I am impoverished

---

1. *Sa Vie et ses oeuvres*, VII, 221–225: Letter MCCXLVIII.

and destitute; I say this sadly, but, as far as I can know myself, it's the absolute truth. And I tell you this, Sir, so that you may not esteem me better than I am, but, following the teachings of our blessed Father, you may continue to give me your friendship and to accept me in the respectful association you wish to have with the daughters of the Visitation. As of now, following the doctrine of this great Father, I am determined to begin seriously to live his holy teachings with greater fidelity. I am encouraged to do so by virtue of the love and veneration God has given you for his spirit. It is perhaps out of place to tell you this, Sir, but I find myself ready to speak to you in all simplicity and confidence, as if I had had the honor of meeting you and knowing you personally, so much have you opened my heart by the kindness, frankness, and trust with which you have been pleased to speak to me. If I had the ability, I think I could say marvelous things in response to your humility and devotion, but, being inarticulate, I don't know what to say to you, Sir; besides, when God Himself speaks to the heart of His servants, creatures should keep still. I can see that His divine light inspires you and that the warmth of His love animates you.

All that remains then, as our blessed Father would say, is to humble yourself profoundly under God's holy hand, to let yourself be led in the way of His good pleasure and, following that same good pleasure, to offer no resistance to whatever He may wish to do with you and to correspond to His grace by fidelity to the opportunities presented to you by Providence. Our blessed Father valued beyond measure these practices and faithfully observed them. His writings, which you are reading so carefully and lovingly, are full of this doctrine. I am sure, Sir, that you find in them all the satisfaction and instruction your dear, deserving soul needs. I feel such respect and affection for your soul that I could never forget you, Sir, before the divine Majesty. I shall continually pray to Him to preserve what, in His goodness, He has given you, and to perfect it according to His eternal designs, so that after having served Him long and well and increased His glory in this life, you may enjoy the fullness of a blessed eternity.

This is what I shall ever desire for you with all my heart. Before God I resolved to do this in the holy communion I made for your intention. Do not doubt, Sir, that I am yours wholly in this divine Savior, and that I shall faithfully keep your secret, as your goodness and trust deserve. Our dearest Sister Favre has written to me about you in terms that show me plainly that your virtue and devotion have powerfully won her heart and given you authority over her. Nevertheless, since you wish, you may write to her and to our Sister Superior in town [Paris]. I think they are very fortunate to be able to communicate with you in the open and simple spirit of our blessed Father, and to give you some little satisfaction, insofar as our lowliness can respond to the dignity of your great kindness which I value beyond words.

From now on and forever I would like us to reverence and cherish you as our most kind father and most dear lord, and therefore I remain, with much respect and incomparable affection, Sir and honored Father, your very humble and obedient servant in our Lord who is ever praised.

Please excuse this disorganized letter; your indulgence gives me the confidence to send it.

Annecy, 1633[1]

My very dear brother,

I have such complete and devoted concern for your true good that there is nothing at all I wouldn't do or endure to obtain it for you. This good is nothing less than a peaceful, quiet response to the lights and inspirations which our Lord gives you. But, you know, I am not saying this so that you will zealously search out ways to carry out your response. On the contrary, God wants you to temper your overeagerness by calming all this ardor, reducing it to a simple assent of your will to do good quietly—and only because it is God's will. In the same way, yield lovingly to this divine will when it allows you to fail to perform some good deed or to commit some fault. Resign yourself to not being able to resign yourself as completely and utterly as you would like, or as you think our Lord would like.

I don't know if I'm making myself clear. What I mean is that in all your good works you should unite yourself to the will of God's good pleasure, and in your faults and imperfections, you should unite yourself to His permissive will gently, quietly, and with peace of mind. Our blessed Father used to say: "Let us do all the good we can, faithfully, peacefully, and quietly; and when we are unfaithful,

---

1. *Sa Vie et ses oeuvres*, VII, 221–25: Letter MCCXLVIII.

let us make up for this failure by humility, but a humility that is gentle and tranquil." You know this better than I, dearest brother, and I know this is what you do. But one can always do better. Abandon all your desires for advancement and perfection; hand them over completely into God's hands. Leave the care of them to *Him*, and only yearn for as much perfection as He wishes to give you. I beg you, toss away all such desires because they will only cause you worry and disquiet, and even make it possible for self-love to creep in imperceptibly. Have only a pure, simple, peaceful longing to please God, and, as I have said before, this will lead you to act without such impetuosity and overeagerness, but with peace and gentleness. Your chief care ought to be to acquire this spirit; however, this care must be tender and loving, free of anxiety, even as you wait for results with unlimited patience and total dependence on the grace of God. Trust Him to bring about these results at the right time for His glory and your benefit. Do not wish to possess them any sooner. In His goodness, He will be a thousand times more pleased to have you rest in His care, surrendered to His holy will, than to have you suffer all sorts of torments in an effort to acquire that perfection you desire so much.

Well, my very dear brother, these are my poor thoughts and feelings about your dear soul. Oh, and don't tell me so many terrible things about yourself for, you see, I have had such an insight into your soul that I can feel only awe for what God has done in you. I am writing you rather hurriedly, but nevertheless, with great concern for the well-being and consolation of your very dear heart which means so much to me.

Annecy, 1634[1]

My very honored and most dearly beloved brother,

No, truly, before God, you could not give me a more pleasing, precious New Year's gift than your renewed expression of concern for my happiness. To me, my truly dear brother, this is a rich treasure and a protection against the ambushes of my enemies. You wouldn't believe how much comfort it gives me to know that you are praying for me. To my knowledge, I don't think I ever fail to remember you, especially at holy communion, and I never want to

---

1. *Sa Vie et ses oeuvres*, VII, 306–313: Letter MCCXCVII.

fail in this. I am sure that the merit of holy communion is a worthy response to the genuine, incomparable love God has given you for our blessed Father and his dear Visitation, and for myself in particular, it seems, even though I don't deserve it. Really, as imperfect as I am, God has willed to unite my heart intimately with yours, and for this I shall ever bless His goodness.

You can judge, then, from this fact, how moved I am about the way it has pleased our gentle Lord to lead you in your holy and happy retirement so that it may be to His greater glory, the benefit of others, and, what is most unusual, to the satisfaction of your relatives. Oh dearest brother, how wonderfully God's hand has been guiding you! Yet, I notice that your humility prompts you to give all the credit to the prayers of the Visitation Sisters and to the advice of those dear sisters who have the good fortune of having more frequent, delightful and profitable communication with you. This is how, in all things, you are increasing your spiritual riches. God be praised for all His graces, especially for having given you a heart which, in my opinion, is fashioned after His own most sacred one. In truth, my very dear brother, your good heart is capable of touching ours by its incomparable love. Apparently, you have drawn this love from the inexhaustible love of our divine Savior, for neither human considerations nor the power of nature could bring about anything like it. It is the most precious gift imaginable. I believe it was obtained for you from the fatherly heart of God through the tender love that our blessed Father has for his dear Visitation.

Furthermore, my true brother, I look upon you very affectionately as the visible guardian angel of our Congregation, a grace for which we can never be thankful enough, either to divine Providence or to you, my very dearest brother. But I know that all you wish from us is fidelity to our vocation and, by this means, a deep union of our hearts with yours. This, surely, is my great wish and I bless God that I personally feel its effects in my life. But why should I tell you all this, dear brother, since God has allowed it to be this way ever since we first met? I hadn't thought about it when I started this letter, but it has come to me because I feel it very intensely, even though I can never quite express it in words.

It's true, beloved brother, that I didn't answer your last letter very satisfactorily because when I did have the chance to write you, I was in such a hurry that I had time only for a note; and imperfect as I am, by the time another opportunity came along, I had been so busy for some months, that I forgot things I should have remembered. Yet, in your kindness, dear brother, it seems that you saw this forgetfulness as nothing else than what I have just explained very sincerely.

But to get back to your retirement, which is the result of God's all-powerful grace: and so it is, dearest brother, because only He, through your faithful cooperation—which is another gift of His kindness—only He could break the ties and overcome the great obstacles which were inevitable in your condition. So it happened that with divine gentleness, he loosened your chains and smoothed away the difficulties in such a way that your passage from one extreme to the other was made almost without difficulty, at least without upsetting or frightening anyone. What is amazing is the satisfaction, the mild reaction, the approval of everyone. This is, and should always be, a very real, tangible sign of God's plan for you in this second vocation of yours. And what greater grace and consolation could there be for your dear and deserving heart than the sense that you are doing God's will by spending the rest of your days in this peaceful, blessed retirement?

Besides, my very dear brother, your state of soul, which you describe so artlessly in your letter, is incomparably better and more solid than if you were filled with consolations and felt you had great courage. At a time of such radical change, it is impossible for nature not to be upset. But this interior peace, this unwavering dependence on God, these inspirations—slight as they seem—which assure you without words that you are solidly planted where God wants you, all these are infallible signs of the reign of God in you and should give you great hope that God, in His goodness, wishes to set you on a path of integrity and simplicity of mind. This is why, most beloved brother, I think that you could not do better than to avoid all introspection as far as possible. Instead of being preoccupied with weighty thoughts, *just gaze at God and let Him do what He wills*—these are the words of our blessed Father—because since our divine Savior is the only object of your love and aspiration, and the sole comfort of your dear, beloved heart, you will find in Him all you need. In the beginning, especially, you must put this into practice in all simplicity. This will strengthen you in the higher part of your soul and calm the passions of nature. However, you, dearest brother, know how to do this better than I can express it; but your humility and my affection give me confidence to tell you everything that comes to me.

I am more consoled than I can say about the satisfactory meeting you have had with those ecclesiastics. Such good relations would certainly be to the liking of our blessed Father. He did not approve of anyone's living in too great a solitude, but rather thought that a life of retirement should have well-regulated exercises of devotion that can be practiced at home, as well as ways of practicing charity toward the neighbor, such as visiting the sick or those in distress. So, after you have told me in detail what you plan to do in your retirement, I shall be informed and maybe I'll remember all kinds of things I heard our blessed Father say, things that could be useful to you. If God finds me worthy of consoling you somewhat, you may be sure, dearest brother, that I shall gladly do so. God in His goodness, gives me such great love for your dear, precious soul, that I can think of nothing to compare with the satisfaction I would have in doing something pleasing and comforting to you. But how much I am obliged by your dear, deserving heart, for after our blessed Father, no one will ever have such affection for the Visitation as you. I beg our great Saint to obtain for us the grace to cooperate in this [friendship], according to his spirit and wishes.

I have always loved dearly and had great respect for our house in the city [the first monastery of Paris], and everyone here knows that of all our houses in France, this one and the one at Bellecour in Lyons, hold first place in my heart. I have so many reasons for being attached to them that I don't think I could ever let go of them; but the tender affection with which you are recommending this blessed house to me will, with God's help, bear wonderful fruit. I assure you, dearest brother, that I believe all the good things you tell me about it, without a shadow of a doubt, for I know the two Mothers there and consider them two solid pillars of the Visitation, especially my very dear Angélique.[2] I am aware also of the great number of fine, virtuous, capable sisters that make up that community. You may be sure, I make a point of never speaking of our houses unless the subject comes up. Recently, the Mother of Moulins wrote me at

---

2. M. Hélène-Angélique Lhuillier of the first monastery and M. Marie-Jacqueline Favre of the second monastery.

great length about our two houses in Paris, describing their differences very clearly, as if she knew what she was talking about. She didn't leave out a single good thing she had to say about the house in town. I answered her briefly that she had judged very well and that I was surprised that in such a short visit, she had arrived at such a thorough acquaintance with matters in these communities which I already knew to be true. That was saying everything, without further explanation, for I don't dare tell everyone all my thoughts, as I do to you. I have to be careful not to arouse jealousy and coldness, so I maintain the cordial understanding and confidence that have always existed among us by showing equal love to all and a concern for peace in all hearts. If I were near you I would say a lot more about this. Here I am at the bottom of my fourth page and still my heart hasn't said everything! I feel such joy and satisfaction in speaking to you with perfect confidence! [. . .]

I've been afraid that during this time of retirement, you might want to take on new austerities. No, I beg you, my dearest brother, don't do that. And, please, see to it that, because of your age and the frailty of your health, you have what you need for your physical well-being, and also what is suited to your [social] condition. The thought came to me to tell you this, and I do so very simply. . . .

[Annecy, 1634][1]

What happiness, my true Father, to be thus totally dedicated and surrendered to the supreme Majesty [of God]! About your desire to make some return to God for the exceptional graces He has bestowed on you, in my opinion, very dear Father, His divine light penetrates right through these graces to the bottom of your soul, and He will be satisfied if you hold on to them without taking the trouble to do great things or to search out occasions to do so. Simply be ready to carry them out when His divine will presents them to you. It seems to me that the most perfect, profitable thing for you to do is simply, reverently, and lovingly to bind your heart to our divine Savior, uniting yourself to the oneness of God in unaffected, pure love. The calm that this will give your soul will allow you to understand more clearly the inspirations and lights that the Holy Spirit will communicate to your soul. Try to perform your actions as per-

---

1. *Sa Vie et ses oeuvres*, VII, 354–355: Letter MCCCXVII.

fectly as you can, without constraint or anxiety. When you find yourself committing some fault or other, just humble yourself quietly before God by a simple acknowledgement of the fault, and think no more about it. Our holy Founder, whom you wish to imitate, used to say that since God did not make us angels, we must put up with our human nature and be satisfied with the level of purity which, humanly speaking, we can achieve.

[Annecy] 14 August [1634][1]

My very honored and most dear Father,

Well, my dear Father, I see you have fallen into the condition where I've always feared your great fervor would bring you. And even so, you tell me that you're afraid of flattering yourself, yet do not fear enough your own fears. Oh, for the love of God, dearest Father, do not make such reflections. Take my word for it, our Lord is more pleased with our accepting the relief our body and spirit require, than by all these apprehensions of not doing enough and wanting to do more. All God wants is our heart. And He is more pleased when we value our uselessness and weakness out of love and reverence for His holy will, than when we do violence to ourselves and perform great works of penance. Now, you know that the peak of perfection lies in our wanting to be what God wishes us to be: so, having given you a delicate constitution, He expects you to take care of it and not demand of it what He himself, in his gentleness, does not ask for. Accept this fact. What God, in His goodness, asks of you is not this excessive zeal which has reduced you to your present condition, but a calm, peaceful uselessness, a resting near Him with no special attention or action of the understanding or will except a few words of love, or of faithful, simple surrender, spoken softly, effortlessly, without the least desire to find consolation or satisfaction in them. If you put that into practice, my dear Father, in peace and tranquility of mind, I promise you, it will please God more than anything else you might do.

Just one more word: do believe me when I say that instead of spending four or five hours on your knees, you should try just one hour—a quarter of an hour after rising; another, in preparation for holy Mass; the same, in thanksgiving; and a short quarter of an hour

---

1. *Sa Vie et ses oeuvres*, VII, 392–95: Letter MCCCXXXVI.

for the evening examination of conscience. That's enough. And try, for love of God, to restore your former strength by getting enough rest, physically and mentally, and by taking plenty of good, nourishing food. This I beg of you, my dear beloved Father, by all that you hold most dear in heaven and on earth. If it weren't that I felt impelled to request this, I wouldn't be writing so soon. I hope that in the great kindness and fatherly affection you have for us—for our consolation—you will not neglect to do whatever you can to regain your health. [. . .]

[Annecy] 18 July 1638[1]

Very honored and dear Father,

Blessed be forever our most gentle Savior who draws His glory and the happiness of souls out of circumstances that, according to human judgment, are so bizarre and hopeless. What has taken place in this affair [of the Ursulines of Loudon], especially as regards the dear Mother Prioress, is a marvel of His all-powerful and infinite mercy.[2] We have seen the holy Names which are imprinted on her hand renewed, by which means it has pleased God's goodness to manifest the power He has placed in the intercession of our blessed Father. For us it is especially meaningful and we are boundlessly grateful. You must have noted the fine qualities God has given this good Mother. I consider her a chosen soul, humble, open, simple, intelligent, and very honest. Her way of prayer is, I think, very good; it is informal and yet solid. We have often spoken of you, dear Father. She respects you, has great regard for your piety, and has told me how much you comfort her. This is understandable. Your heart is unusually devoted to those whom you love and who return that love which is so entirely in God and for their good. The ardor

---

1. *Sa Vie et ses oeuvres*, VIII, 56–60: Letter MDLXX.

2. "The extraordinary circumstances of the possession of the Ursulines of Loudon belong to history. We will only recall here the facts regarding the journey of Mother Jeanne des Anges to Annecy. As is well-known, this religious was possessed of devils who tormented her, and from whom she was only delivered after having made a vow to visit the tomb of St. Francis de Sales. Constrained to obey the exorcisms of Père Surin, S.J., the spirits of darkness, upon quitting her, left imprinted on the left hand of Mother Jeanne des Anges, the names of 'Jesus, Mary, Joseph, Francis de Sales,' so that all, says a contemporary author, might be persuaded of the reality of the possession and of the submission of the demons to the holy Church of Christ." Footnote found in *The Spirit of Saint Jane Frances de Chantal as Shown in Her Letters*, Longmans, Green, and Co., London, 1922, p. 282.

of your own dear soul increases more and more through your contact with others who are seeking God alone. Really, had you come, the feast would have been complete. I would have been delighted, as would several persons of distinction. But I no longer hope for such a pleasure and honor. The frailty of your health, and all the good work you are doing for God, have taken away all my expectations. However, I trust that through the infinite Goodness and the incomprehensible merits [of our Lord], we shall meet each other in heaven and there bless and praise God forever. So be it. Amen.

I admire the intensity with which you are serving God and seeking your perfection: such a grace is a great gift from God. This present attraction you have to strip yourself of all earthly possessions is noble and deserves serious study to help you discern whether it is a divine inspiration and the will of God who really desires its outcome, or whether it is only a readiness on your part to carry out what may later prove to be His will. Sometimes when our Lord asks us to do some good work, all He really wants is our willingness to do the work, and not its accomplishment. Since in your humility and great kindness you want me to speak openly and simply to the good Mother [Ursuline], I've shared all my thoughts on this subject with her and she can tell you about them. I am not capable of making a decision in such a serious matter where everything consists in discerning, by means of your interior impulses and lights, what it is God wishes, for once His will is clear, there should be no reason to doubt or to fear to carry it out. In His goodness, He provides all that is necessary, clears up doubts, and removes all difficulties. Our communities will offer special prayers and communions for this intention, for you know how much we are yours.

As for the business about the Temple, we haven't begun the novena yet because of all the bustle of the crowds who have come to see the Mother Prioress.[3] We've hardly had time to get together, but we have often talked about your plan for the Temple which is so evidently for the glory of God that I can't imagine that He will not see to its accomplishment. As a rule, there is opposition to the works of God, and the more they are meant to succeed for His glory,

---

3. Commander de Sillery was thinking at this time of founding, in connection with the Order of the Knights of Malta of which he was Commander, seminaries for the instruction of priests as well as lay students. The Grand Prior of France had even named him his Vicar-General. But the opposition to his project was so strong he was forced to abandon it.

the more opposition they meet. As you know, our blessed Father used to say: "We have to have strong, unshakable, long-winded courage, when we undertake the good works committed to us by God, and as long as we see His holy will in them, we must never grow slack; and should He wish us to cease trying, even if the work has failed, we must be ready to let go, gently and peacefully." Our Saint was admirable in this practice. Oh! my dear Father, even if it should please our Lord that the Temple project progress no further—which I don't think will be the case—His divine Goodness would take into account the plan you had for it and the determination you had to carry it out. Besides, this plan has already been the means of countless benefits for others, as well as for your own dear soul which, I am sure, has been greatly enriched by it. If for no other reason than this final act of humility and serene self-surrender on your part, the endeavor would be worth more than a thousand little projects. [. . .]

May God make you all His own and very holy. Remember me before His divine majesty. I beg Him to take care of you. And you, very dear Father, consider me your very humble, obedient, and dutiful daughter and servant in our Lord.

[Annecy, 1640][1]

My very honored and worthy Father,

I have been more than repaid for the delay in receiving your delightful letters because you have taken the trouble to write at such length, and in your own dear handwriting, of your heart's intense, sincere desires and of all your holy projects. I had no doubt but that the delay was due to your many occupations and your absence from home.

It certainly would be impossible not to feel the loss of so much spiritual good as could have been expected from the foundation begun at the Temple. Certainly some day God will raise up some kind souls to [finish the work].[2] But His divine Providence, which encouraged you so prudently to undertake this project for His glory, will not leave you unrewarded. He will place such value on your humble acceptance of His will, that some day, my dearest Father,

---

1. *Sa Vie et ses oeuvres*, VIII, 135–40: Letter MDCXX.
2. Refer to note on Temple given with letter 1570.

you will see by His grace that this act will have made you grow in perfection and detachment more than you can imagine. And I believe that it was God who inspired you not to follow the advice you received to go on with your plan. In this, I assure you, you have certainly followed the true spirit of our blessed Father, for, as you know, he wished us to be courageous in our undertakings, and flexible in letting them go when God, in His good pleasure, indicated that we should. Oh! this disappointment is a treasure for your soul, dear Father! I have no doubt but that God is going to help you benefit from this experience! I see that on every side His Providence is offering you tangible opportunities where, according to the spirit you so love and esteem, there is nothing for you to do but to endure quietly the suffering you find in them. Do not stop to analyze them or fight them or attempt to overcome them, but divert your mind and remain at peace.

You must do the same with regard to mental preoccupations. Without worrying about them, try to remain calm amid this warfare of distractions and be satisfied, most dear Father, to spend the appointed time of prayer quietly and peacefully, doing nothing in God's presence, content simply to be there without wishing either to feel His presence or to make an act [of devotion], unless you can do so easily. Just sit there, in inner and outer tranquility and reverence, convinced that this patience is a powerful prayer before God.

You should not be surprised to find yourself in this state. It is the inevitable result of your intense, continual and varied activities of the last two or three years. It happens to everyone, and even did to our blessed Father, as I've already told you. When he would return from his visitations, which lasted only four or five months at a time, he used to find his poor soul so distracted, so worn out, that he had pity on it. He set about reviving it, not with force, but, rather, took it in hand gently, then patiently, slowly, without effort, restored it [to health]. . . . Above all, he recommended that we cut short our introspections, overeagerness, and the longing to be delivered from such inconveniences, and that we be patient in enduring them. You will find this doctrine in several of his *Letters* and *Conferences*. I hope that by following it, dearest Father, you will, before long, be your old self. To sum up, we must be as satisfied to be powerless, idle and still before God, and dried up and barren when He permits it, as to be full of life, enjoying His presence with ease and devotion. The whole matter of our union with God consists in being content either way.

I think, beloved Father, I see you renewing yourself and re-fashioning yourself in the spirit of our blessed Father, and in this practice (by the help of your renunciation of the burden of all worldly things) to spend the rest of your days in great serenity and true devotion. Your age and your health no longer allow you to be active, but only to give yourself over completely to loving and resting in God. I believe that this plan of yours will bring greater glory to God, enrich your dear soul, and benefit others. You could not give a more striking example of genuine piety and total disregard of those things the world values so much. In His goodness, may God grant that many others will imitate you. I wish the Archbishop of Bourges would make the same resolution.[3] He is a perfectly good soul who longs to retire in order to serve the Lord better; but whenever he goes to his abbey, he is frequently interrupted and distracted by visitors and worldly problems, and he is so good-natured and available that he can never say *no* to those who want to see him.

I shall now answer your other letters; I ask God to inspire me to do so according to His good pleasure. My true and loved Father, I wasn't able to finish this letter nor take the time (I've been so terribly busy) to read the last two where, truly, I find evidence of the abundance of holy consolation with which God is filling your soul. For this I bless and thank His everlasting goodness. You can see, dearest Father, how this divine Spirit never ceases to pour out the influence of His grace on minds that are distracted, dried up and weak, when all their troubles stem from the difficulties met with in works undertaken for His glory alone, as is the case with you. That's how it happens that from all this, God, in His infinite goodness, draws out great profit for your soul, and consolation for my poor spirit. I can assure you, I am consoled and satisfied by your attitude which, in my opinion, is truly inspired by God and reflects perfect charity. [. . .]

I am delighted to see the fullness of devotion which our kind

---

3. André Frémyot, her brother. See introduction to the next correspondent.

Savior has poured into your soul, and to see also how divine Providence is using you to establish so many good works that lead others to eternal salvation, and so extend His glory.

May the Author of such holy thoughts be forever blessed; and may you, my very dear Father, always fully possess the riches of His divine Goodness.

LETTERS TO THE ARCHBISHOP OF BOURGES
(ANDRÉ FRÉMYOT)

Her letters of direction to her brother André Frémyot (1573–1641) are somewhat more instructional than those addressed to Noël Brulart. Brother and sister did not begin their real spiritual correspondence until 1625, fifteen years after Jane had entered religious life and more than twenty after André had taken up his post as Archbishop of Bourges. Until that time the younger Frémyot had executed his duties with the genial but "worldly" spirit of a gentleman administrator.

Before entering the priesthood he had studied law at Padua. He chose a Parliamentary career and was a counsellor to the Burgundian Parliament. While still a subdeacon he was appointed Archbishop of Bourges. He and Francis de Sales soon became close friends, and Francis sent the younger bishop a magnificent letter on the art of preaching. He governed his diocese wisely. However, implicated in political intrigue, he was obliged to leave Bourges in 1621, but retained the title of Archbishop of that city. He lived in Paris and held high positions at the court of Louis XIII.

In 1624 a severe illness prompted him to reexamine his pastoral responsibilities as well as the state of his own soul and to reach deep into his own capacity for dedication to the life lived in God. He made three vows: to observe chastity, to say Mass every day, and to make a pilgrimage to thank God for his cure. At this transitional moment he turned to his sister whose reputed and evident holiness now attracted him in a new way. She offered him a plan of devotion to sustain his newborn resolutions. Her counsels are similar to those given to Noël Brulart. Love of God is foremost; abandonment to God's will, especially in times of temporal loss, is stressed. As the years progressed, the friendship of brother and sister, now turned

into a mutual quest for perfect love, grew, ending only with his
death a few months before her own.

Live ⁺ Jesus!

[Chambery, 1625][1]

My very dear Lord,

Since God, in His eternal goodness, has moved you to conse-
crate all your love, your actions, your works, and your whole self
to Him utterly without any self-interest but only for His greater
glory and His satisfaction, remain firm in this resolve. With the confidence of a son, rest in the care and love which divine Providence
has for you in all your needs. Look upon Providence as a child does
its mother who loves him tenderly. You can be sure that God loves
you incomparably more. We can't imagine how great is the love
which God, in His goodness, has for souls who thus abandon themselves to His mercy, and who have no other wish than to do what
they think pleases Him, leaving everything that concerns them to
His care in time and in eternity.

After this, every day in your morning exercise, or at the end of
it, confirm your resolutions and unite your will with God's in all
that you will do that day and in whatever He sends you. Use words
like these: "O most holy Will of God, I give You infinite thanks for
the mercy with which You have surrounded me; with all my
strength and love, I adore You from the depths of my soul and unite
my will to Yours now and forever, especially in all that I shall do
and all that You will be pleased to send me this day, consecrating to
Your glory my soul, my mind, my body, all my thoughts, words
and actions, and my whole being. I beg You, with all the humility
of my heart, accomplish in me Your eternal designs, and do not allow me to present any obstacle to this. Your eyes, which can see the
most intimate recesses of my heart, know the intensity of my desire
to live out Your holy will, but they can also see my weakness and
limitations. That is why, prostrate before Your infinite mercy, I im-
plore You, my Savior, through the gentleness and justice of this
same will of Yours, to grant me the grace of accomplishing it perfectly, so that, consumed in the fire of Your love, I may be an ac-

---

1. *Sa Vie et ses oeuvres,* V, 399–403: Letter DCIII.

ceptable holocaust which, with the glorious Virgin and all the saints, will praise and bless You forever. Amen."

During the activities of the day, spiritual as well as temporal, as often as you can, my dear Lord, unite your will to God's by confirming your morning resolution. Do this either by a simple, loving glance at God, or by a few words spoken quietly and cast into His heart, by assenting in words like: "Yes, Lord, I want to do this action because You want it," or simply, "Yes, Father," or, "O Holy Will, live and rule in me," or other words that the Holy Spirit will suggest to you. You may also make a simple sign of the cross over your heart, or kiss the cross you are wearing. All this will show that above everything, you want to do the holy will of God and seek nothing but His glory in all that you do.

As for the will of God's good pleasure, which we know only through events as they occur, if these events benefit us, we must bless God and unite ourselves to this divine will which sends them. If something occurs which is disagreeable, physically or mentally, let us lovingly unite our will in obedience to the divine good pleasure, despite our natural aversion. We must pay no attention to these feelings, so long as at the fine point of our will we acquiesce very simply to God's will, saying, "O my God, I want this because it is Your good pleasure." Chapter 6 of Book IX of the *Love of God* throws a clear light on this practice and invites us to be courageous and simple in performing it. Whatever good or evil befalls you, be confident that God will convert it all to your good.

As for prayer, don't burden yourself with making considerations; neither your mind nor mine is good at that. Follow your own way of speaking to our Lord sincerely, lovingly, confidently, and simply, as your heart dictates. Sometimes be content to stay ever so short a while in His divine presence, faithfully and humbly, like a child before his father, waiting to be told what to do, totally dependent on the paternal will in which he has placed all his love and trust. You may, if you wish, say a few words on this subject, but very quietly: "You are my Father and my God from whom I expect all my happiness." A few moments later (for you must always wait a little to hear what God will say to your heart): "I am Your child, all Yours; good children think only of pleasing their father; I don't want to have any worries and I leave in Your care everything that concerns me, for You love me, my God. Father, You are my good.

My soul rests and trusts in Your love and eternal providence." Try to let yourself be penetrated by words like these.

When you have committed some fault, go to God humbly, saying to Him, "I have sinned, my God, and I am sorry." Then, with loving confidence, add: "Father, pour the oil of Your bountiful mercy on my wounds, for You are my only hope; heal me." A little later: "By the help of Your grace, I shall be more on my guard and will bless you eternally," and speak like this according to the different movements and feelings of your soul. Sometimes put yourself very simply before God, certain of His presence everywhere, and without any effort, whisper very softly to His sacred heart whatever your own heart prompts you to say.

When you are experiencing some physical pain or a sorrowful heart, try to endure it before God, recalling as much as you can that He is watching you at this time of affliction, especially in physical illness when very often the heart is weary and unable to pray. Don't force yourself to pray, for a simple adherence to God's will, expressed from time to time, is enough. Moreover, suffering borne in the will quietly and patiently is a continual, very powerful prayer before God, regardless of the complaints and anxieties that come from the inferior part of the soul.

Finally, my dear Lord, try to perform all your actions calmly and gently, and keep your mind ever joyful, peaceful and content. Do not worry about your perfection, or about your soul. God to whom it belongs, and to whom you have completely entrusted it, will take care of it and fill it with all the graces, consolations and blessings of His holy love in the measure that they will be useful in this life. In the next life He will grant you eternal bliss. Such is the wish of her to whom your soul is as precious as her own; pray for her, for she never prays without you, my Lord.

[Annecy, 8 May 1625][1]

My very honored and beloved Lord,

May the divine Savior, who ascends, glorious and triumphant, to sit at the right hand of His Father, draw to Himself our hearts and all our affections, in order to place them in the bosom of His love! How consoled I was when I read your letter and saw the graces

---

1. *Sa Vie et ses oeuvres*, V, 432–34: Letter DCXXII.

and mercy that this good Savior has granted you! I have blessed Him and thanked Him for this; I do so again with all my heart, and I shall continue to thank Him unceasingly.

It is good when a soul loves solitude; it's a sign that it takes delight in God and enjoys speaking with Him. Don't you see, my dearest Lord, this is where the divine sweetness communicates its lights and more abundant graces. How great is the grace you have received in this self-examination and the renewal of your soul which you have made with such preparation! Now you experience the fruit of this: peace and contentment in your conscience which is so well prepared that God will be pleased to fill it with His most holy, precious favors. How strongly I feel about this and what great hope I have that it will lead you to utter integrity and perfection! You must respond faithfully to the lights that God will give you, no matter what it costs you, for really, the love which God, in His goodness, has for you, and which He manifests so openly by such excellent, solid graces, requires a reciprocal love, according to the measure of your weakness and poverty. This means that you must refuse nothing you recognize to be His will. This perfect abandonment of yourself in the arms of divine Providence, this loving acceptance of all that He wishes to do with you, and with everything, this peace of conscience, this holy desire to please Him by all kinds of virtuous acts, according to the opportunities He will give you, and especially acts of charity and humility—all this is the wood that will feed the fire of sacred love which you feel in your heart and continually desire. And in this holy exercise, do not forget me, my very dear Lord, so that some day—God knows when—we may see each other in that blessed eternity where we shall love Him and praise and bless Him with all our strength. . . .

Pont-à-Mousson, 1 June 1626[1]

My very dear and very honored Lord,

I thank and praise our good God for the blessing He is pleased to have given us through the exchange made possible by our perfect friendship; for I assure you that if my letters enkindle in you the flame of love for the supreme Good, your very dear letters arouse the same feelings in me and make me wish more and more that our

---

1. *Sa Vie et ses oeuvres*, V, 612–16: Letter DCCXXV.

hearts be totally and constantly united to the good pleasure of God which we find so kind and favorable. Let us love this good pleasure, my dearest Lord, and let us see it alone in all that happens to us, embracing it lovingly. May this exercise be our daily bread. It can be practiced everywhere, and is particularly necessary for you because of the variety of obligations and contacts which you cannot avoid; for, in everything, by God's grace, you seek only Him and His most holy will.

Oh! how satisfying it is to read and reread what you tell me, my very dear Lord—of how you continue to practice your spiritual exercises with the same fervor and love you had when you began them, and how you keep your resolutions vigorous, despite the bustle of the court.

Confident of the Lord's goodness, I trust you will never retreat but will continually advance. Your assurance and testimony about this give my soul consolation and peace. That's why I beg you, my dearest Lord, always to mention something on this subject when you write to me. And don't think that this desire comes from mistrust, certainly not. I have no fear of that, now that your year of "novitiate" is over; and I have never doubted that God would grant you a holy perseverance, for the grace of your vocation in the service of His pure love is too extraordinary and abundant. Let us both appreciate and love this grace well, my very dear Lord, since it is the source of eternal life for us. It is so precious to me that I rank it second among all the God-given graces which impel me most strongly to do good and to long to see our life totally bound with Jesus Christ and hidden in God.

Do not think that by this I mean for us to retire into solitude, or to flee those occupations and legitimate contacts necessary to our vocations; oh, no, for I very much like each one to stay in his state of life and not throw himself into the excesses of a hermit's devotion, especially you, my dearest Lord, for whom this would be most inappropriate. But what I do mean is that we must want, above all, to adorn our souls with the virtues of our Savior, Jesus Christ, and also with that secret, intimate union of our hearts with God, which causes us to long for Him everywhere, as you are doing. As for that humility of heart which makes you think of yourself as a blade of hyssop in comparison to her whom you consider a cedar of Lebanon—though, in truth, she is but a shadow and lifeless image of virtue—my dear Lord, this is the humility which attracts God's Spirit to our souls and fills them with the treasure of all virtues. It is through humility that we live a hidden life, for she manages her good works in secret and holds in security, in the shelter of her protection, the little good that we do.

I didn't intend to write so much, dearest Lord, but that's how my heart always opens up to you. And certainly it is very softened by the holy and incomparable love God has given it for you. Always love this heart of mine well and continue to recommend it to the divine mercy. Be assured that I never cease desiring for you the fullness of His best graces in this life and a very high place before the throne of His glory and only desirable eternity. But all this, no doubt, I do with infinite love and affection.

[Annecy, 1633][1]

My very honored Lord,

Should we not adore God's will in profound submission, and lovingly kiss the rod with which He reproves His elect? Of course we should, and, despite nature's repugnance, we should praise and thank Him a thousand times because He is our good God who sends us both sorrows and joys with the same love, and ordinarily even has us draw more spiritual profit from affliction than from prosperity.

But how does it happen that, having this knowledge and experience, we still feel so keenly the death of those we love? I must admit, my dear Lord, that as I read the little note telling me of the death of our dearest darling daughter, I was so overcome that, had I been standing, I think I would have fallen.[2] I can't remember that any grief ever gripped me this way. But when I read your letter, oh, Lord Jesus! My dear Lord, what a blow it was to my poor heart and how much your sorrow added to mine! It is understandable that you should feel this loss as you do, and at your age; what a sweet support you have lost in this daughter who so devotedly looked after your health and your every want. All this has touched me more than I can say, for whatever affects you affects me acutely. But when I con-

---

1. *Sa Vie et ses oeuvres*, VII, 239–41: Letter MCCLVIII.
2. Marie de Coulanges, Baronesse de Chantal, was Jane's daughter-in-law. She died on August 20, 1633, only a few years after her husband's death. She was buried in the vault of the first monastery of Paris, rue St. Antoine, where Celse-Bénigne was buried.

sider that by means of these privations, lovingly accepted, God wishes to be Himself everything to us, that the least progress we make in His holy love is worth more than the whole world with all its consolations, and that in the most bitter trials which strip us of our greatest satisfactions, God treasures, above all, the union of our wills with His. When I consider all this, then, truly, my dear Lord, I find so many advantages to affliction, that I can't help admitting that the more we suffer, the more we are favored by God. I hope that by now you yourself will have perceived this and found comfort in this truth. Such is my wish for you, and I pray God with all my heart to grant you this grace.

My beloved and dearest Lord, our first reactions are inevitable, and our gentle Savior is not offended by them; but I hope that afterward He will fill you with a thousand delicate, holy consolations. This is what I continually beg of Him, just as I beg you, my dear Lord, to divert yourself as much as you can, and to find strength in the confident hope that we shall all be united in the joy of a blessed eternity. Surely, the virtuous life and saintly death of this very lovable daughter gives us hope that, by God's mercy, she has already attained this bliss. This should console us, for, in the end, dearest Lord, we are in this world only to attain such happiness, and the sooner we reach it, the better. I'm amazed that this truth still doesn't prevent our feeling so profoundly the death of our loved ones.

I am writing to M. and Mme. de Coulanges to whom this terrible loss must have been a great shock. I believe that the love they have always had for the poor little orphan will continue unchanged.[3] When my thoughts turn to this child, I have to check myself. I trust that God, to whom I confide her, will be Father and Protector to her, and I give her over to the care of the Blessed Virgin with all my heart.

On this occasion, the sisters in both houses [Paris] have omitted nothing. Besides their own love for the dear deceased, they have felt keenly your sorrow and mine in this bereavement. I find some comfort in knowing that she will be buried in the very place where the heart of my poor son is kept. [. . .]

---

3. "The poor little orphan" referred to is Jane's granddaughter, the future Madame de Sévigné.

[Annecy, 1639][1]

My Lord,

I have learned, through our dear Sister Superior in Paris, how God has allowed you to share in the calamity with which, in His Providence, He has chastised His people, and how your gentle, loving acceptance of this affliction has touched everyone.[2] No words can express the consolation this gives me; I see in it the special care that our Lord has for your progress in His holy love.

It is clear that through your temporal loss, you are richer in spiritual treasures, the least of which is worth more than the ownership of the entire world. I always remember what our blessed Father used to say: "An ounce of virtue practiced in time of tribulation is worth more than a hundred thousand pounds exercised in prosperity, because that is where real virtue is shown." Blessed be God forever, who has, in His mercy, visited you! How fortunate you are, my dearest Lord, to be able to say with so much courage and indifference: "The Lord gave me those abbeys, and the Lord has taken them away: blessed be the name of the Lord!" It is His grace that gives you this disposition. Once again, I bless and thank Him for it.

In your last letter, you were telling me how our Lord is asking you to move into the retirement you have felt drawn to for some time. Oh! how it comforts me to hear that! I hope you are taking care of your affairs so that you may do this in the manner you think will be most pleasing to God; but, I beg you, do not in any way alter your plan for a reasonable retirement, unless you come to see clearly that our Lord is asking something else of you.

I am forever in His love, yours, etc. . . .

LETTERS TO MADAME DE TOULONJON
(FRANÇOISE DE CHANTAL)

Both of the sets of letters to the two men reveal Jane as a director of those already embarked upon a spiritual journey and desirous of a pure love of God. The letters to the two women, her daughter

---

1. *Sa Vie et ses oeuvres*, VIII, 205–06: Letter MDCLXII.
2. The reference is to a recent epidemic.

208

Françoise and Marie-Aimée de Morville, are of a different ilk, especially in their early phases. Françoise, Madame de Toulonjon (1599–1684), was Jane's third child, her second daughter, whose independent temperament rendered her a worry to her mother from the outset. When she was just a child, Jane considered sending her to a strict convent school, a practice which was at the time considered salutary for youngsters with more a the fair share of strong temperament and will. As it turned out, Françoise went with her mother to the early Visitation where she resided as a boarder until she was old enough to return to society under the protection of other relatives. Never malicious, she was nonetheless excessively fond (in her mother's eyes) of personal adornments, affluence and position in society. She showed little of the docility expected of a young woman at that time for a marriage arranged by a parent. She refused one man who did not have the status and fortune she was longing for. However, she did accept a second match arranged by her mother. Jane's letters to her, which begin with her contemplated engagement to the older but very devoted Antoine de Toulonjon, show Jane in a multifaceted light. On the one hand, she accepts the principle, which she so radically lived out for herself, of a life of selfless and "unworldly" activity as being the way to be for Christ. Yet she never saw the call to the cloister as universal nor did she see secular vocations as incompatible with a deep love of God and a sincere devotion. In this she is at one with Francis de Sales. Early on she recognized that Françoise had no taste for life in religion, and so concentrated her efforts on encouraging her daughter to discern the inner dimension of her life as wife and mother and a woman of means in French society. With motherly anxiety tempered by prudence and real affection, she constantly urged Françoise to avoid excessive luxury, not to have her head turned by her husband's advancements in society, to keep her focus upon love of God and neighbor. The natural chastisement of the years, including the death of children and husband, eventually brought mother and daughter into a close relationship. Françoise was widowed at the age of thirty-three at the peak of her worldly glory; her husband had served the king in the army and died governor of Pignerol. Françoise gave birth to their only surviving son a few hours before the death of her husband. She returned to France with her baby and eleven-year-old daughter to be with her mother in Annecy. One of Jane's *last letters to Françoise shows her as a director for widows—a state the mother herself bore—counseling the simplicity, humility, and unexceptional yet sincerely loving devotion so expressive of the Salesian spirit.*

Live ⁺ Jesus!

[Paris, 1620][1]

Darling, since M. de Toulonjon is free for eight or ten days, he is hurrying off to see you to find out first-hand whether you think he is suitable for you or not. He hopes his personality will not displease you. As for me, frankly, I see nothing to find fault with in him; in fact, I couldn't wish for more. Our Lord has given me so much satisfaction about this match that I can't remember ever having had such a good feeling about a temporal matter. I am not so much attracted by his good background and refinement, as by his intelligence, pleasant disposition, sincerity, sound judgment, integrity, and good reputation. In a word, dear Françon, let us thank God for such a match.

Out of gratitude, dear, try to love and serve God better than you ever have, and don't let anything stop you from continuing to go frequently to the sacraments or from trying to be humble and gentle. Take the *Devout Life* for your guide; it will lead you safely. Don't waste time fussing about jewelry and fashions. You will be living in plenty, but, my darling, remember always that we are meant to use the good things God gives us without being attached to them. Such is the attitude we should have toward all that the world values. From now on, try to live honorably, modestly, sensibly, in the new way of life that is before you.

I'm certainly very happy that your relatives and I arranged this marriage without you, for this is how things should be, and, dearest, I want you always to follow my advice. Moreover, your brother, who has good judgment, is delighted about your engagement. True, M. de Toulonjon is about fifteen years older than you, but, darling, you will be much happier with him than with some rash, dissolute, young fool like the young men of today. You are marrying a man who is not at all like this; he is not a gambler, has lived honorably

---

1. *Sa Vie et ses oeuvres*, IV, 390–91: Letter CCXXXVII.

at court and on the battlefield, has received high appointments from the king. You would be lacking the good sense I believe you to have if you didn't accept him cordially and sincerely. I beg you, dear, accept him graciously, and be assured that God who has been mindful of you will not forget you if you abandon yourself to His tender care, for He guides all those who place their trust in Him.

Paris, 13 April [1620][1]

My dearest daughter,

Praise God who so far has guided you so well in these preliminary steps toward your coming marriage! I hope this divine goodness will give you complete peace. I must say, darling, that I myself am more and more pleased about the match. In my opinion, M. de Toulonjon is as fine a man as one could find anywhere. He has returned as happy as can be, and we have every reason to feel the same. Truly, dear Françon, you have pleased me very much by placing such total confidence in me; but if you only knew how much I have prayed and longed to see you happily settled, and how much more keenly I feel your concerns than my own. Of course, I shall always prefer your happiness to my own. There's no doubt about that. You may be sure that on this occasion I acted with great affection because I saw it was for your happiness. We owe everything to the goodness of our Lord who has watched over you and me and heard our prayers. You can see by the enclosed letter how much the Archbishop of Bourges wants this marriage also. So, stand fast if you are disturbed by fears and imaginings; shut the door upon them, and do not let such feelings enter, under any pretext whatever. In everything use common sense and follow my bit of advice. It is for your good, and if you continue to follow it, you will not regret it. Write me, as you have promised, all the feelings in your heart. And if, as I hope, God Himself has bound you to M. de Toulonjon—for that is what I desire above all else—then I trust that God will have blessed your first meeting. For my part, darling, I tell you frankly, I find him altogether to my liking, as I have already said. Really, I like him very much. All our relatives and friends who know him couldn't ask for more.

As to your rings, M. de Toulonjon is very busy about them and

---

1. *Sa Vie et ses oeuvres*, IV, 401–04: Letter CCXLIII.

wants to have lots of precious stones from Paris sent to me so that I may buy as many as I like for you. I would prefer that you not buy any at all, for, frankly, dear, ladies of rank here no longer wear them; only the townswomen do. However, you can make your own choice when you get here. But I don't know how to make M. de Toulonjon understand this, for he begs me, at least for now, to let him send you pearls, earrings, and a locket covered with diamonds, which is what all the ladies are wearing on the front of their gowns. Dearest, we mustn't let M. de Toulonjon be extravagant about buying so many things for you. He has such an intense desire to please you in every possible way, but we mustn't allow it. If ever there was a perfectly happy woman, it is you; but don't you see, dearest, you must be very discreet and hold him back in this. It will be better to put aside a little of your money and spend it more usefully than to squander it on such trinkets and vanities. For my part, I hope that my Françon will not be swept off her feet by all this. My reputation would be at stake, for since you are my daughter, you are expected to be circumspect and to conduct your affairs wisely and prudently.

I can just picture you as a lady, mistress of the heart and home of our very dear M. de Toulonjon! That's why it will be up to you to manage your affairs carefully. Since he wants you to send me a design of the dress you like, do so, but I am going to allow only one gown to be sent to you, for, more than one, considering all the other things he is getting for you, would be unreasonable. You yourself, if M. Coulon[2] wants to help you, may also have one made, though I would prefer he simply send you the money for it. We could have it made in today's style and out of fashionable fabric so that it could be worn anywhere.

See to it that Foretz is sold.[3] Moreover, you shouldn't have a wedding dress made; today that appears ridiculous among both the ladies at court and the gentry. Besides, I want you to have a quiet wedding; and I want you to trust me in this. M. de Toulonjon tells me that you don't want to be married in May. Good heavens! don't be scrupulous about this, for it's only a superstition. However, I don't think a May wedding is possible anyway, even though he would like that very much. That's because he

---

2. Coulon oversaw Françoise's estate; correction of Plon edition by Burns.
3. Foretz was Françoise's property.

wants to please you at any cost. I'd be in favor of a May wedding too if it meant your getting rid of your scruple about it. He wrote you about how he was prevented from coming here as soon as he had hoped, but he didn't tell you how he did get here. It happened that while he was waiting at the relay station, a friend of his, a State Councilor, was going by in his carriage. M. de Toulonjon jumped right into the carriage without his sword. He hadn't had time to eat but came just as he was. He was sorry not to have been able to send you anything today, but he will on Thursday. Really, the more I see this man, the more I like him and the more I realize how much you and I should praise God for this fortunate match. Write him a courteous, warm answer and speak honestly and openly with him, returning his affection. The time to stand on ceremony is over. His man is waiting downstairs for my letter. Dearest Françon, I want you to love your fiancé perfectly. May you be as happy as you have reason to be happy. As for me, I am completely happy, and with good reason. Goodbye, dearest love. Write to me quite openly.

P.S. A thousand greetings to our dear relatives. Goodbye again, darling. Let us love wholeheartedly him whom God has given us.

[Chambery, 1625][1]
Although I won't be seeing the Archbishop of Bourges as soon as we thought, still, I know my joy will be great when I do. Since his recovery and because of the graces our Lord has granted him, I feel extraordinary affection for him and I can't (nor do I want to) stop praising and thanking God for this great grace. He has written me nothing of what you tell me he did for my son, although he writes very often.[2] When I see him, I shall speak to him about this and I'll watch for an opportunity to put in a good word for you with him. I've always thought he was very fond of you, dearest. I don't think he owns much more than his furniture, but I really don't know. Darling, even if it were true that this good prelate had quite

---

1. *Sa Vie et ses oeuvres*, V, 413–15: Letter DCX. *[1625]*
2. Madame de Toulonjon was very hurt when she learned that her uncle, the Archbishop of Bourges, had favored her brother, the Baron de Chantal, in his will. By way of justifying her reaction, she wrote to her mother that her uncle had an obligation to provide for the future of his sister's children.

forgotten you, is that reason enough for you to give yourself over to sadness and resentment? Oh! Don't do that again; you might offend God. You are too attached to things of this life; you take them too much to heart.

What are you afraid of? That having many children you may not have the means of bringing them up in a style suited to their social background and to your courage? I beg you, don't worry about that. You underestimate the wise Providence of Him who gives you these children and who is good and rich enough to provide for them in a way befitting His glory and their salvation. This is what we should want for our children, rather than social ambition in this sad, mortal world.

And so, dearest, welcome very lovingly, as coming from the hand of God, these little ones that He gives you; take good care of them; cherish them tenderly, and bring them up in the fear of the Lord, and not in a spirit of vanity. If you do this, and if you entrust all your anxieties to God, you will see that His Providence looks after all your needs very nicely and that all you have to do is bless Him and rest in Him totally. Take my word for this, dearest. This is what you must do: serve God, let go of pride, live in harmony with the husband God has given you, take good care of your household; work at all this, and from now on, try to live like a real mother.

If I hadn't had the courage to do this at the beginning of my marriage, we would not have made ends meet for we had less income than you, and a debt of 15,000 crowns besides.

Courage, then, dearest; use your mind and your time, not to worry and fear, but to serve God and your household, for this is God's will for you. You will see how many blessings will flow from this undertaking.

I wanted to speak to you at length about all this. I hope that you will benefit from what I tell you with so much love and concern and that you will reread this letter often so as to put it into practice. I ask God to grant you this grace. In His goodness, may He shower His best blessings on you and all your dear family whom I greet affectionately. You know, my darling, that you are my one and only beloved, dearest daughter, and that I am your very humble and very loving mother who wants you to be completely happy.

LETTERS OF SPIRITUAL DIRECTION

[Annecy, 1626][1]

My dearest daughter,

I have just heard of the death of your son.[2] May God, in His infinite kindness, make up for your loss by filling you with an abundance of spiritual and temporal graces! I am sure you have accepted this visitation from God with patience and a loving submission to His good pleasure, for in this valley of tears we must expect much sorrow and little consolation. Raise your mind often to the thought of eternity, and aspire to and long for this happiness. You will see that there is no real rest anywhere else; so love it and place all your hope in it. Teach this lesson early to your little Gabrielle.

[Annecy, 1633][1]

My dearest daughter,

I hear God has blessed you with another pregnancy. I want to believe, for my own consolation, that you are grateful for this grace, as well as for all the prosperity you enjoy, and that you see all these gifts as coming from the hand of God. He sends them to you, not for show, not to be used out of vanity, but rather to help you advance in humility and a loving fear of Him from whom they come. Tell me frankly and truthfully, dearest, where do you stand in this matter? I am always a little afraid that the abundance of the advantages and honors of this world may obscure your vision by their smoke, perhaps even choke you if you are not on your guard or mindful of their inconstancy and the uncertainty of the time of our departure from this life when we have to leave all that behind us. Think often of our passage from this life, my darling, and of the eternity that awaits those who have valued lasting happiness more than life's fleeting moments. Take care to impress these truths on your daughter's heart; this is the most valuable legacy you can obtain for her and bequeath to her. Teach her to fear offending God and to value the happiness of living in love and fear of Him.

You know, darling, that ever since you were little I have tried to imprint this love of God on your heart and have always recommended that you obey His will, especially in rendering to your hus-

1. *Sa Vie et ses oeuvres*, VI, 10: Letter DCCLX. *[1626]*
2. This was an infant son whose death left little Gabrielle, then four years old, as the only surviving child.
1. *Sa Vie et ses oeuvres*, VII, 219–20: Letter MCCXLVII.*[1633]*

215

band those duties required of you by God. I urge you to make him as happy as possible. Let me know also how you feel about this. Dearest, you shouldn't be solemn and pompous because of the wealth and honor that are yours. I'm told that you are becoming a scoffer. Believe me, dear, it would be better for you to attract attention by your modest, Christian manner and by the sweet and gracious affability you show everyone in your various relationships. Making fun of others is unbecoming in a woman of your social condition and age. Try to distinguish yourself and attract hearts by the means I have just mentioned. Above all, be prudent and reserved in your actions.

Receive this advice as coming from your mother who loves you dearly and who wants you always perfect in your state of life. God grant you this grace.

[Annecy, 1634][1]

I was deeply moved by your letter, my darling, which tells me how keenly you are suffering.[2] Truly, your sorrow is great, and, when looked at only in terms of this earthly life, it is overwhelming. But if you can look beyond the ordinary and shifting events of life and consider the infinite blessings and consolations of eternity, you would find comfort in the midst of these reversals, as well as joy in the assured destiny of him for whom you mourn. Oh, when will we learn to be more attentive to these truths of our faith? When will we savor the tenderness of the Divine Will in all the events of our life, seeing in them only His good pleasure and His unchanging, mysterious love which is always concerned with our good, as much in prosperity as in adversity? But, imperfect as we are, we somehow transform into poison the very medicine the Great Physician prescribes for our healing. Let's stop behaving in such a manner. Rather, like obedient children, let's surrender ourselves lovingly to the will of our heavenly Father and cooperate with His plan to unite us intimately to Himself through suffering. If we do that, He will become all for us: our brother, son, husband, mother, our all in all. Courage! May you find strength in these thoughts.

---

1. *Sa Vie et ses oeuvres*, VII, 340–41: Letter MCCCXII.
2. Françoise's husband, the Count de Toulonjon, died on September 20, 1633, the day she gave birth to a son. Now, in 1634, she is still grieving.

I beg our Lord to help you find the rich treasure which His Goodness has hidden at the very core of the pain that comes to you from His hand. [. . .]

Advice to the Countess de Toulonjon[1]

My dearest,
   You wanted to have my advice in writing, so here it is. My greatest wish is that you live like a true Christian widow, unpretentious in your dress and actions, and especially reserved in your relationships, having nothing to do with vain, worldly young men. Otherwise, dear, even though I am very sure that your conduct is above reproach—I feel more sure about it than of my own—others could question and criticize it if you entertained such persons in your house and took pleasure in their company. Please trust me in this, for your honor and mine, as well as for my peace of mind. I know very well, darling, of course, that we can't live in the world without enjoying some of its pleasures, but take my word for it, dearest, you won't find any really lasting joys except in God, in living virtuously, raising your children well, looking after their affairs and managing your household. If you seek happiness elsewhere, you will experience much anguish, as I well know.
   I am not against the legitimate pleasure you can derive, by way of diversion, from healthy relationships with good people. But visits should be infrequent, considering the condition of life in which God has placed you. In other words, dearest, check your inclinations and surrender them to God for His glory dwelling in you, for the respect and love you owe to the memory of your beloved husband, the preservation of your good name, and the benefit of your daughter who, undoubtedly, will model herself after you. This surrender of your inclinations to God will be advantageous to you and to your dear children, and appropriate to your background, your present state in life and the consolation of your relatives. You will find strength to

---

1. *Sa Vie et ses oeuvres*, VII, 340–41: Letter MCCCXII. When the Countess came to Annecy shortly after her husband's death, her mother offered advice and direction in person. On request she put the same reflections in writing so that her daughter could return to them often.

do this, darling, if you follow faithfully the little devotional practices we spoke of and which I shall now write out for you.

First, upon awakening in the morning, turn your thoughts to God present everywhere; place your heart and your entire being in His hands. Then think briefly of the good you will be able to accomplish that day and the evil you can avoid, especially by controlling your predominant fault. Resolve, by the grace of God, to do good and avoid evil. Then kneel down, adore God from the bottom of your heart and thank Him for all the benefits and graces He has given you. If you think about it for a moment, you will realize how He has surrounded you with His grace and taken special care of you. This thought should touch your heart which you ought to offer Him with all your good resolutions, affections, thoughts, words and deeds of that day, in union with our Divine Savior's offering of Himself on the tree of the cross. Ask Him for His grace and assistance to guide you throughout the day. Ask also for His blessing, that of the Blessed Virgin, your good angel and your patron saints by a simple turning to them in your heart. All this can be done in the space of two *Paters* and *Aves;* then get dressed quickly.

As far as possible, assist at Holy Mass every day as attentively and devoutly as possible, using such considerations as are given in *The Devout Life.* If you can't be present at Mass, at least be there in spirit, as suggested in the same book which ought to be your favorite spiritual guide.

Either during Mass, if you can't do otherwise, or at some other time in the morning, withdraw to some quiet place to pray from your heart for about a quarter of an hour. Place yourself before God or the Blessed Virgin, like a daughter in the presence of her father or mother, conversing with them with humble, filial trust, either by meditating on some mystery of faith, or else, following the promptings of your heart, by simply talking to them about the concerns you have right now. Always conclude your prayer with a strong desire to love and please God, renewing your good resolutions and asking for His grace. Above all, try to have a pure intention in all that you do; frequently offer your actions to God. Often call to mind His goodness and make loving aspirations, according to either His inspirations or the inclinations of your own heart.

Every day read for a quarter or half hour from some spiritual book, preferably from *Philothea*.[2] Before supper, withdraw a bit, or while walking, place yourself in God's hands and make a few aspirations. Before going to bed, examine your conscience and, kneeling in God's presence, adore Him, thank Him, and offer Him your soul. If you can, add the litany of our Lady and have your servants answer the invocations. Receive holy communion at least on the first Sunday of each month, on the major feasts of our Lord and our Lady, and on the feast of Saint Joseph to whom I would like you to have devotion.

In conclusion, dear one, try to calm your passions and inclinations and live according to sound reason and the holy will of God. Otherwise, you will always be anxious and perturbed. But if you are fortunate enough to accept with patience and gentleness the sorrows and difficulties of this life, which God sends to those He loves for their growth and progress toward blessedness, then even in this life you will begin to get a little taste of the delights of a glorious eternity. You may be sure of this, darling. But you must sincerely turn to God and love Him in all the manifestations of His good pleasure. By obeying God's will, we prefer it to our own will, desires and inclinations. May God, in His kindness, grant us this grace, dearest. This is what I pray for constantly, for I love you so specially and with all my heart.

LETTERS TO MADAME DU TERTRE
(MARIE-AIMÉE DE MORVILLE)

The correspondence with Marie-Aimée de Morville (1598–1632) reveals Jane as a guide for those whose perspective is thoroughly "worldly." This young widow became the secular foundress of the Visitation of Moulins and took the religious habit as a result of familial pressure. Her case is one of the few examples of the reception of a candidate into the Visitation on other than purely spiritual grounds. Apparently, the young Madame du Tertre was relegated to the cloister to avoid the scandal raised by a romantic liaison following her widowhood. Her high-placed family, two car-

---

2. *Introduction to the Devout Life.*

dinals, and a leading Jesuit of the day, asked Francis de Sales to give her asylum in one of his monasteries, preferably not in the nascent Visitation community in Paris. She took the habit and was professed at Moulins.

Although she professed a desire for the values of religious life, the ambivalent novice could not for a long time bring herself to conform her behavior to the code that such a life implied. She insisted on retaining for herself the privileges reserved for foundresses who had not received the habit, and continually enlarged her sphere of independent operation. She dressed grandly, entertained visitors in the elegantly appointed house she occupied on convent grounds, several times tried to set fire to the house, and stirred up rivalry between two towns by promising and then withholding money for a new foundation of the order, thus involving Jane and Francis (quite without their consent or knowledge) in awkward diplomatic machinations. She made life so difficult for the community that Jane was obliged to write her stern letters and even go to Moulins herself in 1623 to try to reason with her. The young woman solicited and obtained a papal brief granting her secularization. Jane encouraged her to do this, knowing that she was not in her place and upsetting the community. But Marie-Aimée's efforts to return to secular life were blocked by the Paris Parliament. Jane knew it was useless to struggle against this all-powerful machine, yet at the same time she upheld the legitimate claims of the community to their rightful lifestyle, and so she applied her efforts to the gradual conversion of Marie-Aimée.

For thirteen years she troubled and taxed Jane's ingenuity and generosity. Then, fifteen months before her early death, she had a dream of such vividness that she underwent a dramatic conversion, tore up the document which had secured her privileges as foundress and entered the novitiate with sincere heart and intentions she clung to tenaciously for the brief remainder of her life.

The tremendous patience of Jane's directorial sensibilities are clearly shown in her letters to Marie-Aimée de Morville. She attempts to turn the girl from her headstrong ways by encouraging her brief aspirations for holiness, by holding out the ideal of religious perfection in a compelling and inviting way, and finally by celebrating with open arms the reluctant Visitandine's final conversion.

Live + Jesus!

[Paris] 3 September 1619[1]

Didn't I promise you, my very dear Sister, that you would find in her [Mother Jeanne Charlotte de Bréchard] a person who would completely satisfy and console you? I ask God to grant that through this dear Mother you may receive the strength to grow in divine love. I advise you, in fact, I urge you, my dearest daughter, to be very open with her so that she may, by understanding your heart's weaknesses, bring to it appropriate remedies. If you do this, you will receive a great deal of satisfaction . . . and consolation, beside your spiritual benefit which you should seek above all else, for, my dear, life is short and the hour of our departure from it is always uncertain. Let us work then while we still have time so that we may someday reach a blessed eternity. This is what my heart desires for yours which I dearly love. I am all yours, my very dear Sister, your most humble sister and servant in Our Lord.

[Paris] 11 August 1620[1]

My very dear daughter,

Since I have time to write this note, I beg you, in God's name, to settle this business according to the recommendations of the Bishop of Geneva to whom you have referred the matter. Or at least, let what was so clearly given to Nevers remain there. It should make no difference to you, my dear Sister, so long as you have what you want from us. Why should you be concerned about how we dispose of your gift since there remains a sufficient fund to provide for your needs?

At least, my dear daughter, if you wish to carry out your plan of living completely for God in our midst, please, satisfy the Bishop of Geneva and trust him. As for us, we want neither dispute nor lawsuit; we would rather give up a hundred times the amount you gave us, for we value peace with holy poverty incomparably more than all the wealth in the world with the least unpleasantness. The Bishop of Geneva would agree with what I am saying to you, and I am a little surprised that since his answer arrived, we have heard no more about it, except for what the Bishop of Nevers tells me about our sisters there being pressured to give back what they received.

---

1. *Sa Vie et ses oeuvres*, IV, 339: Letter CCIII. *[1619]*
1. *Sa Vie et ses oeuvres*, IV, 458–59: Letter CCLXXVI. *[1620]*

And so, my dear daughter, if you persevere, as I believe you will, let us, please, say no more about this matter, now that you know the feeling of the Bishop of Geneva and have his advice. Our dear sisters of both houses are distressed to hear things they are not used to hearing. They esteem peace above everything else. Give it to them, I beg you, and believe me always yours. . . .

[Paris, July 1620][1]

Oh, my dearest daughter, be courageous and say firmly: "I can do all things in Him who strengthens me."[2] Yes, my dear, He who has given you the desire to sacrifice yourself to His eternal love will take care to perfect His work. But you must have a filial, child-like confidence in this good, heavenly Father. He has done you the favor of withdrawing you from hell (for that's what I call the world), in order to place you in His house, in His garden of delights, like a loved plant, loved by His divine Heart, so that later He may transplant you to His heavenly garden where you will enjoy His glory for all eternity. O my daughter, how precious is this grace! Yes, I beg you, sacrifice yourself to all those tasks which your nature fears, and which might cause you to suffer. There is such happiness in giving to our Savior labor for labor, life for life, love for love insofar as our littleness allows.

Courage, then, my dear, and use this courage to bear your disappointment that your relatives will not be present at your reception of the habit. Their excuse is legitimate, because the movement of war troops frightens everybody. Don't let that trouble you, dear child: God and His angels are your true relatives and the most Blessed Virgin, your mother; besides, your sisters and your good Mother will be your true mother and sisters. And I will be with you in prayer with all the heartfelt love you could and should desire from me for I am yours unreservedly.

[Paris, January 1621][1]

My very dear daughter,

Praise God, my dearest daughter, that you find comfort and

---

1. *Sa Vie et ses oeuvres*, IV, 464–65: Letter CCLXXIX. [1620]
2. Phil 4:13.
1. *Sa Vie et ses oeuvres*, IV, 503–04: Letter CCCVI. [1621]

encouragement in your religious duties! Have confidence, dear, and journey on as peaceably as possible, under the protection of the Son of God our Lord and of His holy Mother. You may be sure that they will never abandon you even though you are frail and your progress is not as great and steady as you would like it to be, nor as your ambition would require. They see only your good will, which will bring forth its fruit in due time and place. I will continue to appeal to their infinite goodness, dearest Sister, for you would never believe how much I love you, nor how much I hope that some day, with the help of divine grace, you will be all that the heart of God wants you to be. God does not call you to pettiness, my child; so, you must respond gently but generously. It seems to me that above everything else, prayer and a frequent lifting of your heart to God are necessary and useful. Once divine love takes possession of your heart, oh! how easy all the rest will be! I shall ask God very specially to give you this grace and shall ask our community to have a general communion for this intention on the feast of St. Anthony. Unite yourself with us, and your dear Mother also, for she has a real desire for your good.

Certainly, Sister, I am encouraged to see that you have confidence in her, for such trust is well-deserved and well-founded. If dear Sister de Frouville can, she will write you. She is good and is doing very well.

Goodbye, dearest daughter. May the infinitely good God fill you with His holy love. Amen. You know that in Him, I am all yours. May His name be blessed.

[Rumilly, 7 October 1625][1]

I cannot resist telling you, my very dear daughter, the great joy I feel at what your Superior writes me about you. How could it be otherwise, my dearest daughter? This is what we should expect from the goodness of your heart which, in truth, is more suited to serve God than the world. Persevere steadily in this holy undertaking, and may your courage increase every day so that you may attain the full enjoyment of the sovereign and only desirable love of our very gentle Jesus. Do not lose the opportunity that His Providence is presenting you. If you take my advice, you will turn your back

---

1. *Sa Vie et ses oeuvres*, V, 497: Letter DCLXV. *[1625]*

on all that can divert you, such as worldly contacts, for it is impossible to enjoy the frivolous pleasures of the world and at the same time to experience true heavenly consolations. O my daughter, I beg you, in God's name, go forward in your search for these higher joys and leave behind everything else, or, rather, let go of what is nothing in order to possess Him who is All. Do guard against turning back, I beg you; I pray God to hold you by the hand. I am, in this love, entirely yours.

[Annecy, 8 June 1632][1]

I have just come from holy communion, my dearest daughter, where I praised and thanked God who in His Infinite Goodness was pleased to call you back to Him so powerfully.[2] I begged Him with all my heart to hold you securely in His hands so that nothing could ever again draw you away from Him. For this, in all humility, I count on His grace and your faithful cooperation, my dear. I am confident that in the goodness of your dear heart you will never forget such abundant mercy. Think often of the sacred counsels given by the Princes of the Apostles, for they frequently exhort us in their letters to work out our salvation in fear and trembling, and to assure our vocation by good works.

Dearest daughter, it seems to me that the experience of your past misery should keep you in holy fear of falling again and make you very watchful over yourself, in order to avoid all dangerous occasions, especially those which have been most harmful, such as conversations, confidences, affections, contact with people from the outside, even with spiritual persons, except for rare and necessary occasions. You would be happiest if you could be satisfied with the instruction of your good Mother [M. Angélique de Bigny] who, besides her capabilities and charity, has a special love for you. And I think that the tears she has shed over you, the fasts, austerities and prayers that she has offered for you, have touched the Divine Heart and helped bring about your conversion. I'm sure that God will show her all that is necessary for your happiness. Never doubt that through her, His goodness will guide you safely. I am convinced

---

1. *Sa Vie et ses oeuvres*, VII, 90–92: Letter MCLXXVII. *[1632]*
2. See introduction to letters of Sr. de Morville for an explanation of her dramatic conversion.

that whoever gives up following the guidance of her Superior stops following that of God as well.

Finally, dearest, I want you to apply yourself to *doing* rather than *learning*. In the Institute, we have a wealth of the most solid instructions that we could ever wish for and which are uniquely suited to lead us to the very high perfection our vocation calls us to. From now on, let your joy be to read and practice these instructions faithfully. I beg you to do this, my dearest Sister, so that by these means you may offer to the Divine Goodness fruit worthy of the graces He has given you, and, by the exact observance of your vows, inspire the whole Institute by your true conversion. This will make up for all the sorrow and humiliation the Institute suffered by your past disorderly life, and we shall be greatly consoled, especially I who even now am comforted by the acts you have so generously performed. It would be impossible for me to harbor the least resentment toward you, my dearest daughter, for the past. You may be sure that I hold you in the very center of my heart, where I want to love you perfectly as my own most dear daughter. Know that you will receive from me, and from the whole Institute, only love and proofs of sincere affection.

I think it would be good if in a few months, persevering in your good resolutions, you let the whole Institute know in a few humble words the sorrow you feel for your misdeeds of the past. You did well, dearest daughter, to give your heart and your entire being unreservedly to God; you will see that His Providence will not fail you and that He will never allow you to want for anything.

[. . .] I pray God to give you the fullness of His grace, and to perfect what He has begun with such tenderness. Believe that with a guileless and sincere heart I am and will always be, my very dear child, your very humble, unworthy Sister and servant in our Lord.

[Annecy, 1632][1]

Praised be forever the Divine Savior who has seen fit to cast a ray of His holy light into your soul! Only He can enlighten us and open our blind eyes. My daughter, if your passions hadn't taken over, you could have perished through vanity and self-love.[2] It

---

1. *Sa Vie et ses oeuvres*, VII, 102: Letter MCLXXXIII. *[1632]*
2. See Introduction concerning her worldly life.

seems to me that for your own happiness, it was necessary that you fall into that bottomless pit toward which you were racing. All the human knowledge in the world would not have been enough to draw you away from your illusions. But, in His great mercy, God took care of you. For the rest of your life you ought to be deeply prostrate before Him, and very humble and docile toward others. Let yourself be guided, without resistance, and love dearly the humiliations that keep you humble. May God grant you this grace. And, imperfect as I am, I am the most devoted, loving friend that my dearest sister has. I ask God, in His most pure, holy love, to sanctify you, as well as all our dear sisters whom I greet with affection.

As to the complaints you make to me about yourself, dear, the cause may be in your own tendency to be slow and put things off. So long as you are careful to direct your intention to do all for God, then you need only have courage and be gentle with yourself in all your frailty.

I am all yours.

Annecy, 22 August 1632[1]

My very dear daughter,

Since God, in His great mercy, received you into His loving arms, converting you to Himself, you must think no more of the past. Instead, faithfully concentrate on nourishing God's gift of conversion with fear and confidence. Make His grace effective in your life so that you may be steady and persevere in your good desires and holy resolutions. As for me, dearest Sister, I can assure you that I will forget the past. If I remember correctly, I was not at all affected by your letter, but rather by the turmoil I knew your house was experiencing. However, let's not speak any more about this. Just know that I feel great maternal love for you and that you will always find me ready to give you all the spiritual help and comfort that I can. But you will have to remain firm, dearest Sister, and no longer waver in your good resolutions, for from now on you cannot be excused. To help you persevere, keep before your eyes all that you owe God. Often reflect on it—on your salvation, your reputation, and that of the Order where God in His grace has placed you, on your peace of mind and the satisfaction of your dear ones.

---

1. *Sa Vie et ses oeuvres*, VII, 124–25: Letter MCXCV. *[22 August 1632]*

And since you ask me what I would like you to do, O dear child, I can only advise you to look on everything perishable as utterly worthless and to renounce it. Yearn only for what is eternal by means of a perfect observance of the Institute you profess. Become very little in your own eyes, my dear, love solitude, and let your happiness be found in God and not in the world. How happy you will be, dearest daughter, if you do this well. I beg God to grant you this grace; and, by this means, may His holy love grow every day in you. In and for this love I am all yours.

[Annecy] 25 October [1632][1]

I had already written the enclosed, my very dear daughter, when I received your last letter. Oh, my true daughter, I'm not going to scold you, but rather heap a thousand blessings on your dear soul which had the strength, by the grace of our Lord, to cast out the enemy who has so cruelly oppressed it. An evil discovered is half healed. From now on, by a thousand eternal praises, may He who has given you this courage be blessed. Don't be surprised at the enemy's attacks; they are his last attempt to get you. And don't be afraid of the apprehensiveness you feel. God willing, you will find comfort as much from divine grace as from the charity of those persons to whom God has entrusted your salvation. No, dearest, don't be afraid of Him who wants to take full possession of your heart, but surrender yourself lovingly into His hands, for He wants to do great things for you. Without forcing or doing violence to you, I hope He will draw you to Himself by bonds of love and gentleness. He held you in His fatherly hand and guided you through the terrible and dangerous narrow passes of your life when you did not want to be completely His. And now, Sister, that you desire ardently only the fulfillment of His divine will in you, don't you think our divine Savior will be very pleased to protect His poor little lamb who had strayed from her gentle shepherd? All you need is a good and generous courage, and soon, my dearest, you will enjoy the sweetness of a holy peace which surpasses all understanding.

I am writing at length to our dear Sister Superior. I won't re-

---

1. This translation is based on a French text, unpublished as yet, provided by Sister Marie-Patricia Burns, editor of the first critical edition of St. Chantal's letters, of which only the first two volumes have appeared. The other unpublished letters will appear in subsequent volumes of this work.

peat here what I am telling her. You must withdraw a bit into solitude to hear what our Lord will tell you on this subject. We shall make a novena here to our blessed Father and offer a general communion. You should talk the matter over in confession. If you weren't so completely drawn by God and determined to abandon yourself totally to Him, I wouldn't advise you to renew your bonds, except under the conditions required to free you from scruples. The priest will help you in this, for this is a matter of doctrine. Have courage, my dearest daughter! Have true confidence in God and you will see His glory in heaven and on earth. You will reap the fruit of the vocation to which His goodness has called you, in spite of yourself.

Goodbye, my dearest, beloved child. I am very eager to hear from you. When everything is settled, let me know. Meanwhile I shall continually pray to God for you so that His good pleasure be accomplished.

I am more than yours in His love. May He be blessed.

The Visitation of Holy Mary was founded in 1610 as a small, quasi-monastic contemplative community. The concerns that occupied its first Superior, Jane de Chantal, were for the most part particular to the first house and its few residents. For the first five or six years of its existence, the Visitation was in the process of acquiring its own self-identity and Jane was learning to govern and to instill in her daughters the particular Salesian spirit. But by 1616 things had changed.

A new phase of Jane de Chantal's life had begun. She had just returned from Lyons and founding the first monastery after Annecy. She had left the very young Marie Jacqueline Favre as superior, and continued to guide her as she took her first steps under fire. The Archbishop of Lyons did not quite understand Francis de Sales's ideal of a community of women consecrated to a life of prayer, without solemn vows, bound only by their love for God which also defined their cloister. Marie Jacqueline was in the delicate position of not offending her bishop, yet remaining faithful to the lifestyle established by Francis at Annecy. Jane suggested how she should act when the archbishop proposed unacceptable changes in the Rule. Mother Jeanne Charlotte de Brechard, although a much more mature woman, was, like Marie Jacqueline, superior of a new foundation, in this case at Moulins. These were the first two off-shoots of the Annecy community. She let both these and other new superiors and novice mistresses act freely, but skillfully reinforced the spirit with which they should carry out their work.

From the superiors of the order she expected an attitude of motherly attentiveness toward all the Visitandines, the kind of care and solicitude for each entrant that a mother might show her own child. While it was required that faults be noted and that advancement in virtue be cultivated, such guidance must never become judgmental and so cause discouragement or intimidation. Sustaining all this maternal caretaking was the very real belief that this most attractive of methods would suit best to draw the sisters into a loving relationship with God. They were to be drawn, attracted to this vocation in a manner that had less to do with rational arguments than with affective response.

LETTERS OF SPIRITUAL DIRECTION

To Mother Marie-Jacqueline Favre
Superior at Lyons

Live ⁺ Jesus!

Annecy, 9 February 1616[1]

What a surprise! M. de Boisy just told me that if I want to write you, my darling, now is a good time because someone will be leaving before dawn; so here I am, before dawn, writing you this quick note. First of all, I must tell you that all your letters delight and please me very much. I can see that God, by His grace and fatherly care, is leading you by the hand and that all you have to do is trust Him, cling to Him, and, under His protection, journey on as humbly and simply as possible. See to it that your little flock advances faithfully, for this is how you can show God your own fidelity. This is why, as I'm always telling you, my very dearest daughter, you must free yourself from too much activity so that, insofar as your duties allow, you can be with your Sisters whenever they are together, to instruct them and encourage them in the performance of their duties, as much by your example as by precept. I find our good and worthy Archbishop's wish on this subject very fair. He is right, believe me, Sister, when he says you have to be both Superior and Mistress. Nevertheless, it is well that you are training our little *cadette* [Sister Marie-Aimée de Blonay] for she has a good mind, though she is a little too reserved in expressing herself, and she is somewhat lazy and given to following her natural inclinations.[2] Still, I hope that with God's help, she will inspire those dear novices more and more every day, both by her good example and by what she has to say as she opens up. She will be a great help to you since you will often be called away. [. . .]

Be at peace about our dearest Péronne-Marie. I never gave a thought to what others said to you, but do not, on that account, hesitate to have the Sisters trained to do the housework, for certainly,

---

1. *Sa Vie et ses oeuvres*, IV, 55–57: Letter XXXVII.
2. "Cadette" in French is a tender, affectionate term, almost a diminutive or nickname often given to a youngest child. In the Visitation M. Aimée de Blonay was often referred to in this way.

we are obliged, in charity, to let Sister get a good rest after she has set the house in order and trained others to do the work.

Dearest, I have such compassion for poor Sister Anne-Marie; undoubtedly, her imagination plays a part in the trouble. If the Archbishop and her confessor show some disapproval of and trim down to size all that she is puffed up about, they should help to cure her. I'll write to her, as to the others, as soon as I have time. Take good care of dear Sister Jeanne-Françoise; try to keep her as happy and busy as possible, and see to it that she eats well and gets enough sleep, for ordinarily an unstable mind is easily carried away by imaginary temptations. So, for that reason, dear Sister, be extremely compassionate, loving, and patient with her. God and time will reveal to us what this is all about.

Day is dawning; I can't think of anything that requires a prompt answer, except to say that, certainly, my darling, God has blessed you in giving you these two great and worthy prelates as fathers. Their remarkable piety is pleasing to God and everyone. I can't tell you how encouraged I am to see how God has united these two men. I believe that this friendship will bring more glory to our Lord than we, with our small minds, can possibly grasp. I feel very satisfied and I praise God for this with all my heart. For a long time now I have prayed that in His goodness, God would bring it about, for I could see clearly that it would benefit everyone, and especially that the Archbishop would receive from it the joy and consolation he so deserves and needs. Our Bishop [Francis de Sales] has high regard for him.

I shall write as much as I can to those dear daughters of mine at my first opportunity. For now, I send them my most affectionate greetings. May our good Jesus fill them with His gentleness, simplicity, and innocence! My respectful and warm remembrance to the Archbishop; best regards also to Father Phillippe, Father de St. Nizier, to your chaplain, and to anyone else you can think of. Don't ever say again to the President [M. Favre] that you never receive letters from me! I never fail to write you whenever I can. Remember me very especially to your dear companions, my daughters and most dear Sisters.

Good morning, dearest love. May Jesus be our all. Amen. Amen.

LETTERS OF SPIRITUAL DIRECTION

To Sister Péronne-Marie de Châtel
at Lyons

[Annecy, 9 February 1616][1]

At last, my dearest daughter, I have your letter before me to answer as best I can. May God inspire me to say what is for His glory and your consolation.

In my judgment, all your reluctance to speak to me, all your aversions and difficulties are for your greater good; so much so that you have an obligation not to act upon such feelings. Every day you should resolve to resist them and fight them. However, should you fall even fifty times a day, never, on any account, should that surprise or worry you. Instead, ever so gently set your heart back in the right direction and practice the opposite virtue, my darling Péronne, all the time speaking words of love and trust to our Lord after you have committed a thousand faults, as much as if you had committed only one. Try to remember what I have so often said to you on this subject, put it into practice for love of God, and know that out of this weakness of yours He will draw forth both His glory and your perfection. Never doubt this. No matter what happens, be gentle and patient with yourself. Once in a while, if you feel particularly weak, without courage, without confidence, force yourself to make affirmations which are the opposite of your feelings. Say with conviction: "My Savior, my All, despite my feelings of misery and distrust, I place all my confidence in You; You are strength for the weak, refuge for the miserable, wealth for the poor; You are indeed my Savior who has always loved sinners." But, dearest, say these or similar words resolutely, without self-pity or tears; then turn your attention to something else. The Almighty will never let you slip from His arms, for He holds you firmly. Don't you see how very gently He comes to your rescue?

I beg you, never forget the teachings you received here and put them into practice wherever and whenever you have occasion to do so. Write to me whenever you like. I shall always answer you promptly from this heart of mine which is all yours. Take care to set a good example, and remember that in order to do this, you should be exact in following the observances, mindful that a well-

---

1. *Sa Vie et ses oeuvres*, IV, 78–81: Letter XLVII.

ordered exterior results from an awareness of God's presence. As far as possible, ask to be relieved of household duties. I've already suggested this to Sister [Favre] who, I think, likes the idea. If she doesn't, then don't ask for this, but it would be well if you could be training those whom you will be assigning to these tasks.

Certainly, my darling love, I am very happy and pleased with the dearly loved Mother there. Everyone tells me how well she is getting along. I am especially happy with all you tell me about her for I know you speak very sincerely. I hope that someday she will be a great servant of God who will do good to many persons. She will have deepened in humility and abandonment: help her, according to your lights, and tell her forthrightly, in all sincerity, whatever seems good both for her and for the community. I know her heart—God knows how much I love her—and I know she will be grateful to you for whatever your conscience prompts you to tell her. I know well, personally, the great help my *coadjutrix* gives me.[2] A coadjutrix is a tremendous help to a Superior who, because she is preoccupied with so many affairs, cannot pay much attention to minor things which, nevertheless, should be corrected.

So, my darling Péronne, once again I am asking you to cheer up our dear Sister and to keep an eye on her health. Without nagging her, do tell her frankly what she should do to stay well. See to it that she follows through on what you tell her. She should yield to your request in this, just as you should obey her quite simply when she orders what she considers necessary for your health. You may correct her humbly, but in such a manner that she will not lose confidence in you and be unhappy; it is better to be too lenient than to work her too hard. And don't be overly anxious about your own problems. Do whatever you can to get well, for it is only your nerves.

I am closing now because I do not feel well. A thousand million greetings to all our darling sisters. I certainly love that little flock with all my heart. I want them to be ever attentive to their Spouse and to live in His presence like pure, sweet, simple and chaste doves. In spirit I embrace them all lovingly and tenderly—everyone, young and old, but, above all the others, my precious beloved Péronne-

---

2. A *coadjutrix* was a sister who acted as an unofficial advisor to the Superior in personal and spiritual matters.

Marie. Our Bishop sends greetings and loves you tenderly also. Live Jesus!

To Mother Jeanne-Charlotte de Bréchard
Superior at Moulins

Annecy, 16 March 1617[1]

May our gentle Jesus fill you with His pure love, my precious darling! We have received all your letters, and you certainly must have received mine. You do well, dearest daughter, to humble your soul under the hand of God and to accept lovingly humiliations and contradictions as suited to our littleness and nothingness. Dearest, while you have the opportunity, I beg you, do try to become truly humble, gentle, and simple, so that your dear heart which I love so tenderly may become a real heart of Jesus. Amen.

I must run, for I have little leisure and my arm and hand are starting to tire and hurt, even though I've just begun to write. I'm not able to do as much as I used to. May God be praised in everything!

Since your sisters are not finding outside the monastery what their hearts desire, dear Sister, may they be satisfied with direction from you. Everywhere we find that it is best to be satisfied with direction from within the house. The Sisters know so well what they have to do; as for the newcomers, you are adequate for them. Follow the way of prudence; you will know how to bring them to a simple trust which is so useful and necessary. Experience teaches us every day that our sisters should be so perfectly simple that they attract young persons by their example.

As for the business with Rome, two points have been granted.[2]

---

1. *Sa Vie et ses oeuvres*, IV, 177–82: Letter XCVI.

2. On July 10, 1616 Francis de Sales wrote to Cardinal Robert Bellarmine in Rome a long letter in which he explains his reasons for asking the Sacred Congregation to grant three permissions which until then were unheard of for monasteries of women:

a. that widows be permitted to spend some time, even several years, in the monastery, following the religious exercises of the sisters, though still wearing their secular clothes, and without any explicit vows or obligations;

b. that women be permitted to come to the monastery to make retreats of a few days' duration, when they have serious, valid reasons for wanting to do so;

c. that the sisters of the Visitation be permitted to recite the Little Office of the BVM instead of the more difficult and lengthy Divine Office. *Oeuvres*, XVII: Letter MCCXIX.

All that is left is the third, the most important one: the Office. We expect to hear about this very soon. They all praise our Rule. And Cardinal Bellarmine wrote to our Bishop that he could leave our Institute as it is, for it is completely conformable to the old Orders. Our Bishop will make a decision as soon as he returns [from Grenoble] a couple of weeks after Easter.

You do well to communicate more frequently with the sisters. This helps to maintain love's gentleness. Dearest, when I said it would be enough if you wrote to me once a month or every six weeks, I still had you here with me and hadn't yet felt the pain of being a long time without hearing from someone who is greatly loved. But, since your absence, sometimes—and even many times—the weeks and months seem very long. True, mail is very expensive, so we have to cut back and only take advantage of opportunities that present themselves, unless there is some pressing matter. We shall ask the Mother at Lyons to watch for favorable occasions, unless we recommend something very specially to her.

My darling, you should not do penances or tell faults, but the professed sisters should. It seems to me that I spoke to them about this in my last letter. Take care that the penances are always performed sincerely. Instead of letting the sisters choose them, you should always arrange them with prudence. Here [at Annecy] some meaningful penances are performed, but rarely. The Rule shows regard for them and recommends that they be continued.

Oh no, you must not fast at all. The rector forbids it; and hasn't experience proved to you that you aren't able to do so? You mustn't speak of this again, any more than we should. We have been forbidden to fast so absolutely that we will never have the nerve to ask to do so again. [. . .] it is absolutely necessary for the whole house that you stay well and strong.

No, my dearest sister, you must not allow the sisters to take unusual postures [in the choir]. They should all turn modestly toward the altar at prayer, and especially during Holy Mass. What impertinence to do otherwise and not look at what we believe to be God and which, in truth, is God! Let's not begin allowing such eccentric customs, I beg you. Since distractions are not voluntary, it's enough if now and then we accuse ourselves of neglecting to push them aside.

Right, it is not wise to reprimand the sisters for every little fault. The mind grows weary of that and gets so used to it that gradually it becomes insensitive to correction. When you need to correct someone, it is better to put it off a little and make the correction in private and with kindness.

No one should be permitted, under pretext of their charge, to go poking about the house. The Superior and the *Procuratrix* have that responsibility, and that's enough.[3] Poor Sister M. Avoye especially does not need that freedom. You must let her finish out her year and help her to keep up her courage. She's terribly sensitive, and yet she's very good. [. . .]

I must close now for I have no more time to write, neither to you nor to our dear sisters whom I greet very warmly through you. I beg them and the dear novices to serve God lovingly, joyously, gently, and humbly, and also by a perfect observance of the Rule.

Goodbye, darling. Greetings to Reverend Father and to your dear mother. May God bless them for their kindness to you. Goodbye, dearest daughter, whom I love entirely and tenderly in our sweet Savior.

To Mother Marie-Jacqueline Favre
Superior at Montferrand

[Annecy, 1617][1]

God will give you His Spirit, dearest daughter, and will Himself be your advisor as regards this good widow. But since you want me to tell you what I think, I pray God to inspire me to tell you rightly. First of all, dearest sister, it occurs to me that generally we shouldn't be too concerned because we sometimes find people who have difficulty understanding our way of life. Certainly, I don't know anyone so stubborn as not to be somewhat moved when they see our spirit of compliance and observance. We must be very tactful about how we get hearts to expand their vision and to love and esteem virtuous living; in this we really imitate our gentle Savior and Master.

---

3. *Procuratrix:* "One of the sisters shall have the care of the whole House as general Procuratrix of the same." (Constitution XXXVI—1626) In other words, this sister is what would be called today the business manager of the house.

1. *Sa Vie et ses oeuvres,* IV, 598–99; Letter CCCLX.

And so, you say, this widow has a strong will, shows great concern about her health, has a mind full of excuses, and a desire to know everything. Heavens, dear, she must be awfully busy! That's why, in my opinion, you should talk at length to her, all the while trying to bring about her healing by gradually showing her her weaknesses, without upsetting her. I would hope that you wouldn't show your displeasure with all this and let her get discouraged. If, however, she is receptive to the light you are trying to bring her, then you can hope, and get her to hope, that through the goodness of God—if she begins to really desire to serve Him by a perfect observance of those words of our Lord: "gentle and humble of heart" which permeate our Rules—she will some day be a great servant of His and promote His glory. But she must resolve firmly and have a clear understanding of her faults; otherwise, she will be disturbed and will disturb the house. Be very kind toward her, show her that you are really concerned for her well-being and let her experience the joy of humble, pliant souls. Give her plenty of time, and have confidence in the advice you receive from Father Rector.

LETTERS TO THE VISITATION
1619—1622

The years 1619–1622 could be termed the Paris years. Much had changed. Jane had founded Bourges in 1618 before being called to Paris by Francis de Sales to found the first monastery in the French capital. She spent these three years far from Francis who was extremely occupied with his diocese in Annecy. He knew her potential and allowed her to test her own strengths in the difficult foundation of Paris. At the same time, she carried on an active correspondence with an increasing number of new and inexperienced superiors and novice mistresses.

The Visitation spirit, Jane de Chantal was convinced, was embodied in the Rule which had been written for the Institute by Francis de Sales. The history of the Rule is complex, yet Jane deemed absolute fidelity to the Rule in all its detail as the one sure touchstone for assimilation into the Visitation charism. Over and over again in her instructions to novices one sees Jane's insistence on absolute fidelity to the Rule. Within the context of any other spiritual milieu, this strict observance might approach legalistic rigidity. However, within a Salesian world, in which liberty of spirit is uppermost, a happy balance between obedience and individual freedom is maintained. Superiors are entrusted with the task of seeing that not only are the Rules diligently followed, but that they are being followed without any experience of constraint or oppression.

To Mother Péronne-Marie de Châtel
Superior at Grenoble

Live + Jesus!

Paris, 22 July 1619[1]

My poor darling! what must you think of my not having written you for so long! It certainly has not been for lack of affection. But there is such terrible turmoil here; besides, we have just moved, have professed one sister and received six novices. All this has kept us quite busy, to say nothing of the continual, daily affairs and inconveniences which around here are endless. I can assure you that I am very happy whenever I hear from you. Oh! if you knew how much you are the precious daughter of my heart!

Don't worry about your way. I see it and I know better than you do that it is a very good one. Trust me in this, I beg you, for God has given me enough light on the matter. Wasn't His infinite goodness our only aim and rest? What further assurance do we need? Dearest, let us stay right there in complete self-effacement. We ought to be content to go on blindly, without knowing or feeling anything; it is enough for us that God is our God, our hope, our desire. I am glad that you will not have much to tell me about your failures when you see me. Once we have humbled ourselves deeply for the faults that God allows us to become aware of in ourselves, we must forget them and go forward. We know you so well; please have no doubt about that. Continue to live at the fine point of your spirit, bearing as calmly as possible those upheavals that you feel in

---

1. *Sa Vie et ses oeuvres*, IV, 329–32: Letter CXCVII.

the inferior part of your soul.[2] Such suffering is, as you say, the paying of a debt and is pleasing to God. Believe me, it is not good for us to be spared from these assaults. [. . .]

I had written the above yesterday when I received your letter. We must show great respect to the confessors and do all we can reasonably to satisfy them, honoring God in them. However, we must not be subject to them in such matters as procuring preachers, having Masses said, receiving holy communion from persons of repute or others whom we may want to please, or to confess ourselves to such persons when it seems suitable. In all such matters you must remain very free, for such decisions rest completely with you. This is what the Rule and our customs specify. And just as we must, with prudence and discernment, make use of the holy liberty that is given us, so we must guard it carefully and jealously, but always with humility. We show these confessors due respect, yet we explain to them very frankly our liberty of action. [. . .]

Good morning, darling. I am all yours in Jesus. Amen.

To the Sisters of the Visitation
at Annecy

[Paris] 30 September [1619][1]
Since our Lord, in His goodness, has gathered our hearts into one, allow me, my dearest Sisters, to greet you all, as a community and individually; for this same Lord will not allow me to greet you in any other way. But what a greeting it is! The very one that our great and worthy Father taught us: LIVE JESUS! Yes, my beloved Sisters and daughters, I say the words with intense delight: LIVE JESUS in our memory, in our will, and in all our actions! Have in your thoughts only Jesus, in your will have only the longing for His love, and in your actions have only obedience and submission to His

---

2. Salesian anthropology assumes that the soul has three parts: inferior, superior illuminated by natural light, and superior illuminated by supernatural light. At the summit of this last was a spiritual faculty known as the "supreme point" or "fine point" of the spirit which did not operate by the light of discourse or reason but only by a simple apprehension of the understanding and a simple orientation of the will by which one acquiesced to faith, hope, and love. It was at the "fine point" that the divine entered the human soul.

1. *Sa Vie et ses oeuvres,* IV, 290–91: Letter CLXXIII.

good pleasure by an exact observance of the Rule, not only in externals, but, much more, in your interior spirit: a spirit of gentle cordiality toward one another, a spirit of recollection of your whole being before our divine Master, and that true, sincere humility which makes us as simple and gentle as lambs. Finally, strive for that loving union of hearts which brings about a holy peace and the kind of blessing we should desire to have in the house of God and His holy Mother.

All this is what I want for you, my dearest daughters, and I urge you to have great devotion to our Lady to whom I beg you to pray for me. Every day of my life I offer all of you to her maternal care. Goodbye, my very dearest Sisters; pray for my needs. Live joyously and serenely with whatever our Lord will do with you and for you. I am yours with all my love.

To Mother Anne-Marie Rosset
Superior at Bourges

Paris, 1620[1]

My dearest daughter, I am writing to the Sisters. You may look at the letter without telling them you have seen it, then moisten the wafer for sealing it and give it to them if you think it wise. You need courage to bear with these petty whims that will soon pass over. No, there is no point in keeping Sister Maurin any longer. Only wait until she shows further signs that her spirit is not suited to our life. I don't think it ever will be. Somehow, God allowed her to receive the habit even though she didn't have the right disposition. That should be a lesson for us and for all the Sisters, never to admit girls who behave in the least way as she did. You can't go wrong if you take counsel of and obey the Archbishop, and you would do well to follow his advice in important matters, as the Rule says, and whenever the rector tells you to, for you should seek his counsel so as not to bother our bishop about trifles. My dearest Sister, as much as possible, consult only these two so that what goes on in the house doesn't get abroad, for it would hurt the reputation of the house if others knew about these little difficulties.

---

1. *Sa Vie et ses oeuvres*, IV, 397–400: Letter CCXLI.

For the love of God, be kind, sincere, trusting, open and communicative with the Sisters, especially with Sister Assistant. And when you find them at times disagreeing with you, consult them simply and bring them around very gently, for in the end they should yield. But, for goodness' sake, dear, win them over through kindness, patience and instruction, asking them to read often our Bishop's conferences, for love wins all. Refer them always to the conferences and to the Rule which teach so perfectly what each of you should do.

Yes, my dear, true charity requires us to forget the faults of others in order not to wish them ill, but not to forget them when this would mean jeopardizing the well-being of a community which depends on the good will and wisdom of those who make up the community. Since that novice knows that you intend to test her, she will be on her guard. But it will be easy to see if she is well-disposed and if God has brought about a change in her. If this is not clear and proven after more than a year, then in no way must there be any bargaining or talk of profession. You should simply tell everything to the Archbishop and the Rector. Don't have any doubts after asking their advice.

Isn't the world hard to figure out! Doesn't it stand to reason that Religious who make the three essential vows under the Rule of St. Augustine be bound by these vows? Is it the manner in which they are pronounced that makes them solemn? Isn't it, rather, the Church's recognition of them that makes them so? And furthermore, do we not declare that it is to God that we make our vows of chastity, obedience and poverty, according to the Rules and Constitutions of this house which are full of references to the obedience due to our ecclesiastical superiors? What can we do except remain at peace and let them talk.

Now I'm afraid that Sister C. Marie is tormenting herself so much about her profession that she is showing clearly her inability to make her vows and confirming the reasons for delaying her profession. Our Bishop sums up in a word all that can be said on the subject: "If she's a good religious, she won't mind waiting." And that's true, for her profession is being delayed only to see if she is humble and pliable. She will show that she is if she acknowledges that she deserves this delay, and if she behaves gently, trusting in God and in the charity of the Sisters.

I hope that my letter will help the Sisters look into themselves, and also stay within the limits of the Rule, for happiness is found in the religious community when neither the Superior nor the Sisters stray from the Rule. Always remind the Sisters of this and gently point out to them the uselessness of private judgment. For the love of God, my darling, govern in such a way that in your house there may be but one heart and one will, and may that be the will of God lived out in a gentle manner.

I am called away so I must close now. Say goodbye to my very dear nephew to whom I wanted to write but couldn't.[2] A thousand greetings also to everyone and to Madame de Jars.

To Mother Paule-Jéronyme de Monthoux
Superior at Nevers

[Paris, 11 April 1621][1]

I had to let the great and holy days pass without writing to you. I beg God to be our joy forever, and I beg you, my dearest daughter, never to let yourself slip into sadness for any reason at all, for that would disturb your community which should be led with great gentleness.

I am terribly sorry to hear that you are on bad terms with dear Sister N***. I'm afraid the sisters will notice, and that she herself will talk about it outside, which would be harmful. But, nevertheless, we must trust divine Providence and rest in it peacefully because all our fears and gloom will only spoil everything and make us sad. Dearest, you take these little contradictions too much to heart; you shouldn't even notice most of these things. If I had corrected a sister once for some fault that doesn't affect the spirit of the house very much, and if I saw that this reproof made her sad, I wouldn't talk about it any more except privately, and by way of a request, and only if I saw that she was open to the correction. You know, my dearest, we must deal with our sisters as we would with our companions, that is, with the older sisters and those given to us as helpers in doing God's work, for, in truth, they are our partners. What could we do by ourselves!

---

2. Jacques de Neufchèzes, later Bishop of Chalon-sur-Saône.
1. *Sa Vie et ses oeuvres*, V, 1–3: Letter CCCLXII.

This is how we should consider them, and when they commit some fault or other, rather than reprimand them sternly, we should correct them privately in a gentle, kindly manner. In fact, this is how we should treat all our Sisters. Our corrections should always be firm and serious, yet they should be made gently and humbly, never sharply.

My dear, I think God wanted me to write this, for I hadn't thought about it beforehand, as it is off the subject of the misunderstanding between you and that Sister. There is much missing in her attitude, so I have resolved to have her and her companion go elsewhere and to bring you Sister M. Constance who is a truly virtuous person. But don't let on about this. Win her by gentleness, but without giving in to her whims which are contrary to the spirit of your house. Patience, dear! I am very pleased that you aren't becoming discouraged. I realize that you are somewhat brusque by nature. Fight against that and try, with God's help, to govern gently and graciously. You will see that all the Sisters advance more joyously and faithfully. I have greatly recommended you to our Lord during these special days, dearest daughter, you and your little flock whom I greet affectionately.

To Mother Paule-Jéronyme de Monthoux
Superior at Nevers

[Paris] 5 July 1621[1]

Indeed! It's true, dearest daughter, that Sister F. Elisabeth is wrong, for a religious should never prefer a particular good over the general, and still less should she be making plans, under any pretext whatever, without her superior's knowledge. But have patience this time; help her to learn from this fault so that she won't commit it again. Often God allows such things to happen in order to teach us to avoid graver failings, and also, dear, to let us learn from experience that we must test and know the vocation of young women before receiving them. In this lies the fruit to be gained from this experience, so don't say that you aren't capable in your charge. You mustn't talk like that. We should humble ourselves under God's will

---

1. *Sa Vie et ses oeuvres*, IV, 552–55: Letter CCCXXXV.

and do whatever good He gives us the light to see, according to the instructions we find in our Rules, the conferences, and similar works.

Before receiving young women, I would like you to have them examined by some good religious—if possible by the Jesuit fathers who are your extraordinary confessors. Of all the actions for which you are responsible, this is the one that you must perform with the utmost care because it is the most important, and the well-being of the house depends on it. So have this young woman examined by some spiritual person, by a Jesuit, for they [Jesuits] are solid and best for our spirit. Tell him, before he speaks to her, all that you know about her; and after he has seen her, take his advice. Then, based on that, you and the Sisters will make a better decision. Before receiving a young woman, you should discern if she has a firm, constant desire for the vocation. If you trust me, you will do what I have just suggested before allowing them to enter the novitiate or giving them the habit or professing them. You will then be better off. I have nothing else to say on the subject, although in conscience I must add that in what concerns the one about whom you have spoken, in no way would I give her the habit, and I would do all I could to see if she really intends to embrace the religious life. This is where the examination of the Jesuit father can help you. [. . .]

God be praised for what you tell me about the young woman from Orléans. Please, do make good choices of candidates and do not hesitate in the least to send them away if they are not suitable. Don't worry about M. Bonsidat's daughter, and leave her free, because as long as she is living in the house peacefully, it would be better not to dismiss her against her will and that of her parents. And yet, in no way should you consider professing her unless God performs a miracle. If the blind girl can meet the spiritual requirements, I would receive her. To have just one like her is nothing, and the house could take on the responsibility of keeping her in the habit, without professing her, if her blindness would be an impediment to her profession.

Dearest, don't be surprised that our dear Father doesn't write to you; he just doesn't have time. The Sisters should be told that there is no need to ask him about matters on which I know his thought and which I can take care of. He won't answer because there is no way that he could handle so many requests.

We have to recall a couple of Sisters from Moulins, but don't talk about it. I should like to know how many you will be two months from now, for if you take so many all at once, you can't possibly give them an adequate formation. [. . .]

You must cut short all useless talking and teach these Sisters not to waste time on such nonsense; you must lead them to exact obedience. Be careful not to open the door of your house through such trifles. In all humility, remain firm in this. That priest is a good man, but is still young and impulsive. You should, if possible, get help from Father Rector. They [the Jesuits] are always the best. Darling, do walk steadfastly but humbly in the way by which God is leading you, and where He has placed you. Without wavering, hold on to the Rule and to the counsels given us in the conferences; read them often and have your Sisters read them too.

Every month I have one or two of the conferences read at table. Thanks be to God, the family [community] is doing well here.

Good night. Please give my respectful salutation to the Bishop and to your good spiritual father. Warmest greetings to all our dear Sisters. You know how much I am yours.

To Mother Marie-Madeleine de Mouxy
Superior at Belley

[Dijon] 19 September 1622[1]

God be praised eternally, my dearest daughter, for now you are Mother! I beg His divine goodness to give you the spirit that is proper to spiritual mothers who, with a tender and cordial love, see to the advancement of souls, and who are never overeager, especially about temporal matters. The trust they place in the providence and love of their Spouse relieves them of all kinds of anxieties and makes them confident that He will see to all their needs, provided that they try to please Him by a perfect observance and trust in His goodness. That's the disposition I want for you, dearest; I can assure you that it will bring you many blessings. If it were necessary, I would even swear to you that if you do what I have just recommended, you will have an abundance of everything.

---

1. *Sa Vie et ses oeuvres*, V, 57–58: Letter CCCXCVIII.

We have had so much experience with souls who abandon themselves to the loving providence of God, who surrender to Him all their concerns, and who care about nothing except pleasing Him by a faithful observance, that we could never have any doubt about it and, in fact, have difficulty in imagining the contrary. Oh, I know perfectly well, dear, that you have always been attracted to this way; follow it, my dearest daughter, with holy joy.

I send loving greetings to all the Sisters, especially to you, very dear Sister, for I am all yours.

Please pray, and ask the Sisters to pray, for my daughter who needs prayers.

LETTERS TO THE VISITATION
1623—1641

As foundations spread swiftly, Jane continued her ministry to superiors, novice mistresses and other Sisters. Her situation changed dramatically after the death of Francis de Sales in 1622. She began to shoulder alone the full responsibility for the rapidly growing order. Her prime concern was its consolidation. Juridical status had been acquired in 1618 when the new congregation was erected into a religious order. But she felt it necessary, in 1624, to call a meeting of the first Mothers and Sisters who had known Francis personally, to establish the rules and customs on a solid basis. And the means of maintaining union and conformity among the monasteries would haunt her until her death.

For her Sisters the hopeful foundress painted an ideal representation of a Visitation community: the superiors, perfectly surrendered to the spirit of the Institute as expressed in its Rules, with great sisterly affection and maternal attentiveness would lead and guide a household of women likewise united in heart and mind in a spirit of abundant "douceur." In practice, the historical record often resembles more a canvas in progress than a finished work. Yet Jane de Chantal had a genius for spiritual direction which made that continuing work a viable and commendable one.

In her more mature years Jane counseled superiors and Sisters with the same affection—although sometimes there is less spontaneity in its expression—understanding and firmness. Her letters

*frequently betray her fatigue. But nothing quells her ardent quest
for God for herself and those confided to her care.*

To Sister Anne-Marie Rosset
Assistant and Novice Mistress at Dijon

Live ⁺ Jesus!

[Annecy, 1623][1]

God knows the pain I feel in my heart over the misunderstanding that exists in your house. I ask Him to take it in hand. In the end, if a reconciliation doesn't occur, you will have to find a way of sending away the sister who is the cause of it all. No good ever comes from the sisters' wanting to control the Superior; if they were humble and submissive, all would go well. Indeed, my very dear Sister, she who governs there has done so very successfully elsewhere, and this ought to keep the Sisters at peace. Help them to understand this as far as you can so that there may be humble and cordial submission in the house. Help Sister N*** to unite herself to her Superior and to be sincerely open with her. Oh! is this behavior the way to honor the memory of him who so often recommended to us peace and union! What a dangerous temptation! May God, in His goodness, straighten this out! And we shall do what we can, with His help, to remedy the situation.

Now back to you. For my part, I would have no problem in professing Sister A.M., for she shows good will, and fails only through forgetfulness. I can't get over how that sister dares to harass her; what nerve! Would to God she were somewhere else. I think that from now on the Sisters should be asked to give their opinion only after they have left the novitiate.

To be sure, I am convinced, and experience has taught me, that nothing so wins souls as gentleness and cordiality. I beg you, dearest, follow this method, for it is the spirit of our blessed Father. Curtness in words or actions only hardens hearts and depresses them, whereas gentleness encourages them and makes them receptive. I think that in no way should the time planned for the reception

---

1. *Sa Vie et ses oeuvres*, V, 175–77: Letter CDLXIX.

of young women be changed; you should wait a year or so for the little niece of Sister de Vigny, though you may go on instructing her. But I shall be seeing her, and I think she is so reasonable that she will make the adjustment.

To return now to the question of Sister N***. I don't say that she should be treated with affection, but cordially and gently; by that I mean without coldness in words or actions. I suggest the same, and even more strongly, in the case of Sister Anne Jacqueline who has to be handled playfully. She is still very much a child and wouldn't have the stomach for eating solid meat, so to speak, and whoever would give her some would ruin her. She has to be led slowly and tenderly, and be brought to observe silence and other obediences, but not as yet to perform penances and mortifications. You see, my dear, we have to cultivate in these young, delicate souls lots of vigor, cheerfulness, and joy, and thus bring them to want those things they would fear or dread if they were led in any other manner.

Dearest, you must be faithful to ask for relief, and be more frank, warm, open and sincere with Mother, speaking to her with an open heart about everything, quite freely. In this way, my dear, and for love of God, you will be giving to our blessed Father the glory of seeing you live according to his spirit of gentleness and trust, even as you bring others to do the same.[2]

Pray for me, and relieve my heart by telling me there is perfect mutual understanding among you. It is under such circumstances that we witness to the purity of our love and serve God according to His liking, practicing virtues for His glory and not our satisfaction.

You know that I am yours unreservedly.

God be praised!

To the Superior at Digne

Annecy, 1625[1]

My very dear daughter,

In the name of our Divine Savior, I beg you, and urge you, to govern according to His Spirit and that of our vocation, which is a

---

2. "Blessed Father" refers to Francis de Sales. He died in December 1622.
1. *Sa Vie et ses oeuvres*, V, 513–14: Letter DCLXXII.

humble, gentle spirit, supportive and considerate of all. In order to govern in this manner, my dear, you must not act according to the willfulness of your own nature, nor according to your inclination to austerity. What we are asking of you, my dearest daughter, and without further delay, please, is to be most gentle in spirit, word and action, and to treat your own body and those of your Sisters better than you have been doing.

What good will it do to put bread on the table when they don't have teeth to chew it or stomachs to digest it? So, I urge you once again not to let us hear any more talk about your harshness and severity with the Sisters and yourself. Your minds and bodies will be wrecked if you stubbornly refuse to accept humbly what we are saying and begging you to do in the name of God and of our blessed Father. He greatly feared such harshness in his Institute, which he established for those who are delicate and where he wanted a spirit of humility and gentleness to reign. This is what he so recommended everywhere.

Sister, the sincere affection I have for you prompts me to write to you in this way for I am confident that you will not ignore my request nor the humble lessons I have given you before God and in His name. I beg Him to help all of you accomplish what I tell you. I am all yours, and I send greetings to all the Sisters and earnestly ask for their prayers.

God be praised!

To Sister Anne-Catherine de Sautereau
Novice Mistress at Grenoble

Annecy, c. 12 December 1626[1]

My dearest daughter,

As you wished, and in God's presence, I shall tell you what His goodness will inspire me to say to you, for I ask Him to help me. First of all, it seems to me, my dear Sister, that you should try to make your own devotion, and that of your novices, generous, noble, straightforward, and sincere. Try to foster that spirit in all those whom God will ever commit to your care—a spirit

---

1. *Sa Vie et ses oeuvres*, V, 546–47: Letter DCXCI.

founded on that deep humility which results in sincere obedience, sweet charity which supports and excuses all, and an innocent, guileless simplicity which makes us even-tempered and friendly toward everyone.

From there, my dearest daughter, move on to a total surrender of yourself into the hands of our good God, so that, insofar as you can, you may help your own dear soul and those you are guiding, to be free of all that is not God. May these souls have such a pure, upright intention that they do not waste time worrying about created things—their friends, their appearance, their speech. Without stopping at such considerations or at any other obstacle they may meet along the way, may they go forward on the road to perfection by the exact observances of the Institute, seeing in all things only the sacred face of God, that is, His good pleasure. This way is very narrow, my dear Sister, but it is solid, short, simple and sure, and soon leads the soul to its goal: total union with God. Let us follow this way faithfully. It certainly precludes multiplicity and leads us to that unity which alone is necessary. I know you are drawn to this happiness, so pursue it, and rest quietly on the breast of divine Providence. Those souls who have put aside all ambition except that of pleasing God alone should remain peaceful in this holy tabernacle.

My dearest Sister, Abraham (how I love this patriarch!) left his country and his family in order to obey God; but the only Son of God accomplished the will of His heavenly Father by working in the country of His birth. So be content, dear, to imitate the Lord, for nothing can equal His perfection. Don't look elsewhere, but carefully try to accomplish lovingly and with good heart all the tasks that Providence and obedience place in your hands. The principal exercises of the novitiate are mortification and prayer.

This is enough—and perhaps too much—for me to be telling a soul who is already enlightened and led by God. I beg Him in His goodness to guide you to perfection in His most pure love. My soul cherishes yours more than I can say; be absolutely assured of this, and pray for her who is yours unreservedly.

God be praised! Amen.

LETTERS OF SPIRITUAL DIRECTION

To Sister Anne-Marie de Lage de Puylaurens
Assistant and Novice Mistress at Bourges

[Annecy, 1626][1]

My very dear daughter,
God has certainly blessed you by giving you the light and the strength to pull away from the dangerous temptation you have had against your very fine, virtuous Mother. The evil spirit did that; he would like to upset both of you by this disunion. May God who set you free from this evil be praised! Be on your guard, dearest, never to fall into it again. Keep yourself ever and invariably united both to your written Rule and to the living one who is your Superior. Even if someday God should permit that you have a very imperfect Superior, remain steadfast. You will find the Spirit of God in her, so do not look for anything else. Surely you will never lose Him if you follow this way and remain faithful to your duty.

True, my very dear Sister, your timidity stems from self-love. Try, for the love of God, to overcome your inclinations and live, as your Rule recommends, according to reason and the will of God. If you don't decide to do this yourself, no one can help you; others may tell you what to do, but nobody can do it for you. Courage then, darling. God asks this of you and calls you to a high perfection. Correspond faithfully by the exact observance of your Institute, for this is your true way and the only one by which you can reach such perfection. Do all this with the holy fervor of a most humble, gentle and simple spirit.

I am pleased to know that you are cutting back on all your self-scrutiny and that you are more peaceful about your desire to make progress. Such eagerness comes from self-love. Always be on your guard against this, I beg you, and in order to unite yourself to God, get into the habit of seeking His will in all things.

Nothing has changed in the Ceremonial. You may take from the Custom Book and the Spiritual Directory whatever you think fit for your novices whom I greet very affectionately. As for you whom my heart loves with a special, warm affection, I encourage you to be kind and generous.

---

1. *Sa Vie et ses oeuvres*, V, 633–34: Letter DCCXXXVIII.

LETTERS OF SPIRITUAL DIRECTION

To a Superior

Annecy, after 1623[1]

Take care, dearest daughter, not to dismiss the novice with the pulmonary disorder. What would our blessed Father say? "But she will die!" you reply. Well, wouldn't she die in the world, and wouldn't she be happy to die as a spouse of Jesus Christ? There is a postulant here at Annecy with the same illness, but she certainly is not being sent away because of that. "It's flesh and blood that gives such advice," our blessed Father used to say. He never wanted candidates to be sent away because of any physical infirmity unless they had a contagious disease. So let us be unyielding in this matter, holding on to what we have received from our holy Founder. I know this is what you really want to do.

I promise you, I do not choose the most capable or most virtuous Sisters to be superiors, but rather those who I see have the God-given talent of governing well. I have put to the test those who are intelligent, attractive in the eyes of the world, and devout, as well as those who are genuinely holy. I found that neither kind was successful unless they knew how to govern or had the true humility, prudence, and sincerity that the Institute calls for. But if they had these virtues, even if they had other imperfections which I saw they were trying to overcome, I didn't hesitate to put them in charge. This is what our holy Father did, with the hope that God would bless them. Still, he did look at the external talents of those whom we thought of making superiors, so that, as he put it, they might satisfy and attract secular persons.

Your answer to the Archbishop is fine, except that instead of submitting to an infringement of this point in the Constitution if he ordered it, you should have asked him very humbly to let you continue the practice which obliges you to show your accounts to the ecclesiastical superior every year when he asks to see them, or to the one making the visitation, but not to anyone else. This is an obligation of the Rule.

My dearest Sister, we must, in all humility, resolve to maintain our observances; otherwise, if we break down on one point, then all the rest will be dissipated. Let us be obedient toward our ecclesi-

---

1. *Sa Vie et ses oeuvres*, VI, 47–49: Letter DCCLXXXIV.

astical superiors in everything that they ask as long as it is not contrary to our Institute; but let us always be faithful to our Founder's recommendations. Our ecclesiastical superiors are there only to see that we observe our Rule, not to destroy it. What would happen if each one of these superiors wanted to make changes? What would happen to the Visitation? It would soon look very different. Dearest, let us be constant in our fidelity; once small irregularities creep in, the big ones follow. Our holy Founder so often advised us not to fail in any detail or soon we would lose everything.

I am writing to our houses to encourage them to persevere in and maintain their holy union. I am doing and saying what my conscience dictates and what I know or feel to be the intention of our blessed Father. Beyond that, I leave the care of it all to Divine Providence. As for people making fun of us—that won't last, for I'm not worthy of such suffering. But we should be careful not to bring on ridicule ourselves.

I greet all your dear daughters, but especially the older Sisters. May God keep each of us according to His heart. Yours, etc. . . .

To Mother Marie-Adrienne Fichet
Superior at Rumilly

[Annecy, 1627][1]

(The first lines are illegible) . . . As for your temptations, pay no attention to them, and do whatever is necessary to keep your mind off them. These efforts, though forceful, must reflect moderation. You see, dear, the way by which you are being led is at once mild yet strong and solid. God hides the prize of eternal glory in our mortifications and the victory over ourselves which we always strive for with gentleness. Otherwise, your impulsiveness would cause you, and others, to suffer. In the end, *gentleness plays a large part in the way we govern.* Every day I notice that kindness, gentleness, and support, as well as generosity, can do so much for souls. You know that God has given me a very special love for your house, and it seems to me that it is like a dormitory or annex of Annecy.

So people are talking, are they, saying that your house is un-

1. *Sa Vie et ses oeuvres*, VI, 49–51: Letter DCCLXXXV.

lucky because you've had so much misfortune.[2] That's the language of the world! God speaks quite a different one. It is a great mark of His blessing when a house is stricken with some tribulation or other which does not offend Him, for instance, the death of the Sisters. On the contrary, He is glorified by this sorrow because these dear souls have gone to heaven to praise Him forever.

Furthermore, be more and more careful that your corrections are not too harsh, for that would be neither beneficial nor useful. Those who are responsible for others cannot always say with St. Paul [sic]: "I am innocent of your blood," that is, of the faults his people were committing. But we, on the other hand, are usually guilty, as much for the faults of others as for our own, either because we over-corrected or tolerated too much, or else, corrected too harshly or neglected to correct; or because we failed to include in our correction the sweetness of holy charity.

Dearest, here is the money for the new habit which you sent me, and please, send me back the one which our Sisters kept. There is nothing that bothers me more than their attachment to these external signs of imaginary holiness in me. These are traps which the devil puts in my way to make me stumble into the bottomless pit of pride. I am already weak enough, and enough of a stumbling-block to myself, without anyone adding another. So I beg all of you not to be an occasion of such temptation for me. If anyone has anything belonging to me, do me the kindness of burning it. If only our Sisters would treat me as I deserve to be treated before God, then I would have some hope of becoming, through these humiliations, what they imagine me to be. But to be presenting me with continual temptations to vanity is intolerable. This brings sadness to my heart and tears to my eyes as I tell it to you.

Dear N. and N. seem to be happy to have to bear so many external humiliations. For this, I love them even more and believe them to be even greater in the sight of God whose judgment is so different from ours. Yours. . . .

---

2. At this time, 1627, many sisters in the young, struggling community of Rumilly (founded on September 29, 1625) were stricken by long, dangerous illnesses. Some townspeople who were against the foundation were saying that all this bad luck was a sign of God's displeasure.

To Mother Marie-Aimée de Rabutin
Superior at Thonon

[Annecy, 1639][1]

My dearest daughter,

[. . .] Concerning the lack of gentleness that you show your Sisters when they bother you for trifles, you know that you must not behave in this way since the Superior has a duty to listen to and answer all who wish to speak to her. After you have listened to the Sisters, you may point out to them that what they say is either trivial or useless, but you must not guard your privacy so jealously that the Sisters don't dare approach you except for very important matters.

I don't foresee any occasion to go to see you. Beside the fact that your house doesn't need my presence, it wouldn't be right for me to leave here so abruptly when I have already been gone so long. Besides, we must be careful not to go out without real necessity. There are persons who really keep an eye on us in this matter. Once I have said what I think, I shall be ready to obey. The Bishop of Geneva is due to come very soon and he will be going to see you. You can tell him then your need either to have me come to your house or to come here yourself. You can imagine what joy it would be for me to see you! But if he does not think it wise, then patience— two years will quickly pass.

You do well to speak to all your Sisters in community about whatever you feel they need to hear, as you have done, for instance, about religious modesty in matters like eating and drinking. But it's better not to be too specific for you could upset those who committed the faults you are mentioning, as would be the case in the example you gave me. It's much better to point out such faults in private.

About those souls who are somewhat difficult: I can't tell you anything more on the subject. You'll have to handle them according to whatever light God gives you, and not torment yourself so much by wondering if you're the cause of their failures. Please, don't tell me about this all over again, and don't think about it so much. Must you continue to be your own cross? I can see that no matter which

---

1. *Sa Vie et ses oeuvres*, VII, 154–156: Letter MCCXII.

way God leads you, you change everything into bitterness and trouble for yourself by constantly examining yourself and brooding over everything. For the love of God, stop behaving like this. You gave your whole being to God and surrendered yourself to His care, so stay that way and replace all this self-scrutiny with a pure and simple glance at His goodness. In that glance, let all your fears and introspections die. I can't help repeating this and telling you that, really, if you don't stop being so hard on yourself, forever in despair over all your problems, I won't answer you again, for I see you wallowing in your misery and choosing to make yourself a martyr.

To Mother Marie-Jacqueline Favre
at the second monastery of Paris

[Annecy, 1634][1]

My *grande fille*, so specially loved,[2]

Your letter touched my heart deeply for you can't imagine how sensitive I am to everything that concerns you. Love draws to my heart all the feelings contained in yours. Oh, my darling, God's plans for you are so wonderful! True, *His ways are painful to nature, but I am sure that you will experience them as sweeter than honey in the depths of your heart.* You do well to keep your eyes fastened on God's tremendous goodness! He will take you out of this furnace pure as gold taken from the crucible. When all is said, *the richness of the soul lies in its being able to suffer much, in peace and love.* If I were what I should be, I wouldn't long for any other happiness.

So you are still sick! I can assure you, dearest, that the Bishop of Geneva did not intend that your health, which is certainly very precious to him, should be exposed to any risks. I think it would be better not to speak of your departure until the right time has come and you can do so unobtrusively and without fuss.

I believe that God has been taking care of things, and that He permitted these obstacles so that His plans, as well as the wish of our blessed Father, would be fulfilled. Anyway, it is time for you

---

1. *Sa Vie et ses oeuvres*, VII, 419–20: Letter MCCCLIII.
2. "Grande fille" is a tender, intimate term given to a first-born daughter. Jane used it for M. Jacqueline Favre, one of the two Visitandines who established the original Annecy foundation with her.

to leave Paris and to return here with the honor and propriety befitting the kind of person God willed you to be. I hope that all will succeed for the sake of His glory and your happiness. In His providence, God will lead you where He has destined you to go. My dearest daughter, I beg you to find joy in your heart. Be as sure of my heart as of your very own, for I tell you, in the presence of God and the angels, that I belong as much to you as I do to myself. The love God has given me for you is most special, faithful and tenderly maternal. I wouldn't spare my own life for your peace and joy. God knows that what I say is true, and that I am yours, etc. . . . .

To a Visitandine

Annecy[1]

I have so much confidence in the kindness of your heart that I think you will receive this note graciously, even though I'm late. You're right, my dear, to say that our beloved Sister [Favre] is a living rule, and I'm comforted to hear of the happiness you had in taking care of her during her illness. It's at such times that real virtue is tested. Praise God who gave her such solid virtue.

You tell me, dear, that you experience God's infinite goodness so intimately present in your soul that you are scarcely aware of yourself. May His divine mercies be ever blessed! This is a great grace. To feel God's presence so intimately and powerfully in oneself that one is no longer aware of self is to have that little drop of water, self, dissolve in the Ocean of Divinity. How blessed are the souls who are so lost in God, for they can truly say with all the ardor of St. Paul: "I live now, no longer I, but Jesus Christ lives in me!" But, you tell me, it's only your soul that attains this intimate union and that you have to do violence to yourself to get your other faculties to move in that direction. Don't be surprised at this, for they're not capable on their own of attaining such simple, profound union. God Himself will calm them when it is expedient to do so. Passions that are stirred up but not desired or followed are for us so many exercises of virtue. Your love for your neighbor is pure since it is totally in God and for Him. Let yourself be guided by obedience

---

1. *Sa Vie et ses oeuvres*, VII, 421–22: Letter MCCCLIV.

as God will lead you. He asks you for absolute dependence on His will and a pure intention. Therefore, you must rid yourself of all that is not God.

I'm glad to see that your thirst for knowledge is satisfied within the Institute. Everything is there, my dearest daughter, I mean, the most excellent means of reaching high perfection. May God grant you the grace of not seeking it elsewhere, and may He fill your dear soul with His most pure and holy love in which I am all yours, with all my heart.

To Mother Claude-Marie d'Auvaine
at Pont-à-Mousson

Annecy, 15 April 1638[1]

My very dear daughter,

May our gentle, kind Savior always be our comfort and your heart's only love! Your letter touched me very much, my dearest daughter, because I saw in it the good condition of your dear community. For this I thank God with all my heart! These Sisters are so fortunate to be advancing like this, peacefully and simply in their holy vocation, without much outside communication. I praise and thank our Divine Savior for having been pleased to give this disposition to almost all the Sisters of the Visitation; it is a good sign if one possesses this spirit. So I have no other wish for our dearest Sisters, your daughters, than to continue to love profound humility and gentleness of heart, which are the two dear virtues of the Institute.

[. . .] May God continue to bless this dear family, and especially you, whom I see filled with holy intentions and resolutions drawn from the writings of our Founder. This teaching truly nourishes our souls; may God always grant us the grace to practice it faithfully. You will experience the usefulness of this [practice] more and more. I'm sure you will follow it more exactly, especially total dependence on and confidence in divine Providence. O my dearest Sister, our self-sufficiency and capabilities are so partial and weak if they are not sustained and guided by God, who is the source of

---

1. Unpublished letter.

all the good He accomplishes. May we adore Him eternally! His graces are so great!

Dearest daughter, I beg you, as well as all our Sisters whom I greet affectionately through you, to remember me often to God's goodness.

[. . .] My very dear Sister, I ask God to fill us with His holy love, in which I am, with all my heart, your very humble and unworthy sister and servant in our Lord.

To Mother Madeleine-Elisabeth de Lucinges
at Turin

[Annecy, 23 September 1639][1]

My dearest daughter,

The other day I received your letters written on the feast of St. Augustine, in which I see you are still having difficulties with Sister Assistant. Really, Sister, I can't help but fear that this is a preoccupation and temptation coming from the evil spirit who wants to disturb your dear heart, taking from it the gentleness you should be showing your Sisters who are, in fact, so good and so eager to please you. To make matters worse, they themselves know that you are not pleased with them; yet, I see that their whole desire is to please you.

It seems to me that what you wrote me about their saying "Mother, you should do this or that" is not disrespectful. I know very well that our Sisters are always telling me what I should or should not do, and similar things—some of which are more important where respect is concerned—but I certainly don't pay attention to that, and wouldn't want them to either, for those little marks of respect in words and actions that are observed in the world are of no importance among us; personally, I couldn't stand them. I see our Sisters giving me their advice and speaking to me as freely and in the same way that they would speak to an officer [of the house], except that they use the little marks of respect that are prescribed for us, like kissing the hand. Among us, true respect is found in love, confidence, and obedience. If they [the Sisters] failed to obey, certainly, my dearest Sister, we would have to reprimand them and

---

1. Unpublished letter.

correct them in a maternal manner, and support and love them. You are their Mother and you should rid yourself of all those petty, narrow-minded impressions and govern with a very expansive heart, in freedom and good faith, living with them in great and sincere liberty.

I told you in my earlier letters that I see you have not yet taken in all that I have been able to tell you. In brief, my very dear daughter, go forward very simply and broadmindedly, have the Sisters do the same, and keep your own spirit and theirs content. You have every reason to do so, for I see that God continues to grant you His special favors and gives your dear soul an ever greater disposition to love and adore His most holy will in all things. May His goodness be eternally blessed!

I have already written you what I think concerning the novitiate. Do in this according to the light God gives you, for we must seek and follow it in everything, rather than our own feelings or inclinations. You are, through God's Providence, Mother and Superior of both the novices and the professed Sisters in that house. Govern them so well and with so much love and care that God will thus be glorified by the progress and perfection of souls and especially of yours. [. . .]

To a Visitation Community

[no date][1]

Here I am back again to greet my very dear daughters whom I love with all my heart. You are, I hope, always striving more earnestly to rid yourselves of all that is displeasing to your sovereign Spouse and to acquire those virtues which please Him. Oh, my dearest Sisters, how deeply is this wish engraved in my heart! What would I not do or suffer to obtain for you a perfect observance of our holy Rules, the kind of observance you promised and vowed to our Lord who now asks you to keep your word. Dear Sisters, I would gladly give my very life to obtain this happiness for you. I

---

1. *Sa Vie et ses oeuvres*, VII, 559–61: Letter MCDXLI.

say this with such intense feeling that my whole soul is filled with this desire on your behalf, if such were God's good pleasure for you.

So, courage, dear ones. May all of you together, and each one in particular, work at this and never grow slack. May you all live in harmony with one heart and mind in God. Do not wish for anything except what your superiors and your Sisters ask of you. Show a childlike trust and gentleness toward one another, supporting each one in mutual charity. Never be astonished at the faults of the community or of any individual Sister, for to be shocked at our Sisters' faults, to pick them apart, examine them, to get all upset about them is the sign of a narrowmindedness which has no insight into human frailty, and very little charity or forbearance. That is why those who are inclined to be so righteous should close their eyes to what is going on around them and remind themselves constantly that charity does not go looking for evil, and when she does come upon it, she looks the other way and excuses those who commit it. This should be our attitude toward our Sisters who are our companions.

As regards submission to your superiors, I refer you to the constitution on obedience: there is to be no criticizing of our superiors or censure of the conduct of those whom God has given us. Never let this happen among you, my dearest daughters, for it offends God too much! Be simple and perfectly open toward all. Accept lovingly to be admonished and corrected, and never complain, murmur, or blame others.

In the name of God, beloved daughters, take my advice, for I speak to you in God's presence and with a most caring, maternal affection.

Do not take me lightly but profit by what I am saying. I repeat with all my strength: be kind to one another, and request one another's opinions. Do not criticize, and, I beg you, interpret everything positively. If you have some difficulty in overcoming your inclinations, look at our Divine Savior in the struggles He endured throughout His life in order to obtain glory for you. If you imitate Him in these little trials of yours and make His divine will rule in you, He will fill you with every blessing, especially with His peace which surpasses all understanding and is the ultimate possession of every person of good will. And lastly, He will fill you with His eternal glory. My very dear Sisters, how worthy of our human efforts are these graces! Let us work to this end with courage. I urge you to this once again, for the love of our Savior and by His precious blood, and with the deep affection of my heart which is all yours in Jesus.

To a Visitandine

[no date][1]

My very dear daughter,

Although I have never met you, I know you and love you very much. Your letter showed me very clearly the state of your soul and the source of its pain and perplexity, which is your overeagerness to attain the true happiness you desire, and your lack of patience and docility to the will of Him who alone can grant it to you. Therefore, if you really want to acquire the spirit of your vocation, you will have to correct this overeagerness. Do everything you are taught in a spirit of gentleness and fidelity in order to reach the goal toward which you are being guided, cutting short all thought of attaining it except in God's good time. It seems to me that you are not satisfied with doing those acts required for your perfection, but that you want to feel and know that you are doing them. You must put an end to that and be content with telling God, without any feeling, "Lord, with all my heart I desire to practice such and such virtue just to please You." Then, set to work, although without feeling, and lovingly resolve to serve God in this way, desiring nothing more. If you do this, you will soon find yourself in that state of tranquility and peace which is so necessary for souls who wish to live virtuously, according to the spirit, and not according to their own inclinations and judgments.

This is what I see to be necessary for your peace of mind and spiritual advancement. May God fill each one of us with Himself, and may He grant you the grace of putting into practice all that she who has the obligation to guide you will advise. I am yours with love.

---

1. *Sa Vie et ses oeuvres*, VIII, 432–34: Letter MDCCXC.

LETTERS OF SPIRITUAL DIRECTION

To Mother Marie-Aimée de Rabutin
Superior at Thonon

[Annecy] 26 June 1641[1]

My very dear daughter,

I bless God who gives you the courage to bear your burden cheerfully, despite the aversion you feel. It becomes clearer all the time that our Lord has destined you to be there for the good and happiness of that house. [. . .]

Do well what I advised you some time ago: help souls along very gently by word and deed and good example, without worrying so much about those who don't seem to profit from your efforts. There is nothing you can do about that. God's interest in these Sisters is greater than yours and He will, in His tender mercy, touch their hearts when He wishes.

Be careful not to put too much stock in what the Sisters say about each other, for often they can be mistaken. [. . .] My dear, you mustn't be so disturbed about the Sisters who resist your leadership. Always tell them what you think is for their good, but do so calmly, without raising your voice. If they follow your advice, praise God! If they don't, remain at peace, pray for them, and turn your attention to the other Sisters. Don't show annoyance or a desire to keep them under control.

This is how God, who is Master and has power to do whatever He wants, deals with us. Don't listen to those Sisters whom you see not acting out of pure charity, and urge all of them to cut back on all gossip, speaking only when charity or necessity requires it.

I see, my darling, that your soul still agonizes when you feel without grace or when you commit some fault that comes from the rigor with which you would like to make progress in a purity that is not to be found in this life. Your failings are not worth bothering about. I still think that the best thing is to stop examining yourself and to remain wide open in a holy confidence and joy, avoiding tension as much as possible.

I'm waiting for your articles in order to answer them. To this end, may God inspire me to say what He wills! Pray for me who am so intimately yours. . . .

---

1. *Sa Vie et ses oeuvres*, VIII, 452–54: Letter MDCCCIV.

LETTERS OF SPIRITUAL DIRECTION

To a Visitandine

[no date][1]

I return your greeting and also wish you a "forever," not of this perishable life, but of a blessed eternity which will be yours to claim after you've led a long, holy life of service to God through a faithful observance of your Rule. Our blessed Father used to say that the best means of grasping the spirit of our vocation was to put into practice the instructions found in our Rules. And you know that the principal ones are humility, self-effacement, and a holy simplicity which of itself does away with all kinds of vanity, self-seeking and self-satisfaction. If you put these virtues into practice, it will become apparent in all that you say, do, and write. Now it is this very simplicity that I especially want for you because it is the distinctive quality of the daughters of the Visitation.

Your indulgent heart, which I love most sincerely, gives me confidence to mention something in passing that I think you won't mind hearing. I find your letter very well written, but, it seems to me, it contains too many expressions that lack simplicity. That's why I hope that the virtues I have just spoken of will be seen in your thoughts, words and deeds, and that there will be nothing in your manner of speaking or writing that smacks of affectation. In truth, I would rather have us appear unskilled in letter-writing than be considered affected. [. . .]

I beg you, my dearest daughter, to pray to God for me. I wish you the attainment of a most holy perfection.

To a Superior

[no date][1]

My dearest daughter,

[. . .] If it appears that a Sister has done something that could lessen the mutual love and confidence that should exist among us, I prefer that before taking the rumor seriously and talking about it, you write to her quite candidly, not as if you believed what was

---

1. *Sa Vie et ses oeuvres*, VIII, 542: Letter MDCCLXIV. *[To a Visitandine]*
1. *Sa Vie et ses oeuvres*, VIII, 556–57: Letter MDCCCLXXII. *[To a Superior]*

being spread, but to learn the truth from her directly and to believe her.

I beg you, my dear Sister, govern your community with great expansiveness of heart: give the Sisters a holy liberty of spirit, and banish from your mind and theirs a servile spirit of constraint. If a Sister seems to lack confidence in you, don't for that reason show her the least coldness, but gain her trust through love and kindness. Don't entertain thoughts against any one of the Sisters, but treat them all equally. Lead them, not with a bustling, anxious kind of concern, but with a care that is genuine, loving, and gentle. I know there is no better way to succeed in leading souls. The more solicitous, open, and supportive you are with them, the more you will win their hearts. This is the best way of helping them advance toward the perfection of their vocation. So be present at the community exercises as often as you can, and let the Sisters know how much you enjoy being with them.

You tell me that you can no longer stand the burden of being Superior. Oh, Sister! please, don't ever let me hear you say that again! Do you want to bury your talents and render useless all the gifts God has lavished upon you? He has given you these graces so that His glory may be increased in whatever houses He confides to your governance. So look beyond your timid, fearful hesitations. Trample them underfoot, my dearest daughter, and keep your eye on God's good pleasure and His eternal plan for you. Surrender all the remaining days of your life to Him and let Him use them for such activities and services as please Him, and not yourself. Finally, place in His hands all your consolations, and believe that I am

Always yours, etc. . . .

To a Visitandine

[no date][1]

My dearest daughter,

It would be impossible for me to flatter you or treat you softly since you show me so much trust and liberty. I think that our Lord has given you a spirit that He wants you to value above everything,

---

1. *Sa Vie et ses oeuvres*, VIII, 651–52: Letter MCMXLIX.

especially above yourself, your passions and inclinations, worthy as these may seem to be. This is the greatest and most agreeable sacrifice you can make to the Lord.

As for that old desire of yours to be a domestic Sister, my dear, take my word for it, our blessed Father's advice to "ask for nothing and refuse nothing" is far superior to this desire of yours or any other practice of humility. I admit that God wants you to be most humble, but in the ways He chooses for you, not in those you would choose. So make good use of the scorn and insults of others and of your own failures and shortcomings. You may be certain that these are the only means by which you will acquire the true and solid humility that He wants you to have.

The core of humility lies in the very center of our being. If we have real self-knowledge and love of our lowliness and our nothingness, and if we accept being overlooked by others, then we can be sure we have true humility. No longer think about—at least, do not dwell upon—these external humiliations, or wish to go anywhere else because of them, since God has destined you for other services.

Nothing can equal the grandeur and dignity of God or of His holy Mother; and nothing will ever equal their humility. So surrender all your yearnings to their care and be at peace. Yours, etc. . . . .

SELECTED BIBLIOGRAPHY

A. Primary Sources

Oeuvres de Saint François de Sales, Evêque de Genève et Docteur de l'Eglise, Edition Complète, d'après les autographes et les éditions originales . . . publiée . . . par les soins des Religieuses de la Visitation du Premier Monastère d'Annecy, 27 vols. Annecy: J. Niérat *et al.*, 1892–1964. Vol. 1: *Les Controverses*. 2: *Defense de l'Estendart de la Sainte Croix*. 3: *Introduction à la Vie Dévote*. 4 and 5: *Traité de l'Amour de Dieu*. 6: *Les Vrays Entretiens Spirituels*. 7–10: *Sermons*. 11–21: *Lettres*. 22–26: *Opuscles*. 27: *Table Analytique*.

St. François de Sales. *Oeuvres*. Ed. André Ravier et Roger Devos. Paris: Bibliothèque de la Pléiade, Editions Gallimard, 1969.

François de Sales. Correspondance: les lettres d'amitié spirituelle. Ed. André Ravier. Paris: Bibliothèque Européenne, Desclée de Brouwer, 1980.

S:e. *Jeanne Françoise Frémyot de Chantal. Sa vie et ses oeuvres*. Edition authentique publiée par les soins des Religieuses du Premier Monastère de la Visitation Sainte-Marie d'Annecy. 8 vols. Paris: Plon, 1874–79. Vol. 1: *Mémoire sur la vie et les vertus de sainte Jeanne-Françoise Frémyot de Chantal*. Par la Mère Françoise-Madeleine de Chaugy. 2 and 3: *Oeuvres diverses*. 4–8: *Lettres*.

Jeanne-Françoise Frémyot de Chantal. *Correspondance*. Edition critique établie et annotée par Soeur Marie-Patricia Burns. Paris: Centre d'Etudes Franco-Italien, Les Editions du Cerf. Vol. I, 1986; Vol. 2, 1987. Vol. I, 1605–1621.

B. Translations

Francis de Sales, St. *Introduction to the Devout Life*. Trans. John K. Ryan. New York: Doubleday. 1982.

———. *Treatise on the Love of God*. 2 vols. Trans. John K. Ryan. Rockford, Illinois: TAN Books and Publ., 1974.

Library of St. Francis de Sales. Trans. and ed. H. B. Mackey. London, 1873–1910. Vol. 1: *Letters to Persons in the World*. 2: *Treatise on the Love of God*. 3: *The Catholic Controversy*. 4: *Letters to Persons in*

Religion. 5: *Spiritual Conferences*. 6: *Mystical Explanation of the Canticle of Canticles* and *Depositions of Ste. Jeanne de Chantal*. 7: *The Spirit of St. Francis de Sales* by his friend Jean Pierre Camus, bishop of Belley.

On the Preacher and Preaching. A Letter by Francis de Sales. Trans. John K. Ryan. Chicago: Henry Regnery Co., 1964.

St. Francis de Sales in His Letters. Ed. by the Sisters of the Visitation, Harrow-on-the-Hill. St. Louis, Mo.: B. Herder Book Co., 1933.

St. Francis de Sales. Selected Letters. Trans. Elisabeth Stopp. New York: Harper and Bros., 1960.

The Spiritual Conferences of St. Francis de Sales. Trans. Abbot Gasquet and the late Canon Mackey. Westminster, Maryland: Newman Bookshop, 1943.

The Sermons of St. Francis de Sales. Trans. by Nuns of the Visitation, ed. Lewis S. Fiorelli, OSFS. Rockford, Ill.: TAN Books and Publishers, 1985—. Vol. 1: On Prayer. Vol. 2: On Our Lady. Vol. 3: Lent. Vol. 4: Advent and Christmas.

St. Francis de Sales: A Testimony by St. Chantal. Trans. Elisabeth Stopp. Hyattsville, Md.: Institute of Salesian Studies, 1967.

The Spirit of Saint Jane Frances de Chantal as Shown in Her Letters. Trans. Sisters of the Visitation, Harrow-on-the-Hill. New York: Longmans, Green and Co., 1922.

Saint Jane Frances Frémyot de Chantal. Her Exhortations, Conferences and Instructions. Trans. from the Paris 1875 ed. Chicago: Loyola Univ. Press, 1928.

C. SECONDARY WORKS

Abruzzese, John A. *The Theology of Hearts in the Writings of St. Francis de Sales*. Rome: Pontifical University of St. Thomas Aquinas, 1985.

Bedoyere, Michael de la. *François de Sales*. New York: Harper, 1960.

Bremond, Henri. *Histoire littéraire du sentiment religieux en France depuis la fin des guerres de religion jusqu'à nos jours*. 3 Vols. Paris: Bloud et Gay, 1921. English trans.: *A Literary History of Religious Thought in France from the Wars of Religion Down to Our Own Times*. 3 Vols. New York: Macmillan Co., 1930.

SELECTED BIBLIOGRAPHY

Calvet, J. *La littérature religieuse de François de Sales à Fénélon.* Paris: Les Editions Mondiales, 1956.

Camus, Jean Pierre (Bishop of Belley). *The Spirit of St. François de Sales.* Trans. C. F. Kelley. New York: Harper and Bros., 1952.

Georges-Thomas, Marcelle. *Sainte Chantal et la spiritualité salésienne.* Paris: Edition Saint-Paul, 1963.

Henry-Coüannier, Maurice. *Saint Francis de Sales and His Friends.* Trans. Veronica Morrow. Staten Island, N.Y.: Alba House, 1964.

Julien-Eymard d'Angers. *L'humanisme chrétien au XVIIe siècle: St. François de Sales et Yves de Paris.* La Haye: Martinus Nijhoff, 1970.

Lajeunie, E.-M. *Saint François de Sales et l'esprit salésien.* Bourges: Editions du Seuil, 1962.

———. *Saint François de Sales. L'homme, la pensée, l'action.* 2 Vols. Paris: Editions Guy Victor, 1964. Trans. by Rory O'Sullivan, OSFS: *Saint Francis de Sales. The Man, the Thinker, His Influence.* 2 Vols. Bangalore, India: S.F.S. Publications, 1986, 1987.

Lemaire, Henri. *Les images chez St. François de Sales.* Paris: Editions A. G. Nizet, 1962.

———. *Lexique des oeuvres complètes de François de Sales.* Paris: Editions A. G. Nizet, 1973.

Liuima, Antanas. *Aux sources du traité de l'amour de Dieu de St. François de Sales.* 2 Parts. Rome: Librairie Editrice de l'Université Grégorienne, 1960.

Muller, Michael. *St. Francis de Sales.* New York: Sheed and Ward, 1937; reprint, Bangalore, India: S.F.S. Publications, 1984.

Murphy, Ruth. *Saint François de Sales et la civilité chrétienne.* Paris: A. G. Nizet, 1964.

Ravier, André. *Jeanne-Françoise Frémyot, Baronne de Chantal, sa race et sa grace.* Paris: Henry Labat, 1983.

———. *Un Sage et un saint: François de Sales.* Paris: Nouvelle Cité, 1985.

Sanders, E. K. *Sainte Chantal, 1572–1641: A Study in Vocation.* London: Society for Promoting Christian Knowledge, 1918.

Schueller, Th. *La Femme et le saint: la femme et ses problèmes d'après saint François de Sales.* Paris: Les Editions Ouvrières, 1970.

Serouet, Pierre. *De la vie dévote à la vie mystique: Ste. Thérèse d'Avila,*

St. François de Sales. Paris: Les Etudes Carmelitaines chez Desclée de Brouwer, 1958.

————. Article "François de Sales" in *Dictionnaire de Spiritualité*, Vol. V. col. 1057–1097. Paris: Beauchesne, 1963.

Stopp, Elisabeth. *Madame de Chantal. Portrait of a Saint*. Westminster, Md.: Newman, 1963.

Wright, Wendy M. *Bond of Perfection: Jeanne de Chantal and François de Sales*. New York/Mahwah: Paulist Press, 1985.

D. BIBLIOGRAPHIES

Brasier, V., E. Morganti, and M. St. Durica. *Opere e Scritti Riguardanti San Francesco di Sales*. Repertorio bibliografico 1623–1955. Turin: Societa Editrice Internazionale, 1956.

Struś, Józef. "S. Francesco di Sales 1567–1622: Rassegna Bibliografica dal 1956," *Salesianum* 45 (1983), 635–671.

Index

*Indicates figure of speech.

INDEX

INDEX

INDEX

sisters, 254; or life, 163; uselessness of details at, 159

Decisions, method of making, 106, 196; of Francis, 144

Defense of the Standard of the Holy Cross, 23

Debris, floating*, 118

Della Casa, Giovanni, 22

Dependence, upon God, 65, 68, 69, 80, 189, 191; upon God as male model of sanctity, 82; Jane's upon Francis, 81.

Depression, about world, 162; after small results from efforts, 98; guard against, 129; of Francis (as youth), 180; of unknown gentleman, 180

Desert spirituality, 44, 44n, 54–56

The Desert and the City: An Interpretation of the History of Christian Spirituality, Thomas Gannon and George W. Traub, 44n

Desire, excellence of Francis's, 186; follow only God, 131; for advancement, 189, 251; for consolation, knowledge, happiness, control, 194, 237, 262, 263; for daughter's marriage, 211; for perfect observance, 260–261; for religious life, 101, 146, 244; for your good, 223; God's graces, 187, 204, 206, 238; like orange trees*, 124; lofty, 95n, 96; love from me, 222; not necessary for perfection, 97; not outside monastery, 234; of heart, 197; over-zealous, 111; passions not of, 257; to be domestic sister, 226; to love, serve God, 31, 102, 104, 108, 148, 168, 172, 180, 193, 201, 208, 226, 227; to please superior, 259; to see dear ones make progress, 110; to see your liberty of heart, 144; to serve you, 127; useless, dangerous, unwise, 162

Detachment, from wordly ties, 137; frustrated plans resulting in, 198; of Francis, 78; of Jane from Francis, 31, 80–83, 144; of Saint John the Baptist, 141; part of "pure love," 50; Salesian, 185

Devil, attacks of, 227; possession by, 195n; response of St. Bernard to, 173; sending distractions, 128; stop arguing with, 131; temptations of, 112, 120, 259; temptations of against faith, 132–134; traps put in way by, 254; wants to keep from fruits of love, 169; wants to upset by disunion, 251

Devos, Roger, "Le testament spiritual de Sainte Jeanne Françoise de Chantal," 33

Devotion, absent in prayer, 118; blessing in one hour, 107; call to, 13; enjoyment of God with, 199; fullness of, 199; generous, noble, sincere, 249; hermit's, 205; honey of*, 167; human, 38; humble, 114; in various circumstances, 45, 55, 56, 102; love and make lovable, 104; matter of relationships, 47; of children, 135–136; plan of, 200; practices of, 218; pretext of 140; salvation

through, 159; simple, 210; society infused with, 27

Devout life. *See* Devotion

Dew*, care of Jane of Maytime, 144–145, 148

Dictionnaire de Spiritualité ascetique et mystique, 28n

Difficult, souls, 255

Difficulties, accept with patience and gentleness, 219; conquer, 107; for greater good, 232; Francis overwhelmed by, 166; hurt reputation, 240; in avoiding sin, 180; in finding spiritual guides, 169; in footsteps of saints, 113; in overcoming inclinations, 261; in works for God's glory, 199; of Francis's sister, 162; smoothed away, 191; understanding way of life, 236; with Sister Assistant, 259

Digne (city), 248

Dignity, of the Commandeur, 186, 188; of God and His Mother, 266; of things willed by God, 111

Dijon, 247; Carmelites of, 84; Francis's preaching in, 25, 102, 177; Jane's home, 9n, 19; Jane's spending time in, 137; meeting of Jane and Francis in, 25, 123n, 132; St. Claude near, 130n; writing via, 147

Dinner, unprepared*, 115

Dionysius the Pseudo-Areopagite, fifth century, influence on Francis, 28

Directee. *See* Spiritual Directee

Direction. *See* Spiritual Direction

Director. *See* Spiritual Director

Discernment, Ignation tradition, 40, 74; inner dimension, 209; of spiritual guides, 169; Salesian approach to, 41–42; serious study, 196; true, 68; use liberty with, 239

Discernment of Spirits, Jacques Guillet, 40n

Disciple(s), 119–120; Jane traditionally viewed as, 11; Jesus admonished, 120; retained some imperfections, 108

Discipline (lash), use in moderation, 134, 135

Discouragement, at reproofs, 164; do not yield to, 115; guidance not to cause, 229, 237; humble self without, 165; pleased at lack of, 243

Disease, contagious, reason to send candidates away, 252

Disinterestedness. *See* Indifference

Distaff and spindles*, 146

Distinctions between Jane and Francis, 70–86

"Distinctive Salesian Virtues, Humility and Gentleness, The" Thomas A. McHugh, 63n

Distraction(s), guarding against intellect, 151; not voluntary, 235; opportunities for growth, 105; remain calm amidst, 198; remedy for, 177; Spirit pours grace on, 199

Disturbance, by fears and imaginings, 211; caused by self-love, 118; not necessary 19, 118;

277

INDEX

INDEX

Geneva, 22, 23, 143

Genoa, 124

Gentleness, acceptance of afflictions with, 208, 219; achieve little by little, 171; acts of, 158; all called to, 64; beg God's help with, 163; communication maintains love's, 235; correct with, 243; divine, 191, 194, 201; effect of freedom, 138; give heart to Lord in, 115, 125; govern with, 241, 242, 248, 249, 253, 255, 259; in cordiality, 240; in prayer, 114, 151, 198; influence daughter with, 136; lead others to God with, 27, 137, 247, 263, 265; let go with, 197; little virtue of, 62–63, 64, 66, 69, 98, 146; misunderstood, 31; of demeanor, 46; of heart, 237; of Jane, 85; of Jesus, 62–63, 66, 69, 99, 231; perform actions with, 203, 251; pursue holiness with, 110, 155, 188, 189, 262; respond to God with, 223; return from distractions with, 177; seek healing with, 115; serve God with, 236; speak with, 176; strength is, 127; support with, 185; toward everyone, 121, 159, 165; toward husband, 179; translations of prayers in, 135; with self, 226, 232

Georges-Thomas, Marcelle, *Sainte Chantal et la spiritualité salesienne*, 70n

Getting up, 176, 194, 218

Gifts of God, differences of, 82; friendship as, 123, 144; in prayer, 52; indifference, 160; humility re: 66; love, 190; of conversion, 226; spirit of Francis, 186; to advance in humility, 216; to Mother Jeanne des Anges, 195, 195n

Gilligan, Carol, *In a Different Voice*, 73n, 74–75, 75n

Gold from crucible*, 256

Good pleasure. *See* Will of God's good pleasure

Good Shepherd, 5

Gospel, 135, 135n

Gossip, 263

Governing, gentleness in, 249, 253; talent for, 252; with expansiveness of heart, 260, 265

Gracefulness, 64; of Francis, 46, 72

Graciousness, affability, 216; *douceur*, 64; govern with, 243; in community, 27; tone of letter, 186; when interrupted in prayer, 138

"*Grande Fille,*" Marie Jacqueline Favre, 256, 256n

Granier, Claude de, Bishop of Geneva (+ 1602), 22–23, 25

Granieu, François de, 166

Granieu, Madame de, Laurence de Ferrus (1579–1652), background, 166; letter to, 5, 166–168; methodless prayer, 51n

Grace(s), awareness of God's presence, 257; blessing God for, 111; cooperation with, 191; correspondence with, 187; dependence upon, 181, 189, 224; desire for, 206; exceptional, 193; feeling without, 263; filled with, 64; filling soul with, 203; for God's glory, 265; fruit worthy of, 225; granted to André Frémyot, 213; greatness of, 259; help of, 203, 223; imperfection as, 176; in distractions, dryness, 99; in self-examination, 204; necessity of, 83; of afflictions, 207; of confidence in God, 222; of doing God's will, 191, 201, 205, 209; of doing good/avoiding evil, 218; of Francis, 186; of heart like God's, 190; of humility, 226; of keeping heart in God's love, 168; of not seeking perfection beyond Institute, 258; of perfection in state of life, 216; of practicing what is advised, 262; of Spirit, 177; placed in Order by, 227; seeing through, 198; stripping impossible without, 81; sufficient, 35; to cooperate, 192; to explain truth, 138; to have affections without reflections, 167; to make up for loss, 215; virtues given by, 154

Grapes*, 148

Gratian, Father Jerome (1545–1614), 126

Gratitude, for extraordinary favor, 195; for pregnancy and prosperity, 215; simplicity in, 97

Greenspan, Miriam, *New Approaches to Woman and Therapy*, 73n

Grenoble, 166, 166n, 235, 238, 249

Grief, acceptance of, 74, 77; at death of daughter-in-law, 206; identification with, 83; identity-shattering, 75; in detachment, 81; offered, 85

Guillet, Jacques, Discernment of Spirits, 40n

Habit, religious, desert spirituality, 54; foundresses without, 220; of Jane as relic, 254; reception of, 222, 240, 244

Hand, busy, 145; hurt, 234; names on, 195, 195n; of God*, 148, 153, 155, 157, 164, 165, 167, 174, 187, 189, 190, 203, 214, 215, 219, 224, 227, 234, 250, 265; punish, 173; take heart, soul in*, 158, 198

Hannivel, Mother Marie de la Trinité, 145, 145n

Harmony, in community, 261; of person, 64; with husband, 214

Happiness, concern for, 189; from God, 202; in care of sick, 257; in God, 215, 217, 227, 250; in humiliations, 254; in instruction of superior, 224; of eternity, 207, 215; of house, 263; of perfect observance, 260; out of difficulties, 195; over marriage, 210; prefer yours to mine, 211; reason for, 212, 213; to be virtuous, 256

Harshness, Francis's fear of, 249; in corrections, 254

Harvest*, 148

Healing, gradual, 237; medicines transformed to poison, 216; of evil discovered, 227; of God, 174, 203; of heart, 115; of illicit love, 149

INDEX

INDEX

INDEX

cludes constraint, 134; theme of, 65; uppermost, 238. *See also*, Freedom

Life (lives), attached to thinge of this, 214; breath of, 175, departure from, 215; devoid of love, 163; disorderly, 225; eternal, 205; full of, 99; giving life for, 222; graces useful in this, 203; in God, 200; long service in this, 187; Lord bringing, 174; made difficult, 220; narrow passes of*, 227; new way of, 210; not of this, 264; of selfless activity of those dear, 144; religious, 220; rest of 220, 226, 266; sorrows, difficulties of, 219; virtuous, 207, 217

Life, Mère de Chaugy, 16n

Light and clouds*, 95

Lilies*, white 111

Limojon, Mme de, Jeanne-Louise de Genton, background, 155; letters to 155–157

Lions with Sampson,* 181

Lisbon, 150n

Little(ness), contradictions, humiliations suited to, 234; gift insofar as allowed by, 222; in own eyes, 227; ordinary virtues suited to, 98; Salesian affinity for, 69; way, 148

Liuima, Antanas, *Aux sources du traité*, 28n

Live Jesus!, and His mother, 153; as Prince of Peace, 65n; because of humility, 66n, 67; by winning heart, 59; engraved on heart, 55, 85; greeting, 239; how? 10; in interior, 57, 57n, 60, 61; in simplicity, 69; in variety of conditions, 45, 56; letter closing, 150, 153, 168; letter heading, 9, 16, 186, 201, 210, 220, 247; proclaimed by faith, hope, charity, 173; relationally, 46; to be said in temptation, 133; through Salesian spirituality, 12, 153

Long-winded courage*, 197

Lord, Commandeur de Sillery, 188; André Frémyot, 201–207

Lord (God), absence of, 154; action of, 240; asking work, 196; direction of, 188, 190, 208, 228; feasts of, 219; giving satisfaction, 210; giving spirit, 265; goodness of, 211, 239; graces of, 213, 227; hope in, 181; in (closing of letter), 197, 221; prayer to, 165, 177, 202, 232, 243; protection of, 223; serving, 180, 199; taste of, 167, transfigured in, 163; virtues recommended by, 163; words of, 158, 175

Loss, acceptance of temporal, 197, 200; of death, 206, 207, 215

Loudon, 195, 195n

Louis of Grenada (1504–1588), 103, 103n

Louis IX, Saint, King of France (1215–1270), 141–142

Louis XIII, King (1601–1643), 200–201

Love, abundance of, 125; actions for, 248, 262; affective, 36; "All through . . . ," advice of Francis, 134; as magnet*, 59; at Cross, 60;

blessing of, 155; bond of, 48, 172, 228, compassionate, 35; consecration, 179, 201; death of those held in, 206; death or, 163; desire for, 96, 208, 239; desire to give, 218, 261; doing all for, 152; effective, 36; equal, 193; eternal, 204, 215; evil spirit deprived of, 169; expression of, 27, 46; filling with divine, 223, 234, 258, 259; fire of God's, 160, 202; for Abraham, 250; for Commandeur de Sillery, 192, 206; for Francis, 121, 137, 187, 194; for Françoise, 214, 216; for grandchild, 207; for Jane, 131, 147; for Mme de Limojon, 156; for Sister Marie-Aimée de Morville, 222–224, 226, 228; for Sister Péronne-Marie de Châtel, 164; for sisters, 231, 240, 245, 256, 260; gentleness of, 235; giving money for, 106; giving self over to, 199; goal, 108, 113; God as your, 166; growth in divine, 221; guiding to perfection in, 250; heart as image of, 57; human drawn from divine, 190; human relationships and God, 46, illicit, 149; imprinting on heart, 215; in (closing of letter), 143; in *Treatise*, 27; lessening of, 264; living in hearts, 114; looking at God for, 152; making up for omissions, 134; more for God, 210; Mutual for God, 27, 131, 195; never stopping, 165; of benevolence, 57, 57n; of complacence, 57, 57n; of conformity, 40, 40n, 41, 50; of fathers, 202; of God in present, 20, 20n; of God and neighbor, 46n; of God's good pleasure, 205; of lowliness, 226; of neighbor, 103, 104, 137, 257; of recommendations, 149; of Saint John the Baptist, 141; of self; 109, 147, 189, 226; of solitude, 204, 227; of submission, 40n, 43; of things on earth; of widowhood, 124; only law or coercion, 146; perfecting humans, 21; plan in God's*, 222; praying through, 175; profound level of, 58; sacrifice to, 222; sanctification in God's, 226; Savior only object of, 191; serving God in, 236; speaking to God of, 232; summer of*, 148; surrender in, 216; taking possession of heart, 223; trust in God's, 245; welcoming children with, 214; winning God's and other's, 156; without method, 167. *See also* Affection, Friendship, Relationship

"Love of Benevolence and Liturgy," Joseph F. Power, 57n

Lowliness. *See* Humility

Luther, Martin (1483–1546), 18

Lucinges, Mother Madeleine-Elizabeth de, letter to, 259–260

Lydwine, Saint (1380–1433), 146

Lynch, Jackie, xii

Lynch, John, Portrait of Francis and Jane, cover, vi

Lyons, 30, 62n, 147, 192, 229, 230, 232, 235

284

INDEX

McCabe, Sister Mary Regina, V.H.M., x

McCarthy, Sister Mary Paula, V.H.M., xii

McHugh, Thomas A., 63n

Mackey, Dom Henry Benedict, *Oeuvres Complètes*, 87

Madame de Chantal: Portrait of a Saint, Elisabeth Stopp, 18n, 61n, 79n, 89

Male, orientation, 72, 77, 82; vis à vis female, 46; Visitation not, 71

Malta, knight of, 185

Man in Love with God: Introduction to the Theology and Spirituality of Saint Francis de Sales, James S. Langelaan, O.S.F.S., 22n, 36n

Marceau, William, CSB, *Optimism in the Works of Saint Francis de Sales*, 34n

"Marketplace Spirituality," Joseph Power, 44n

Marquemont, Denis Simon de, Cardinal Archbishop of Lyons (1572–1626), 30, 229, 230, 231

Marriage, advice to daughter concerning, 38, 209, 210, 211, 214; bond of charity not opposed to, 128; experience of, 74, 78, 157; income during, 214; preliminary steps, 209, 210, 211; prayer life before, 166; shaped by, 72, 78

Married persons, seeking perfection, 102; duties of, 140

Marriage of hearts*, human and divine, 58

Martyrdom*, busyness, 158; choosing for self, 256; detachment of Jane from Francis, 82; of love, 60–61

Mary, Blessed Virgin, "Amen, alleluia" of, 142; as Abbess*, 41; at foot of Cross; blessing of, 218, color of hair, 145; daughter of, 165; devotion to, 240; dignity and humility of, 261; giving orphan to care of, 207; in mystery of Visitation, 56; litany of, 219; Live Jesus and, 153; name of, 195n; not leaving, 164; praising God with, 202; protection of, 223

Mary Magdalene, Saint, 108, 152

Mass(es), called away for, 122; daily, 200; have said, 239; pray during, 218; preparation for, 194; remembrance at, 102, 129, 143; schedule time for, 178; turn to altar during, 235

The Mass of the Roman Rite, Joseph Jungmann, 103n

Master, sculptor, 152; serve, 103–104; our Lord as, 119

"Maternal Thinking," Sarah Ruddick, 72n

Maternal care, 229, 246; correction, 260; experience, 47; gifts, 72; graciousness, 64; love, 26, 257, 261

Maubuisson, Abbey of, 168

Meat*, 248

Medicine*, 216

Medieval Religious Women, Volume II, *Peace Weavers*, 60n

Meditation(s), applying point of, 159; books of, 103, 103n, 135, 135n; copy enclosed, 124; discursive, 69; interruption of, 138–139; note on, 107; on four Last Ends, 135; on mystery, 115–116, 218; virtues of crucified Lord, 112; preparation for service by, 96–97; preparation of points for, 167; prevented by sickness, 121; subject of, 111; type not superior, 51; without sweetness, 118

Memo, 105, 105n

Mercy, abandonment to, 20, 200; confidence in, 68, 125; eternal bliss through, 161, 207; friendship through, 142; gift of, 169, 186, 204; God of, 35; God's care in, 148, 164, 208, 226; greater than human choice, 21; in heart of, 179; infinite, 202; naked before throne of, 80; not to be forgotten, 224; physical pain calling forth, 134; praise of God for, 170, 257; surrendered to, 154; touch hearts in, 263

Mère Angélique et Saint François de Sales, La, Louis Cognet, 31

Midst, in the, theme, 44–48, 162

Mildness, 127, 172

Miller, Jean Baker, *Toward a New Psychology*, 73n, 75n, 77n

Mind, calming objections of, 182; consecration to God, 201; creative, 172; focus in prayer, 177; in distractions, 198, 199; not good at considerations, 202; "one heart and", 170, 246, 261; raise to thought of eternity, 215; reasonable, 157; tranquility of, 194; troubled by fear, 180; wrecked by fasting, 249

Mirot, Albert, *Saint François de Sales et ses faussaires*, 87, 87n

Misery, acknowledge, 98; despite, 232; keep in fear of falling, 224; learn from, 117, 119; wallowing in, 256

Misfortune, 254, 254n

Missionary, 23

Mistletoe,* 151

Misunderstanding, 243, 247

Moderation, education of Françoise in, 136; everything in, 176; fine line of, 170; in efforts against temptations, 253; in spiritual exercises, 112; in penance practices, 56, 134, 135; of outbursts of annoyance, 110

Modesty, as noble woman, 210, 216; at court, 56; of dress, 68; religious, 255

Molina, Luis de, S.J. (1535–1600), *Concord of Free Will with the Gift of Grace*, 21

Monasteries, desert spirituality, 54; direction within, 254; observance of rules, 24; permissions for, 234n; reform of, 29, 116; spirituality not restricted to, 44

Monastic, imagery, 41; rhythm, 29; simplified routine, 26; spirituality not necessarily, 56; tra-

INDEX

Commandeur, 206; of letter, 122; toward all sisters, 261; with fiancé, 213; with superior, 221, 248

Optimism, 34–35, 34n, 83

Optimism in the Works of St. Francis de Sales, William Marceau, CSB, 34n

Orange-flower water*, 118

Orange trees*, 124

Orchard*, 139

Ounce of virtue*, 208

Overeagerness, act without, 189; caused by intensity of desires, 110; cut short, 198; temper, 188; tense diligence is, 159; to attain happiness, 262

Oratorian, 89

Pacatula, 136

Padua, University of, 20, 22, 36, 200

Pain, endure before God, 203; God hidden at core of*, 217; of spiritual childbirth*, 129; over misunderstanding, 247; overeagerness source of, 261; to nature, honey to heart*, 256

Paris, André Frémyot in, 200; Francis in, 168, 177; gifts from, 212; heading of letters, 210, 211, 221, 222, 238, 239, 242, 243, 256; Jane in, 237; novice in, 95; spiritual crisis in, 19–21; study in, 19; superior in, 188, 208; time to leave, 256–257; trip to, 150

Parliament, career in, 200; secularization blocked by, 220

Paschal Lamb*, 132

Passes, narrow and dangerous*, 227

Passion (of Jesus), abjection in, 66; conflict during, 118–119; darkness of, 154; meditation on, 116; peace in, 120

Passions, calming of, 191, 219; disturbance by, 115, 172, 173; in relationships, 4; not mastered immediately, 108; spirit to be valued above, 265–266; stirred up but not followed, 257. *See also* Emotions

Path*, 110–111, 167

Patience, acceptance of sorrow with, 215, 219; as prayer, 198; bearing suffering in, 63, 105, 169, 203; giving greatest assurance of perfection, 96; giving out, 147; growing gradually in, 171; have (or simply, Patience!), 132, 146, 243, 255; in prayer, 101; lack of, 98, 262; of Francis, 102, 147, 168; of Jane, 85, 220; toward self, 96, 108, 158, 160, 165; waiting in, 189; with sisters, 231, 241

Paul, Saint, 11, 11n, 46, 47, 103, 105, 124, 127, 154, 165, 172, 224, 254

Paula, Saint (347–404), 146

Peace, accepting resistance of sisters in, 263; advancing in vocation, 258; assurance bringing, 205; bitterness transformed into, 175; consolation bringing, 170; disturbances filling with,

150; enemies leaving us in, 114; esteemed above all else, 222; Francis as maker of, 65, 65n; God giving, 211; hating faults in, 161; in conversations, 179; in midst of busyness, 64; in prayer, 167, 194; interior, 191; journey in, 223; keeping sisters in, 247; lack of feeling in, 262; letting go in, 197; little virtue of, 69; longing to please God, 189; Lord as Prince of, 119, 120; morning preparation for, 158; of soul, 118; opponents gone home in, 149; praying in, 100, 107; pursuit of perfection leading to, 156; remaining in, 112, 128, 133, 171, 198, 203, 242, 266; response to Lord's lights in, 188; restoration to Chablais, 23; suffering in, 256; surpassing understanding, 227, 261; union of hearts causing, 240

La Pédagogie en France aux XVII et XVIII siècles, Georges Snyders, 37n

Peddler and pack, little*, 98

Pelikan, Jaroslav, *Jesus Through the Centuries*, 65n

Penance(s), desert spirituality, 54; God more pleased with acceptance than, 194; in proportion to sin, 169; of Rule, 235; sea of*, 141; too soon for, 248

Penance, sacrament. *See* Confession

Perfection, acts required for, 262; called to, 251; desire for, 102, 108, 110, 189; friendship of, 204; God glorified by, 260; growth in, 198; height of, 185; hurry to attain, 96; in detachment, 81–83; in state of life, 216; in uniting self to God, 193; mark of, 101; means to attain, 125, 160; memo on, 104, 105, 125; of vocation, 225, 265; of what God has done, 187, 222; out of weakness, 232; preparation, 97, 98; quest for, 26, 79–80, 196; religious, 220; respect for, 121; road to*, 250; vow of, 79n; wishing attainment of, 264; worry about, 203

Perseverance, of André Frémyot, 205; of Sister Marie-Aimée de Morville, 222, 223, 226

Peter, Saint, Apostle, 108, 115, 164–165, 165n

Portraits, 166–167

Philip Neri, Saint (1515–1595), 18

Philippe, Father, probably Philippe de Saint-Jean Baptiste Malabaila (1578–1657), 231

Philosophical Sketches, Susanne Langer, 85n

Philothea, 55, 66, 177n, 178. *See also Introduction to the Devout Life*

Physician, Great*, 216

Piety, exaggerated or mournful, 107; example of, 199; gentle, peaceful, 156; old-fashioned, 3; regard for, 195

Pignerol, 209

Pilgrimage, example of good action, 106; of André Frémyot, 200; sites, 29; to St. Claude, 130, 130n, 142–143

Pillars of tabernacle*, 124

INDEX

Pit, bottomless*, 226

Pleiade edition of *Oeuvres*, St. Francis de Sales, ed. André Ravier, 19–20, 19n, 45n

Plon, edition of *Sainte Jeanne-Françoise Frémyot de Chantal, sa vie et ses oeuvres*, vi, xi, 16n, 87, 87n

Point of meditation, beginners' method, 112; on patience, 159; preparation, yet freedom, 167

Poison, 116; *, 216

Poor, charity to sick, 146; make something for 146; visits to, 27, 56–57; wealth for, 232

Pont-à-Mousson, 258

Port Royal, 67n, 168

Possessions, of God, 224; of heart, 227; stripping of, 198

Possession (demonic), 195n

Possevin, Antoine, S.J. (Posevinus, Anthonius 1533 or 1534–1611), 20, 28

Post-Reformation Spirituality, 25n

Post-Tridentine Church, 70

Postulant, 252

Pounds, 100,000*, 208

Poverty, in midst of wealth, 55; interior*, 204; poor example of, 116; value more than wealth, 221; vow of, 241

Power, Father Joseph, O.S.F.S., vi, ix, 44n, 57n

Power, God's presence in, 257; in intercession of Francis, 195; in patient prayer, 198; of conversion, 224; of God, 263; suffering is prayer of, 203

Prayer, affective, 151, 167; books on, 103; bringing directee into atmosphere of, 58; consecrated to, 229; difficulties in, 68, 99–101; discursive or contemplative, 69; distinction between that of Jane and that of Francis, 84–86; distractions in, 97, 105, 160–161, 177, 198; doing nothing in, 108–109, 152; dryness in, 108, 118; during pregnancy, 115; for André Frémyot, 203; for Commandeur de Sillery, 187; for discernment, 130, 148, 196; for Francis, 99, 126, 166; for Françoise, 211, 222; for intention, 110; for Jane, 189, 203, 249, 263; for love of neighbor, 104; for Sister Marie-Aimée de Morville, 224, 228; freedom in, 124, 134, 138–139; French translation of, 135; from heart, 218; from Psalms, 181; gifts of, 164; God's will manifested in, 41; heard by God, 211; imagination, understanding in, 144–145; inclusion of Jane in, 131, 143; interruption in, 138–139, length of, 115, 178; means of union with God, 102; meditation, 103, 107, 124, 131; method of, 51, 69, 112, 151, 167, 171, 179, 195, 202–203; morning, 218; of beginners, 112; of Visitation Sisters, 190; principal exercise of novitiate, 250; retaking Geneva by, 65; schedule of, 56, 170; spontaneous, 103, 202–203; to live longer, 144; various conditions in, 114

Preaching, advent, 166; art of, 137, 137n, 200; charismatic fervor of, 24; compassion for those, 125; Francis's 12, 58, 88; Lenten, 139, 157, 166; of Lent 1604, 102, 116, 177; of St. Bernard, 173; practicing of, 147

Predestination, Francis's struggle over, 19–21, 34, 49

Pregnancy*, 96; blessing of, 215; shorter prayer during, 116

Presence of God, awareness of, 233; coming into, 167; doing nothing in, 198; felt in guidance, 47; John the Baptist's desire for, 141; kneeling in, 219; place self in 100; practice of, 52; speak in 249, 257, 261; stay short while, 202; staying in different from placing self in, 151

Pride, checking, 67; from immediate mastery of passions, 108; in affection of human fathers, 171; in rank, honor, beauty, 66; let go of, 214; sin rooted in, 73; temptations to, 173, 254

Priesthood, desire for, 22; of Brulart, 185; of Frémyot, 200; rspect for, 45n

Prize*, 109

Procuratrix, 236, 236n

Profession, acceptable because of good will, 247; changing, 106; examination by Jesuits before, 244; not unless well-disposed, 241; of Sister Marie-Aimée de Morville, 220

Protestant Spiritual Traditions, ed. Frank Senn, 10n

Providence, abandonment to, 52, 154, 204, 246; adoring, 154; all within, 42; calling by name, 172; chastisement in, 208; confidence in, 95, 99, 203, 242, 245, 258; dignity in things of, 111; encouragement of, 195; entrusting care, wishes to, 144, 148, 253; following only, 131; God leading in, 257; here because of, 168; holding offices through, 260; never failing, 225; opportunities presented by, 187, 223; resting in, 151, 201, 250; seeing when in grief, 174; thankfulness to, 190; underestimating, 214; understanding from, 177; used by, 200

Provost, 22, 23

Puits d'Orbe, Abbey, 102, 104, 113, 116, 136

Prudence, arrange penances with, 235; anxiety tempered by, 209; expected of Jane's daughter, 212; follow way of, 234; in actions, 216; in undertaking project, 197; spiritual directors with, 169; superiors need, 252; use holy liberty with, 239

Purity, achievable by humans, 194; not found in this life, 263; of gold from crucible*, 256; of heart, 68; speak in honesty and, 132; through confession, 118; weighing things on scales of sanctuary, 111

Puylaurens, Sister Anne-Marie de Lage de, 251

INDEX

Quakers, 65n

Queen Anne of Austria, wife of Louis XIII (1601–1666), 172

Quietly, dismiss distractions, 176, 177; endure suffering, 198; humble self, 158; respond to lights and inspirations, 188; speak to God, 202

Rabelais François (1483 to 1500–1553), 18

Rabutin, Christophe de, Baron de Chantal (1565–1601), 25–26, 143

Rabutin, Guy de, Baron de Chantal (+ 1613), 26, 27, 42, 137

Rabutin-Chantal, Celse-Bénigne de (1596–1627), 25, 83, 136, 143, 206n, 207, 213, 213n

Rabutin-Chantal, Charlotte de (1601–1610), 25, 27

Rabutin-Chantal, Françoise de, Madame de Toulonjon (1599–1684), 25; at Annecy monastery, 27; background, 208–210; education of, 136, 136n; letters to, 89, 210–219; worldly, 83

Rabutin-Chantal, Mother Marie-Aimée de (1608–1678), letters to, 255–256, 263

Rabutin-Chantal, Marie de, Madame de Sevigné (1626–1696), "poor little orphan," 207, 207n

Rabutin-Chantal, Marie-Aimée de, Madame de Sales (1598–1617), 25, 27, 153, 153n

Ravier, André, *Saint François de Sales, Correspondance,* 46n; *Saint François de Sales et ses faussaires,* 87, 87n; *Saint François de Sales, Oeuvres,* 19–20n, 45n; *Un Sage et un Saint,* 11n, 14n, 18n

Ravishment, 79

Reading, instructions in Institute, 225; letters, 205, 214; on life and death of our Lord, 104; *Philothea,* 218–219; *Treatise on the Love of God,* 167, 177; writings of Francis, 187

Reception of habit, 222

Reconciliation, 247

Reflection(s), of not doing enough, 110; on way of life, 217n; prayer better without many, 167, to be avoided, 194

Reform, done by Francis, 12; of Bons, 160, 160n; of Port Royal, 168; of Puits d'Orbe, 116, 136

"...Refuse nothing," advice of Francis, 266

Relationship(s), as woman, 72, 74, 77, 78, 82, 83; healthy, 217; not precluded by spiritual direction, 126; of Francis and Jane, 4, 11–12, 31, 46, 81–82, 89; of mother and daughter, 209; reserved in, 219; spiritual, 4, 14, 31, 46, 47, 89; spiritual direction, 88; various, 216; with God, 79, 85, 229; with ecclesiastics, 192. *See also* Friendship

Relatives, approval of match by, 210, 211; avoid inconvenience to, 104; consolation of, 217; dear to Francis, 137; death of, 105; greetings to, 213; making something for, 146; protection of, 209; retirement satisfactroy to, 190; true, 222

Reprimand, not for every little fault, 235; in maternal manner, 259–260

Repugnance, praise God in spite of, 206; or impatience, 113

Resentment, no reason for, 214; impossible to harbor, 225

Resignation, occasion to practice, 176; over not having, 188; peak of, 154; situations received with, 43; small virtue, 146; to God's providence, 99; to God's will, 101

Resistance, be guided without, 226; not without peace, 120; of temptation, 180–181; offer none to what God wishes, 187; to feelings of aversion, 232; will become weaker, 110

Resolution(s), advancing along way of, 163; drawn from Founder's writings, 258; firmness of, 201; from affections to actions, 145; keeping vigorous, 205; living at fine point of soul, 173; morning, 202; not to act on feelings, 232, not waver in, 226; of superior part of soul, 119; renewing, 218; taking in arms*, 129; to do good and avoid evil, 218

Respect, due to superior, 259–260; of Commandeur Brulart, 186–188; owed to husband, 217

Responses de Notre Sainte Mère Jeanne Françoise Frémyot, Baronne de Chantal sur les règles, constitutions et coutumier de l'Institut, 16n, 28n

Responsibilities, do not abandon, 104, 120

Resting, in God, 112, 122, 159, 189, 194, 199, 214; in heart, 122; in Providence, 203, 242; none except in eternity, 215

Rethinking the Family: Some Feminist Questions, ed. Barrie Thorne, 72n

Retirement, of Commandeur de Sillery, 190, 191, 192, 193; of André Frémyot, 199, 208; into solitude, 205

Retreat of 1616, 80–81, 88

Retreats for laywomen, 27, 234n

Rheno-Flemish spirituality, 28

Ribadeneira, (or Ribera) Pedro de, S.J. (1526 or 1527–1611), 126n

Road to perfection*, 250

Robert Bellarmine, Saint, 234n, 235

Rod (of reproval)*, 206

Roffat, Claude, *Une Spiritualité pour tous,* 9n

Rome, Angélique Arnauld's application to, 168; ambassador to, 185; requests from, 234, 234n

Ronsard, Pierre de (1524–1585), 18

Ropes*, 148

Rose*, 111, 117

Rosset, Sister Anne Marie (1594–1667), letters to, 240–242, 247–248

Rousselot, Paul, *Histoire de l'éducation en France depuis le seizième siècle,* 37n

Royal road*, 117

Ruddick, Sarah, "Maternal Thinking" 72n

289

INDEX

Rue Saint Antoine (First monastery of Paris), 206n
Rue Saint-Jacques (Carmelite monastery), 95
Rule(s), instability changing, 139; living (superior)*, 251; not needed in prayer, 51; of community as will of God, 71; of congregation permeated by gentleness, humility, 237; of congregation praised, 235; of congregation to be observed, 64, 174, 175, 236, 238, 239, 240, 241, 242, 244, 245, 246, 251, 252, 253, 260, 264
Rumilly, 157, 253
Ryan, John K., trans., *Introduction to the Devout Life*, 16n; *On the Preacher and Preaching*, 58n, 137n; *Treatise on the Love of God*, 16n

Sacraments, frequent reception of, 210; means of union with God, 102; reverence for, 128
Sacred Congregation, 234n
Sadness, at lack of sweetness, 118; attacks of, 163; devotion without, 156; heart filled with, 180; none at deprivation, 138; not reason for, 214; not to slip into, 242; of soul, 181; physical, 161; temptations to vanity bringing, 254
Sage et un saint, François de Sales, Un, André Ravier, 11n, 14n–15, 18n
Saint(s), blessing of, 218; footsteps of, 113; "if I were...," 177; praise and bless God with, 202; resounded with Amen, 142
Saint-Cyran, M. de (Jean Duvergier de Hauranne, 1581–1643), 168
"Saint Francis de Sales at Clermont College," Elisabeth Stopp, 19n, 40n
Saint Francis de Sales, Selected Letters, Elisabeth Stopp, 15n, 38n, 88n
Saint Francis de Sales and his Friends, Maurice Henry-Coüannier, 89n
Saint François de Sales, Directeur d'âmes: l'éducation de la volonté, Francis Vincent, 14n
Saint François de Sales et la civilité chrétienne, Ruth Murphy, 64n
Saint François de Sales et ses faussaires, André Ravier and Albert Mirot, 87, 87n
Saint François de Sales: Oeuvres, André Ravier, 19n, 20n
Saint François de Sales, L'homme, la pensée, l'action, E. J. Lajeunie O.P, 18n, 19n, 21n, 23n, 65n
Saint François de Sales, "Traité de l'amour de Dieu" und seine Spanishchen Vorlaufer, 88n
"Saint Jane de Chantal's Guidance of Women,"Wendy M. Wright, 37n, 72n
Saint-Nizier, Nicolas Ménard de, (1581–1629) first spiritual father of Visitation at Lyons, 231
St. Peter, Church of, 22
Sainte Chantal, Henri Bremond, 18n

Sainte Chantal et la spiritualité salesienne, Marcelle Georges-Thomas, 70n
Saint Jeanne de Chantal: Correspondance, ed. Sister Marie-Patricia Burns, 87, 89n, 227n
Sainte Jeanne-Françoise Frémyot de Chantal, sa vie et ses oeuvres,; Plon Edition, vi, xi, 16n, 87, 87n
Saiving Valerie, "The Human Situation: A Feminine View." 73n
Sales, Bernard de, Baron de Sales et de Thorens (1583–1617), 27, 153n
Sales, Château de, 143n
Sales, Saint Francis de (1567–1622), bibliographical works, 87; biography, 9–33; comparison with Jane, 70–86; death of, 246; distance of Jane from, 237; example of, 198; friendships of, 200, 231; giving asylum, 220; greetings from, 234; lack of time, 244; letters from, 95–182; love for, 190; name of, 195, 195n, 249; novena to, 228; recommendations of, 221, 222, 252, 253; requests from Rome, 235; similarity of Jane's spirituality, 185–186; spirit of, 188, 192, 198, 209; teachings of, 187, 241, 258; wish of, 256; words of, 191, 194, 197, 208, 239, 264
Sales, Jean-François, Bishop of Geneva (1578–1635) 130, 147, 147n, 255, 256
Salvation, and predestination, 34–35; desires not of essence of, 110; lead others to, 200; lights for Jane's, 142; little virtues significant for, 63; Live Jesus, word of, 55; of children, 214; of fathers, 137; of pastors and preachers, 125; personal cooperation in, 49; persons to whom entrusted, 227; what matters most, 159; work out in fear and trembling, 224
Samson, 181
Sanctification, of Commandeur de Sillery, 185; of Sister Marie-Aimée de Morville, 226; process of, 71
Satan, *See* Devil
Sauce*, 109
Sautereau, Sister Anne-Catherine de (1591–1652), letter to, 249–250
Savior, belonging entirely to, 154; calling on, 115; for love of, 262; gentle, 63, 207, 236, 258; giving heart to, 156; God revealed as, 21; in name of, 248; in struggles, 261; love of, 190; near Saint John the Baptist, 141; only object of love, 191; praise to, 225; prayer to, 201, 232; protecting lamb*, 227; response to, 222; union with crucified, 116; uniting death with, 161; uniting hearts to, 193, 203; virtues of, 205; yours in, 187
Savoy, 9, 9n, 18, 19, 22, 26, 29, 89
Scales of sanctuary*, 111, 111n, 148, 148n
Scandal, 140, 219
Schueller, Theophiler, O.S.F.S., 66n, 68n

INDEX

Scripture, favorite passage of, 163n; place where God's will manifest, 41; reminder in, 134; source of revelation, 40; study of, 19

Scrupulosity, avoiding, 125, 128, 129, 133, 134, 170; freeing from, 228; gifts not preventing, 164; of women, 129; others trying to give, 126; over superstition, 212–213; undue self-concern, 68; vow regarded as, 79n

Sculptor*, 152, 155–156

Scupoli, Lawrence, *The Spiritual Combat*, 27

Scythe*, 127

Sea of penance*, 141

Seamstress*, 69

Seasickness*, 98, 118

Seasons in the soul*, 148

Secret, keep faithfully, 187; not to be revealed, 176; of sacrament of Penance, 128; union of hearts, 205

Seeds, sowing*, 110

Select Letters of Saint Jerome, trans. F.A. Wright, 136n

Self-, assertion, 73; complacency, 119; confidence, 98; consecration of, 201; denial, 148; deprecation, 73; drop dissolved in Ocean of Divinity*, 257; effacement, 238, 264; examination, 124, 204, 256, 263; identity, 74; interest, 201; knowledge, 266; love, 109, 110, 114, 118, 119, 172, 173, 176, 189, 225, 251; mastery, 156; pity, 232; satisfaction, 264; scrutiny, 251, 256; seeking, 264; sufficiency, 119, 258; will, 110

Senn, Frank C., *Protestant Spiritual Traditions*, 10n

Senses, interior and exterior, 15, 97

Seraphim, 97

Serenity, contradictions fill with, 150; effect of freedom, 138; in self-surrender, 197; spend last days in, 199

Serpents, hissing*, 179

Servant(s), answering litany, 219; at prayer*, 100; not to be inconvenienced, 104; of God*, 186, 187, 233, 237; your*, 112, 142, 221

"Serve God well today . . . ," advice of Francis, 170–171

Service, by turning heart from evil conversations, 179; desire for, 180; destined for other, 266; detachment in, 141; distant things in, 171; freedom for, 53; long life of, 264; maternal quality of, 64; of directee, 157; of Francis for Jane, 4, 127; of God, 107, 113, 163, 187, 196, 214, 223, 262; of God in neighbor, 139; of king in army, 209; of neighbor, 97; preserving physical strength for, 174; progress in, 102, 110, 136

Shadow*, 108–109, 205–206

Shelter in Lord's wounds*, 129

Ship*, 162

Shoulders of charity*, (St. Bernard), 122

Sickness, care for those in, 104, 106, 139, 146; prayer not to be missed except in, 170; risks not wished, 256

Signs (of God's will), 130, 133, 191

Silence, in prayer pleasing to God, 101; observance of, 248

Sillery, Commandeur de. *See* Brulart, Noël

Simplicity, consulting with, 241; curing temptations, 165, 175; exact observance with, 251; filling with, 231; glance of, 106, 202, 256; going forward in, 174, 191, 230, 258, 260; in prayer, 151, 167; innocent, guileless, 250; little virtue of, 146; longing to please God in, 189; obedience in, 233; of Francis, 149; placing self before God in, 203; reporting on prayer with, 171; Salesian virtue, 210, 264; seeking, 234; soul of, 164, 195; speaking in, 187, 193; spirit of Francis, 188; surrender, 194; toward all, 261; union of, 257; writing in, 137, 156, 177

Sin(s), fleeing from, 180; Francis's view of self, 169; Jesus carried on Cross, 129; Job's lack of, 117; mortal, 138, 142; repentance at, 203; Savior's love for those with, 232; surprised at our, 119; weaknesses rather than, 161; yield in everything not, 138

Sincerity, calling on Francis in, 128; liberty and, 144; letter written in, 126; of affection, 249; of Antoine Toulonjon, 210; of desires, 197; speaking to God with, 202; speaking with, 233; turning to God with, 156, 219; with sisters, 241; with superior, 248

Sionnaz, Françoise de, Mme de Boisy. *See* Boisy

Sister, 45, 102, 116, 121, 153, 153n, 162, 163, 200

Skin*, 120

Sleep, children alone, 136; in arms of God*, 151; Mother and child*, 152; six hours of, 171

Smoke*, 215

Snyders, Georges, *La Pédagogie en France aux XVIIe et XVIIIe siècles*, 37n

Society, behavior in, 216; children brought up according to, 214; return to, 209; woman in, 209

Solitude, assaults of, 45; draw into, 228; love of, 204, 227; not only source of living Jesus, 46; not too great a, 192, 205

Solomon (author of Wisdom books), 108, 114, 127

Son, confidence of*, 201; of Françoise, 209, 215, 216n; of Jane, 25, 83, 136, 143, 206n, 207, 213, 213n

Song(s), assure Lord in, 154; bundle of, 147, 147n

Song of Songs, 19, 28, 50n

Sorrow, acceptance of, 219; at death, 206, 215, 216; *douceur* in midst of, 64; endure before God, 203; over religious wars, 83

INDEX

Superior(s), religious, at Digne, 248; at Moulins, 227; burden of being, 265; coadjutrix help to, 233; correspondence with, 237, 246; in Paris, 185, 188, 208; Jane's life as, 27, 70–71, 73, 79, 229; letter to, 252, 264; meeting of, 246; Mother Anne-Marie Rosset, 240; Mother Claude-Marie d'Auvaine, 258; Mother Jeanne-Charlotte de Bréchard, 221, 223, 229, 234; Mother Madeleine-Elisabeth de Lucinges, 259; Mother Marie-Adrienne Fichet, 253; Mother Marie-Aimée de Rabutin, 255, 263; Mother Marie-Angélique de Bigny, 224; Mother Marie-Jacqueline Favre, 229, 230, 233, 236, 256, 257; Mother Marie-Madeleine de Mouxy, 244; Mother Paule-Jéronyme de Monthoux, 242, 243; Mother Péronne-Marie de Châtel, 238; need to govern with expansive heart, 260; sisters' efforts to control, 247; submission to, 261; temptation against, 251

Surin, Père Jean-Joseph, S.J. (1600–1665), 195n

Surrender, days of life, 265; giving value to project, 197; into hands of God, 227, 250; of consolations, 143–144; of heart of God, 62; to God, 80, 160, 194, 217, 256; to mercy of providence, 154; to will of God, 85, 189, 216; yearnings, 266

Sweetness, absent in meditation, 118; douceur, 64; in relationships, 216; in solitude, 204; of holy charity, 254; of holy peace, 228; of honey*, 167, 256

Swine, herding*, 109

Tabernacle*, 250

Tablet, blank*, 51

Tabor, Mount*, 163

Tauler, Johann (1294–1361), 135, 135n

Tears, brings to my eyes, 254; shed for you, 224; speak without self-pity or, 232

Temperament, active, 176; differences of, 82; independent, 209; resemblance to Jane in, 157; suited to cherishing relationships, 83

Temple, project of Commandeur de Sillery, 196, 196n, 197, 197n

Temptation(s), against faith, 132–134; bringing us back to God, 115; distrust of capacity to resist, 181; disunion with sister, 259; disunion with superior, 247, 251; diverting mind from, 253; in anxious thoughts, 120; to classify role of Francis, 126; to evaluate at prayer, 160; to return to world, 112; to vanity, 254

Tenderness, cherish children with, 214; of Francis toward his sister, 162; of God, 201, 211, 216, 225; with self, 171; without feelings of, 118

"Tendresse de Ste Jeanne de Chantal, La," Sister Patricia Burns, 72n

Teresa of Avila, Saint, ("Mother Teresa" 1515–1582), 18, 28, 65n, 84, 109, 109n, 121, 125, 126, 126n

Tertre, Mlle du. See Morville, Sister Marie Aimée de

"Testament spirituel de Sainte Jeanne-Françoise de Chantal et l'affaire de visiteur apostolique, Le," Roger Devos, 33n

Thanks, after Mass, 194; for afflictions, 206; for conversion, 208, 213, 224; for friendship, 204; for gifts to Visitation, 190; for God's grace, 194, 199, 201, 204; for good match, 210; in daily prayer, 218, 219

Thibert, Sister Péronne Marie, V.H.M., vi, ix

Theology of Hearts in the Writings of Saint Francis de Sales, The, John A. Abruzzese, 57n, 59n, 60n

Theotimus, 177, 177n

"Thérèse of Lisieux from a Feminist Perspective," Joann Wolski-Conn, 82n

Thomas Aquinas, Saint (1225–1274), 21, 21n

Thonon, 255, 263

Tied up, hand and foot*, 142

Tietz, Manfred, Saint François de Sales "Traité de l'amour de Dieu und seine Spanishchen Vorlaufer, 88n

Timidity, accusation can cause, 174; from self-love, 251; in face of contradictions, 164; look beyond, 265

Tomorrow, no care about, 98–99, 171

Torment(s), God prefers dependence to, 189; of devils, 195n; useless thoughts cause, 178; with thought of causing failures, 255; with thought of death and judgment, 180

Toulonjon, Antoine, Count de (1574–1633), 209, 210, 211, 212, 213, 214, 216n, 217, 217n

Toulonjon, Françoise de. See Rabutin-Chantal, Françoise de

Toulonjon, Gabrielle de (1622–1646), 215

Tours (city), 178

Toward a New Psychology of Women, Jean Baker Miller, 73n, 75n, 77n

Traité sur oraison, attributed to Saint Jane de Chantal, 16n

Tranquility, humility in, 189; in prayer, inner and outer, 198; necessary for virtuous living, 262; of mind, 194

Transference (in helping relationship), 5

Transfiguration, 162n, 163

Translation, in English, 88; in French of prayers, 135

Transplant*, 222

Traub, George W. and Thomas Gannon, The Desert and the City, 44n

Treatise on the Love of God, 9n, 11n, 16n, 27, 28, 35, 40n, 57n, 106n, 167, 177, 177n, 202

Trees*, bearing fruit, 109; of desire, 123–124

293

INDEX

Trent, Council of, 18, 23, 30, 103n

Trials, blessing to be struck with, 254; calm self in, 134; God treasures union of wills in, 207; imitate Savior in, 261; interior, 153; mutual support in, 123; no doubt of God's will in, 105; present in affection during, 117

Tribulations. *See* Trials

Trouble, at absence of relatives, 222; caused by vanity, 175; change everything into, 256; from work for God, 199; in fear of death, 180; no need in seeking God, 119; over temptations, 164; place resolutions in Lord's wounds*, 129; progress in spite of, 107

Trust, after faults, 232; help to those with, 45, 211; in blessing on meeting, 211; in Francis, 127, 221; in Jane, 187, 217, 265; in prayer, 218; in providence, 99, 203, 242, 245; in tribulations, 117; living in spirit of, 248; love of our Lord and our Lady for, 165; of own experience, 82; with sisters, 241; writing with, 125

Truth, about eternity does not prevent sorrow, 207; comfort in, 207; impress on daughter, 215; learn, 265; letter written in, 126; speaking, 146, 154, 166; that God gave Francis to Jane, 132, 153

Turbulence of sea*, 118

Turin, 9n, 166, 259

Under fire*, 181

Understanding, mutual, 248; of inspirations of Holy Spirit, 193; of sisters, 246; of way of life, 236; peace which surpasses, 227; spiritual life not primarily about, 58; temptations against faith go to, 133; use of in prayer, 145, 167, 194

Union, among monasteries, 246, 253; goal, 250; invitation to, 35; means of, 103; of hearts, 190, 240; of hearts with God, 205; of soul, not other faculties, 257; of wills with God's, 207; with God through suffering, 216; with neighbor, 103; with offering on Cross, 218; with superior, 247

Upset, at being upset, 115; at failing, do not be, 158, 165; at missing spiritual exercises, 138; change made without, 191; desires good because they do not, 146; strengthen minds against thoughts which, 178

Ursulines, 29, 195, 195n, 196

Valley of tears*, 215

Vanity, beautiful, 163; could have perished through, 225; from instant conversion, 108; gifts of God not for, 215; humility without, 97; in illness, learn of one's, 117; of worldly young men, 217; problem for females, 68, 136; spirit

of, 214; squander money on, 212; temptations to, 254; tendencies to, 173; thoughts of, 175

Villars (or Villers), Mlle Jeanne Humbert de, 128

Vincent de Paul, Saint (1581–1660), 32

Villesavin, Mme de, Isabelle Blondeau (1687), background, 177; letter to, 178–179

Vincent, Francis, *Saint François de Sales, Directeur d'âmes: l'éducation de la volonté*, 14n

Vines pruning*, 155

Violence, God draws without, 227; to self in moving toward God, 257; weakness as pleasing as, 194

Virtue(s), acquiring solid, 186; acquisition of religious, 71; burden of duties opportunity for, 158; cultivating advancement in, 229; daughter-in-law's life of, 207; esteeming, 236; for governing, 252; humble gentleness, virtue of, 179; humility and gentleness, of the Institute, 258; humility attracts other, 206; in tribulation, 208; joy in, 217; need for winter to practice*, 148; no delight in practice of, 154; no need for sign of possessing, 181; not produced by outward repose, 163; opportunity in temptation for practice, 134; opposite to failings, 232; ordinarily not to be neglected, 139; pleasing God by acts of, 204, 262; Salesian, 63, 264; Solomon self-assured by, 114; striving to acquire, 260; tested during illness, 257

Virtues, little, beautiful, 148; ordinary, suited to our littleness, 98; theme of Salesian spirituality, 62–69

Visitation of Holy Mary, (Congregation of the, until 1618; Order of the, after 1618), affection for, 190, 192; benefactor of, 185; boarder at, 209; characteristics of, 26–27, 47, 56, 59, 61, 64, 84; conformable to old Orders, 235; daughters of, 187, 264; fear of harshness in, 249; first members of, 164; foundations of, 157, 174, 174n, 219–220; houses of, 80; instructions in, 225, 258; Jane's influence on, 12; letters to, 229, 237, 246; motto of, 9n; observances of, 227, 250, 251; publications by, vi, 10n, 87, 87n; sisters of, ix, xi, 186; structure of, 47–48, 47n, 67, 71; superior of, 73, 79; transfer to, 168, virtues called for by, 252

Visits, infrequent, 217; interruptions by, 199; of Francis to Angélique Arnauld, 168; to elegant house on convent grounds, 220; to Lord, 141; to poor, 27, 56–57; to sick, 27, 136, 192

Visitations, by bishop, 160, 198, 252

Vive Jesus! *See* Live Jesus!

Vocation, advancing in, 258, 265; assure by good works, 224; attracted to with love, 229; contacts necessary to, 205; desire for, 244; devout in, 107; duties of, 105; fidelity to, 190; freedom

INDEX

Wood for fire of love*, 204

Word(s) beyond expression in, 190, 208; express sorrow in few, 225; few of love, 194; of Francis, 191; of God, preaching, 58; offering to God, 218; prayer better than with many, 167; prayer without, 85; sample for prayer, 201, 202; simplicity in, 264; take mine for it, 217

Work(s), consecration of, 201; get from poor horse*, 171; God perfects His, 222; good, 178, 185, 196, 197, 200; more than realized, 107; of humility in secret, 206

World, called hell, 222; children of this, 178; frivolous pleasures of, 224; happiness not in, 227; honors of, 215; language of, 254; marks of respect in, 259; more worth than, 207, 208; not attached to, 151; pleasures of, 217; rank in, 186; sad, mortal, 214; stirrings of passion in, 173; things of, 159, 163; values of, 199, 210; with vanities and superfluities, 156

Worldliness, activity opposite to, 209; conversations of, 169; diversions of, 146; renunciation of, 199; vanity and, 185; young men filled with, 217

Worry, caused by desire for perfection, 189; Françoise to Jane, 209; not about created things, 250; not about means for children, 214; not about unresponsive souls, 263; not at distractions, 198; not over falling, 232; not while waiting, 150; put in God's care, 202

Wounds, healing of, 174, 203; in Lord's*, 125, 129

Wright, F. A., trans. *Select Letters of Saint Jerome*, 136n

Wright, Wendy M., ix; *Bond of Perfection*, 11n, 26n, 32n, 46n, 68n, 79n, 88n, 136n, "Saint Jane de Chantal's Guidance of Women," 37n, 72n; "Jeanne de Chantal: Two Faces of Christ," 60n

Writing advice in, 217, 217n, 218; affectation in 173, 264; of Francis, 187, 258

Yielding, in everything not sin, 104, 138

Zeal, calming excessive, 188, 194; virtues lost through excessive, 111

Zwingli, Ulric (1484–1531), 18

296

Other Volumes in this Series

John Climacus ● THE LADDER OF DIVINE ASCENT
Francis and Clare ● THE COMPLETE WORKS
Gregory Palamas ● THE TRIADS
Pietists ● SELECTED WRITINGS
The Shakers ● TWO CENTURIES OF SPIRITUAL REFLECTION
Zohar ● THE BOOK OF ENLIGHTENMENT
Luis de León ● THE NAMES OF CHRIST
Quaker Spirituality ● SELECTED WRITINGS
Emanuel Swedenborg ● THE UNIVERSAL HUMAN AND SOUL-BODY INTERACTION
Augustine of Hippo ● SELECTED WRITINGS
Safed Spirituality ● RULES OF MYSTICAL PIETY, THE BEGINNING OF WISDOM
Maximus Confessor ● SELECTED WRITINGS
John Cassian ● CONFERENCES
Johannes Tauler ● SERMONS
John Ruusbroec ● THE SPIRITUAL ESPOUSALS AND OTHER WORKS
Ibn 'Abbād of Ronda ● LETTERS ON THE SŪFĪ PATH
Angelus Silesius ● THE CHERUBINIC WANDERER
The Early Kabbalah ●
Meister Eckhart ● TEACHER AND PREACHER
John of the Cross ● SELECTED WRITINGS
Pseudo-Dionysius ● THE COMPLETE WORKS
Bernard of Clairvaux ● SELECTED WORKS
Devotio Moderna ● BASIC WRITINGS
The Pursuit of Wisdom ● AND OTHER WORKS BY THE AUTHOR OF
    THE CLOUD OF UNKNOWING
Richard Rolle ● THE ENGLISH WRITINGS